BEHOLD THE HERITAGE

*Foundations of Education
in the Dominican Tradition*

BEHOLD
THE HERITAGE

*Foundations of Education
in the Dominican Tradition*

✛

Edited by
Sister Matthew Marie Cummings, O.P.
Sister Elizabeth Anne Allen, O.P.

Angelico Press

First published in the USA
by Angelico Press
© Sister Matthew Marie Cummings, O.P.
and Sister Elizabeth Anne Allen, O.P. 2012
© Libreria Editrice Vaticana, 2012

Excerpt from Thomas C. McGonigle and Phyllis Zagano,
The Dominican Tradition © 2006 by The Order of Saint Benedict, Inc.
Published by Liturgical Press, Collegeville, Minnesota.
Reprinted with permission.

"A Dominican Philosophy of Education,"
by Father Philip A. Smith, O.P., and "The Healing Work of
Teaching: Thomas Aquinas and Education," by Father
Vivian Boland, O.P., in *Towards the Intelligent Use of Liberty:
Dominican Approaches in Education*, Gabrielle Kelly and
Kevin Saunders (eds), Adelaide, Australia: ATF Press, 2007.
Reprinted with permission.

978-1-62138-007-8 paperback
978-1-62138-008-5 cloth
978-1-62138-570-7 case
For information, address:
Angelico Press, 4619 Slayden Rd., NE
Tacoma, WA 98422
www.angelicopress.com

Front cover image: Fra Angelico, *Virgin and Child
with Sts. Dominic and Thomas Aquinas*, completed in 1445.
Gallery: The Hermitage, St. Petersburg.
Back cover image: Fra Angelico, *The Mocking of Christ*
(detail of St. Dominic) 1440–41, Convento di San Marco, Florence.
Cover design: Cristy Deming

TABLE OF CONTENTS

Introduction 1

Declaration on Christian Education (*Gravissimum Educationis*)
    Second Vatican Council, 1965 6

On Evangelization in the Modern World (*Evangelii Nuntiandi*)
    Pope Paul VI, 1975 18

The Catholic School
    Sacred Congregation for Catholic Education, 1977 64

Lay Catholics in Schools: Witnesses to Faith
    Sacred Congregation for Catholic Education, 1982 88

The Religious Dimension of Education in a Catholic School:
    Guidelines for Reflection and Renewal
    Congregation for Catholic Education, 1988 119

On Catholic Universities (*Ex Corde Ecclesiae*)
    Pope John Paul II, 1990 162

The Catholic School on the Threshold of the Third Millennium
    Congregation for Catholic Education, 1997 187

Consecrated Persons and Their Mission in Schools:
    Reflections and Guidelines
    Congregation for Catholic Education, 2002 198

Educating Together in Catholic Schools: A Shared Mission
    Between Consecrated Persons and the Lay Faithful
    Congregation for Catholic Education, 2007 234

The Dominican Tradition
    Father Thomas C. McGonigle, O.P. 254

A Dominican Philosophy of Education
    Father Philip A. Smith, O.P. 261

The Healing Work of Teaching:
    Thomas Aquinas and Education
    Father Vivian Boland, O.P. 274

About the Editors 282

BEHOLD THE HERITAGE

Introduction

"Behold, my children, the heritage I leave. Have charity for one another, guard humility, make your treasure out of voluntary poverty." This statement is the last will and testament of Saint Dominic de Guzman. By using the word *Behold*, it calls our attention to something beyond the ordinary, something of great significance. The object we are called to *behold* is the heritage left to us by Saint Dominic.

What is this *heritage* we are called to *behold*? It is the glorious heritage of working for the salvation of souls through preaching and teaching in the Dominican tradition. Many sources refer to Saint Dominic as being "*in medio ecclesiae*" or "in the midst of the Church." This also describes Dominican education, a tradition rooted "*in medio ecclesiae*." Father Philip Smith, in his work *A Dominican Philosophy of Education*, states, "...the Dominican tradition should be rooted in and shaped by the broader intellectual, spiritual, and cultural tradition of the Church from which it emerged" (page 261). That is why the Church documents must have pride of place in a collection of works on Dominican education.

The documents included in this volume have a scope, spanning over forty years (1965-2007) and touching virtually every level of Catholic education. Taken collectively, the variety of topics considered has great breadth: Catholic education in general, its direct relation to evangelization, the nature and purpose of the Catholic school specifically, and the significant roles of both laity and religious in the Church's educational efforts. Throughout, there is a clear and direct sense of the importance of teaching and the impact it has on both individuals and the mission of the Church. The documents are presented in this work in chronological order to make apparent the care and thoroughness with which the Church treats the subject of education.

The *Declaration on Christian Education*, issued by Vatican Council II in 1965, maintains that education is both a right and a duty. Education, as a human right, is linked to the dignity of the human person (page 7). Education as a duty is shared among the parents, the state and the Church, each having distinct but complementary roles (page 9). The role of the teacher in all types and levels of schools is especially valued: "Beautiful indeed and of great importance is the vocation of all those who aid parents in fulfilling their duties and who, as representatives of the human community, undertake the task of education in schools" (page 11).

In 1975, Paul VI issued *On Evangelization in the Modern World*, in which he relates evangelization, the initial proclamation of the Gospel, to the life of the

Church in three ways: by asserting that evangelization is the essential mission of the Church (page 23), by emphasizing the incorporation of those who have received the message of the Gospel into a community which then itself has the mission of evangelizing (page 22); and by insisting that catechetical instruction, including that carried out in schools, is itself a form of evangelization (page 36). The significance and role of teachers in this process is repeatedly stressed in the document, as in the clear expression, "Modern man listens more willingly to witnesses than to teachers, and if he does listen to teachers, it is because they are witnesses" (page 35).

The stated intention of the Sacred Congregation for Catholic Education (1977) in writing *The Catholic School* is to develop the ideas of the Vatican Council's *Declaration on Christian Education* with an exclusive focus on the schools (page 64). A significant portion of the document deals with the identity of Catholic schools, enumerating those qualities which make the Catholic school distinctive from other types of schools. At the same time, the attributes and responsibilities which are proper to all schools are examined.

Lay Catholics in Schools: Witnesses to Faith (1982) concerns all Catholics who serve as educators in primary or secondary schools, regardless of the sponsorship of those schools. Recognizing the theological basis for the participation of the laity in the field of education, the document asserts that it is the laity in the schools who will "substantially determine whether or not the school recognizes its aims and accomplishes its objectives" (page 88). The role of the teacher as witness to the faith is given considerable attention throughout the document, since "the more completely an educator can give concrete witness to the model of the ideal person that is being presented to the students, the more this ideal will be believed and imitated" (page 100). Lay teachers, above all, are charged to help bring about "the integration of temporal reality with the Gospel" (page 118).

Building on the theme of the existence of a community climate in the Catholic school, a theme originally noted in the *Declaration on Christian Education,* the Congregation for Catholic Education in *The Religious Dimension of Education in a Catholic School* (1988), explains that the religious dimension is that single characteristic which makes the Catholic school distinctive (page 119). The religious dimension, in turn, is constituted by "the educational climate, the personal development of each student, the relationship established between culture and the Gospel, and the illumination of all knowledge with the light of faith" (page 119). Attention is given to the significant process of human formation and to the teacher's role in that process (page 119ff).

Just as *The Catholic School* considers the distinctive qualities and role belonging to Catholic elementary and secondary schools, so *Ex Corde Ecclesiae* (1990) examines the characteristics of and purposes served by Catholic institutions of higher learning. The words "ex corde ecclesiae" mean "from the heart of the Church," and it is with this phrase that Pope John Paul II begins his constitution on Catholic universities. These words also indicate the relationship of the Catholic university with the Catholic Church as John Paul II saw it: the Catholic university, as an institution, was "born from the heart of the Church" and shares in the Church's mission to teach (page 162). The vocation of the Catholic university is summarized as "dedication to research, to teaching and to the education of students who freely associate with their teachers in a common love of knowledge" (page 162). The document identifies characteristics which should mark all Catholic colleges are identified and makes subsequent applications to teaching, learning, research and community. The document also affirms the importance of the Catholic university in culture, to humanity and to the evangelization mission of the Church (pages 174–180).

In *The Catholic School on the Threshold of the Third Millennium* (1997), the Congregation for Catholic Education recognizes the past accomplishments and present challenges of the Catholic school and acknowledges its particular value in the current times. The school is seen especially as a place in which the human person has centrality and is also viewed in terms of cultural and ecclesial identities. The vocation of the teacher is assigned great importance, not only in terms of achieving institutional goals, but in terms of relating to each student: "... for the teacher does not write on inanimate material, but on the very spirits of human beings" (page 196).

Consecrated Persons and Their Mission in Schools (2002) is a companion document to *Lay Catholics in Schools: Witnesses to Faith*. The consecrated life is linked with the evangelizing purpose of education and gives special emphasis to the value of the educational apostolate. Designating service in education a "prophetic choice" (page 231), the Congregation for Catholic Education acknowledges circumstances which have contributed to the abandonment of schools by many congregations of consecrated persons (page 200). Religious are urged to participate in the mission of education where they are able to give witness to the community and communion at the core of their vocation.

Educating Together in Catholic Schools: A Shared Mission between Consecrated Persons and the Lay Faithful (2007) examines the distinctive gifts that both consecrated persons and laity bring to the Catholic school. The school is characterized in this document by its ecclesial dimension, seen as sharing in the Church's mission and being a place of "integral education of the human person ... directed at creating a synthesis between faith, culture and life" (page 235). The Catholic school is viewed as both an "educating community" and a "Christian community, that is, a community of faith" (page 238). In order to make this community a reality, teachers—lay and consecrated persons alike—must be witnesses as well as teachers (page 239).

The function of documents issued by the Church is pastoral in nature. Such documents are to instruct the faithful and to clarify Church teachings so that they may be better understood. One can see from the collection of documents presented here the importance of Catholic education.

When a Catholic education is handed on by those in a school affiliated with a religious order, that education has a special character or tradition of its own. How does one learn to teach in the Dominican Tradition? For those living in a Dominican religious community, the tradition is learned through the formation that is received by the faithful handing on of what has been bestowed down through the centuries. Together with the dedicated service of countless lay persons teaching together with religious in Dominican schools, the Dominican tradition of education endures.

Father Thomas McGonigle's work on *The Dominican Tradition* serves as a cornerstone for understanding the Dominican approach to education. In this text, we are introduced to Saint Dominic and the circumstances which led him to found the Order of Preachers. The four pillars of Dominican life, prayer, study, community and preaching, are clearly iterated as are the vows of poverty, chastity and obedience. Father also acquaints us with the different members of the Dominican family, namely the friars, nuns, sisters, and laity.

In *A Dominican Philosophy of Education*, Father Philip Smith articulates how the Dominican tradition is made manifest in a school to make it a *Dominican* school. He concretizes the Dominican philosophy of education by demonstrating its presence in the work at Providence College.

A companion piece to Father Philip Smith's *A Dominican Philosophy of Education*, is *The Healing Work of Teaching: Thomas Aquinas and Education* by Father Vivian Boland. Thomas Aquinas, modeled after Christ the master teacher, ". . . was himself a good teacher, and his preferred analogy for what the teacher does is the work of the medical doctor. Just as the medic cannot replace nature but can assist it in various ways, so the teacher cannot replace the student's intellectual processes but can assist them in various ways. . . . The teacher cannot do the students' understanding for them, and so the students' appreciation of truth is not identical with the teacher's appreciation of truth. And for Thomas, this means that a real change comes about through teaching" (page 276). Father Boland also conveys to us that "[f]or Thomas human flourishing can only come about through the living of a theological life. Wisdom, the tasted knowledge of truth-goodness-beauty that human beings seek, is found, he believed, in the knowledge of Jesus Christ" (page 280). Thus we are led back to the Master Teacher whom we encounter in the Living Word of God.

It is our desire that we help to form these educators in the Dominican tradition by providing them with some foundational texts to serve as inspiration for the important vocation in which they share—namely, the salvation of souls. The collection of documents cited here gives abundant evidence of the importance attached to the mission of education and testifies to the esteem in which teachers are held by the Church. The Dominican tradition has served in this apostolate of preaching and teaching for over 800 years, seeing it as an expression of the Order's purpose: "to praise, to bless, to preach."

This text is dedicated to all those men and women who have handed on the Dominican tradition of education to us, those who have gone before us, those we have known and been influenced by directly and those who will come after us, and to all those students we have had the privilege of helping to form and who have also formed us as educators. Saint Dominic, pray for us!

DECLARATION ON CHRISTIAN EDUCATION
GRAVISSIMUM EDUCATIONIS

PROCLAIMED BY HIS HOLINESS POPE PAUL VI ON OCTOBER 28, 1965
Second Vatican Council

Introduction

The Sacred Ecumenical Council has considered with care how extremely important education is in the life of man and how its influence ever grows in the social progress of this age.[1]

Indeed, the circumstances of our time have made it easier and at once more urgent to educate young people and, what is more, to continue the education of adults. Men are more aware of their own dignity and position; more and more they want to take an active part in social and especially in economic and political life.[2] Enjoying more leisure, as they sometimes do, men find that the remarkable development of technology and scientific investigation and the new means of communication offer them an opportunity of attaining more easily their cultural and spiritual inheritance and of fulfilling one another in the closer ties between groups and even between peoples.

Consequently, attempts are being made everywhere to promote more education. The rights of men to an education, particularly the primary rights of children and parents, are being proclaimed and recognized in public documents.[3] As the number of pupils rapidly increases, schools are multiplied and expanded far and wide and other educational institutions are established. New experi-

1. Among many documents illustrating the importance of education confer above all apostolic letter of Benedict XV, *Communes Litteras*, April 10, 1919: *AAS* 11 (1919) p. 172. Pius XI's encyclical letter, *Divini Illius Magistri*, Dec. 31, 1929: *AAS* 22 (1930) pp. 49–86. Pius XII's allocution to the youths of Italian Catholic Action, April 20, 1946: Discourses and Radio Messages, vol. 8, pp. 53–57. Allocution to fathers of French families, Sept. 18, 1951: Discourses and Radio Messages, vol. 13, pp. 241–245. John XXIII's 30th anniversary message on the publication of the encyclical letter, *Divini Illius Magistri*, Dec. 30, 1959: *AAS* 52 (1960) pp. 57–59. Paul VI's allocution to members of Federated Institutes Dependent on Ecclesiastic Authority, Dec. 30, 1963: Encyclicals and Discourses of His Holiness Paul VI, Rome, 1964, pp. 601–603. Above all are to be consulted the Acts and Documents of the Second Vatican Council appearing in the first series of the ante-preparatory phase. vol. 3. pp. 363–364; 370–371; 373–374.

2. Cf. John XXIII's encyclical letter *Mater et Magistra*, May 15, 1961: *AAS* 53 (1961) pp. 413–415; 417–424; encyclical letter, *Pacem in Terris*, April 11, 1963: *AAS* 55 (1963) p. 278ff.

3. Declaration on the Rights of Man of Dec. 10, 1948, adopted by the General Assembly of the United Nations, and also cf. the Declaration of the Rights of Children of Nov. 20 1959; additional protocol to the Convention Safeguarding the Rights of Men and Fundamental Liberties, Paris, March 20, 1952; regarding that universal profession of the character of human laws cf. encyclical letter *Pacem in Terris*, of John XXIII of April 11, 1963: *AAS* 55 (1963) p. 295ff.

ments are conducted in methods of education and teaching. Mighty attempts are being made to obtain education for all, even though vast numbers of children and young people are still deprived of even rudimentary training and so many others lack a suitable education in which truth and love are developed together.

To fulfill the mandate she has received from her divine founder of proclaiming the mystery of salvation to all men and of restoring all things in Christ, Holy Mother the Church must be concerned with the whole of man's life, even the secular part of it insofar as it has a bearing on his heavenly calling.[4] Therefore she has a role in the progress and development of education. Hence this sacred synod declares certain fundamental principles of Christian education especially in schools. These principles will have to be developed at greater length by a special post-conciliar commission and applied by episcopal conferences to varying local situations.

1. *The Meaning of the Universal Right to an Education*

All men of every race, condition and age, since they enjoy the dignity of a human being, have an inalienable right to an education[5] that is in keeping with their ultimate goal,[6] their ability, their sex, and the culture and tradition of their country, and also in harmony with their fraternal association with other peoples in the fostering of true unity and peace on earth. For a true education aims at the formation of the human person in the pursuit of his ultimate end and of the good of the societies of which, as man, he is a member, and in whose obligations, as an adult, he will share.

Therefore children and young people must be helped, with the aid of the latest advances in psychology and the arts and science of teaching, to develop harmoniously their physical, moral and intellectual endowments so that they may gradually acquire a mature sense of responsibility in striving endlessly to form their own lives properly and in pursuing true freedom as they surmount the vicissitudes of life with courage and constancy. Let them be given also, as they advance in years, a positive and prudent sexual education. Moreover they should be so trained to take their part in social life that properly instructed in the necessary and opportune skills they can become actively involved in various

---

4. Cf. John XXIII's encyclical letter, *Mater et Magistra*, May 15, 1961: *AAS* 53 (1961) p. 402. Cf. Second Vatican Council's Dogmatic Constitution on the Church, no. 17: *AAS* 57 (1965) p. 21, and schema on the Pastoral Constitution on the Church in the Modern World, 1965.

5. Pius XII's radio message of Dec. 24, 1942: *AAS* 35 (1943) pp. 12-19, and John XXIII's encyclical letter, *Pacem in Terris* April 11, 1963: *AAS* 55 (1963) p. 259ff. Also cf. declaration cited on the rights of man in footnote 3.

6. Cf. Pius XI's encyclical letter, *Divini Illius Magistri*, Dec. 31, 1929: *AAS* 22 (1930) p. 50ff.

community organizations, open to discourse with others and willing to do their best to promote the common good.

This sacred synod likewise declares that children and young people have a right to be motivated to appraise moral values with a right conscience, to embrace them with a personal adherence, together with a deeper knowledge and love of God. Consequently it earnestly entreats all those who hold a position of public authority or who are in charge of education to see to it that youth is never deprived of this sacred right. It further exhorts the sons of the Church to give their attention with generosity to the entire field of education, having especially in mind the need of extending very soon the benefits of a suitable education and training to everyone in all parts of the world.[7]

2. *Christian Education*

Since all Christians have become by rebirth of water and the Holy Spirit a new creature[8] so that they should be called and should be children of God, they have a right to a Christian education. A Christian education does not merely strive for the maturing of a human person as just now described, but has as its principal purpose this goal: that the baptized, while they are gradually introduced the knowledge of the mystery of salvation, become ever more aware of the gift of Faith they have received, and that they learn in addition how to worship God the Father in spirit and truth (cf. *Jn* 4:23) especially in liturgical action, and be conformed in their personal lives according to the new man created in justice and holiness of truth (*Eph* 4:22–24); also that they develop into perfect manhood, to the mature measure of the fullness of Christ (cf. *Eph* 4:13) and strive for the growth of the Mystical Body; moreover, that aware of their calling, they learn not only how to bear witness to the hope that is in them (cf. *1 Pt* 3:15) but also how to help in the Christian formation of the world that takes place when natural powers viewed in the full consideration of man redeemed by Christ contribute to the good of the whole society.[9] Wherefore this sacred synod recalls to pastors of souls their most serious obligation to see to it that all the faithful, but especially the youth who are the hope of the Church, enjoy this Christian education.[10]

---

7. Cf. John XXIII's encyclical letter, *Mater et Magistra*, May 15 1961: *AAS* 53 (1961) p. 441ff.
8. Cf. Pius XI's encyclical letter, *Divini Illius Magistri*, 1, p. 83.
9. Cf. Second Vatican Council's Dogmatic Constitution on the Church, no. 36: *AAS* 57 (1965) p. 41ff.
10. Cf. Second Vatican Council's schema on the Decree on the Lay Apostolate (1965), no. 12.

3. *The Authors of Education*

Since parents have given children their life, they are bound by the most serious obligation to educate their offspring and therefore must be recognized as the primary and principal educators.[11] This role in education is so important that only with difficulty can it be supplied where it is lacking. Parents are the ones who must create a family atmosphere animated by love and respect for God and man, in which the well-rounded personal and social education of children is fostered. Hence the family is the first school of the social virtues that every society needs. It is particularly in the Christian family, enriched by the grace and office of the sacrament of matrimony, that children should be taught from their early years to have a knowledge of God according to the faith received in Baptism, to worship Him, and to love their neighbor. Here, too, they find their first experience of a wholesome human society and of the Church. Finally, it is through the family that they are gradually led to a companionship with their fellowmen and with the people of God. Let parents, then, recognize the inestimable importance a truly Christian family has for the life and progress of God's own people.[12]

The family which has the primary duty of imparting education needs help of the whole community. In addition, therefore, to the rights of parents and others to whom the parents entrust a share in the work of education, certain rights and duties belong indeed to civil society, whose role is to direct what is required for the common temporal good. Its function is to promote the education of youth in many ways, namely: to protect the duties and rights of parents and others who share in education and to give them aid; according to the principle of subsidiarity, when the endeavors of parents and other societies are lacking, to carry out the work of education in accordance with the wishes of the parents; and, moreover, as the common good demands, to build schools and institutions.[13]

Finally, in a special way, the duty of educating belongs to the Church, not merely because she must be recognized as a human society capable of educating, but especially because she has the responsibility of announcing the way of salvation to all men, of communicating the life of Christ to those who believe,

---

11. Cf. Pius XI's encyclical letter *Divini Illius Magistri*, 1, p. 59ff., encyclical letter *Mit Brennender Sorge*, March 14, 1937: *AAS* 29; Pius XII's allocution to the first national congress of the Italian Catholic Teachers' Association, Sept. 8, 1946: Discourses and Radio Messages, vol. 8, p. 218.

12. Cf. Second Vatican Council's Dogmatic Constitution on the Church, nos. 11 and 35: *AAS* 57 (1965) pp. 16, 40ff.

13. Cf. Pius XI's encyclical letter *Divini Illius Magistri*, 1, p. 63ff. Pius XII's radio message of June 1, 1941: *AAS* 33 (1941) p. 200; allocution to the first national congress of the Association of Italian Catholic Teachers, Sept. 8, 1946: Discourses and Radio Messages, vol. 8, 1946: Discourses and Radio Messages, vol. 8 p. 218. Regarding the principle of subsidiarity, cf. John XXIII's encyclical letter, *Pacem in Terris*, April 11, 1963: *AAS* 55 (1963) p. 294.

and, in her unfailing solicitude, of assisting men to be able to come to the fullness of this life.[14] The Church is bound as a mother to give to these children of hers an education by which their whole life can be imbued with the spirit of Christ and at the same time do all she can to promote for all peoples the complete perfection of the human person, the good of earthly society and the building of a world that is more human.[15]

4. *Various Aids to Christian Education*

In fulfilling its educational role, the Church, eager to employ all suitable aids, is concerned especially about those which are her very own. Foremost among these is catechetical instruction,[16] which enlightens and strengthens the faith, nourishes life according to the spirit of Christ, leads to intelligent and active participation in the liturgical mystery[17] and gives motivation for apostolic activity. The Church esteems highly and seeks to penetrate and ennoble with her own spirit also other aids which belong to the general heritage of man and which are of great influence in forming souls and molding men, such as the media of communication,[18] various groups for mental and physical development, youth associations, and, in particular, schools.

5. *The Importance of Schools*

Among all educational instruments the school has a special importance.[19] It is designed not only to develop with special care the intellectual faculties but also to form the ability to judge rightly, to hand on the cultural legacy of previous generations, to foster a sense of values, to prepare for professional life. Between pupils of different talents and backgrounds it promotes friendly relations and fosters a spirit of mutual understanding; and it establishes as it were a center

---

14. Cf. Pius XI's encyclical letter, *Divini Illius Magistri*, 1 pp. 53ff. and 56ff; encyclical letter, *Non Abbiamo Bisogno* June 29, 1931: *AAS* 23 (1931) p. 311ff. Pius XII's letter from the Secretariat of State to the 28th Italian Social Week, Sept. 20, 1955; *L'Osservatore Romano*, Sept. 29, 1955.

15. The Church praises those local, national and international civic authorities who, conscious of the urgent necessity in these times, expend all their energy so that all peoples may benefit from more education and human culture. Cf. Paul VI's allocution to the United Nations General Assembly, Oct. 4, 1965: *L'Osservatore Romano*, Oct. 6, 1965.

16. Cf. Pius XI's motu proprio. *Orbem Catholicum*, June 29 1923: *AAS* 15 (1923) pp. 327–329; decree, *Provide Sane*, Jan. 12, 1935: *AAS* 27 (1935) pp. 145-152. Second Vatican Council's Decree on Bishops and Pastoral Duties, nos. 13 and 14.

17. Cf. Second Vatican Council's Constitution on the Sacred Liturgy, no. 14: *AAS* 56 (1964) p. 104.

18. Cf. Second Vatican Council's Decree on Communications Media, nos. 13 and 14: *AAS* 56 (1964) p. 149ff.

19. Cf. Pius XI's encyclical letter, *Divini Illius Magistri*, 1, p. 76; Pius XII's allocution to Bavarian Association of Catholic Teachers, Dec. 31, 1956: Discourses and Radio Messages, vol. 18, p. 746.

whose work and progress must be shared together by families, teachers, associations of various types that foster cultural, civic, and religious life, as well as by civil society and the entire human community.

Beautiful indeed and of great importance is the vocation of all those who aid parents in fulfilling their duties and who, as representatives of the human community, undertake the task of education in schools. This vocation demands special qualities of mind and heart, very careful preparation, and continuing readiness to renew and to adapt.

6. *The Duties and Rights of Parents*

Parents who have the primary and inalienable right and duty to educate their children must enjoy true liberty in their choice of schools. Consequently, the public power, which has the obligation to protect and defend the rights of citizens, must see to it, in its concern for distributive justice, that public subsidies are paid out in such a way that parents are truly free to choose according to their conscience the schools they want for their children.[20]

In addition it is the task of the state to see to it that all citizens are able to come to a suitable share in culture and are properly prepared to exercise their civic duties and rights. Therefore the state must protect the right of children to an adequate school education, check on the ability of teachers and the excellence of their training, look after the health of the pupils and in general, promote the whole school project. But it must always keep in mind the principle of subsidiarity so that there is no kind of school monopoly, for this is opposed to the native rights of the human person, to the development and spread of culture, to the peaceful association of citizens and to the pluralism that exists today in ever so many societies.[21]

Therefore this sacred synod exhorts the faithful to assist to their utmost in finding suitable methods of education and programs of study and in forming teachers who can give youth a true education. Through the associations of parents in particular they should further with their assistance all the work of the school but especially the moral education it must impart.[22]

20. Cf. Provincial Council of Cincinnati III, a. 1861: *Collatio Lacensis*, III, col. 1240, c/d; Pius XI's encyclical letter, *Divini Illius Magistri*, 1, pp. 60, 63ff.

21. Cf. Pius XI's encyclical letter, *Divini Illius Magistri*, 1, p. 63; encyclical letter, *Non Abbiamo Bisogno*, June 29, 1931: *AAS* 23 (1931) p. 305, Pius XII's letter from the Secretariat of State to the 28th Italian Social Week, Sept. 20, 1955: *L'Osservatore Romano*, Sept. 29, 1955. Paul VI's allocution to the Association of Italian Christian Workers, Oct. 6, 1963: *Encyclicals and Discourses of Paul VI*, vol. 1, Rome, 1964, p. 230.

22. Cf. John XXIII's message on the 30th anniversary of the encyclical letter, *Divini Illius Magistri*, Dec. 30, 1959: *AAS* 52 (1960) p. 57.

7. *Moral and Religious Education in All Schools*

Feeling very keenly the weighty responsibility of diligently caring for the moral and religious education of all her children, the Church must be present with her own special affection and help for the great number who are being trained in schools that are not Catholic. This is possible by the witness of the lives of those who teach and direct them, by the apostolic action of their fellow-students,[23] but especially by the ministry of priests and laymen who give them the doctrine of salvation in a way suited to their age and circumstances and provide spiritual aid in every way the times and conditions allow.

The Church reminds parents of the duty that is theirs to arrange and even demand that their children be able to enjoy these aids and advance in their Christian formation to a degree that is abreast of their development in secular subjects. Therefore the Church esteems highly those civil authorities and societies which, bearing in mind the pluralism of contemporary society and respecting religious freedom, assist families so that the education of their children can be imparted in all schools according to the individual moral and religious principles of the families.[24]

8. *Catholic Schools*

The influence of the Church in the field of education is shown in a special manner by the Catholic school. No less than other schools does the Catholic school pursue cultural goals and the human formation of youth. But its proper function is to create for the school community a special atmosphere animated by the Gospel spirit of freedom and charity, to help youth grow according to the new creatures they were made through baptism as they develop their own personalities, and finally to order the whole of human culture to the news of salvation so that the knowledge the students gradually acquire of the world, life and man is illumined by faith.[25] So indeed the Catholic school, while it is open, as it must be, to the situation of the contemporary world, leads its students to promote efficaciously the good of the earthly city and also prepares them for service in the spread of the Kingdom of God, so that by leading an

---

23. The Church considers it as apostolic action of great worth also when Catholic teachers and associates work in these schools. Cf. Second Vatican Council's schema of the Decree on the Lay Apostolate (1965), nos. 12 and 16.

24. Cf. Second Vatican Council's schema on the Declaration on Religious Liberty (1965), no. 5.

25. Cf. Provincial Council of Westminster I, a. 1852: *Collatio Lacensis,* III, col. 1334, a/b; Pius XI's encyclical letter, *Divini Illius Magistri,* 1, p. 77ff.; Pius XII's allocution to the Bavarian Association of Catholic Teachers, Dec. 31, 1956: *Discourses and Radio Messages,* vol. 18, p. 746; Paul VI's allocution to the members of Federated Institutes Dependent on Ecclesiastic Authority, Dec. 30, 1963: *Encyclicals and Discourses of Paul VI,* 1, Rome, 1964, 602ff.

exemplary apostolic life they become, as it were, a saving leaven in the human community.

Since, therefore, the Catholic school can be such an aid to the fulfillment of the mission of the People of God and to the fostering of the dialogue between the Church and mankind, to the benefit of both, it retains even in our present circumstances the utmost importance. Consequently this sacred synod proclaims anew what has already been taught in several documents of the magisterium,[26] namely: the right of the Church freely to establish and to conduct schools of every type and level. And the council calls to mind that the exercise of a right of this kind contributes in the highest degree to the protection of freedom of conscience, the rights of parents, as well as to the betterment of culture itself.

But let teachers recognize that the Catholic school depends upon them almost entirely for the accomplishment of its goals and programs.[27] They should therefore be very carefully prepared so that both in secular and religious knowledge they are equipped with suitable qualifications and also with a pedagogical skill that is in keeping with the findings of the contemporary world. Intimately linked in charity to one another and to their students and endowed with an apostolic spirit, may teachers by their life as much as by their instruction bear witness to Christ, the unique Teacher. Let them work as partners with parents and together with them in every phase of education give due consideration to the difference of sex and the proper ends Divine Providence assigns to each sex in the family and in society. Let them do all they can to stimulate their students to act for themselves and even after graduation to continue to assist them with advice, friendship and by establishing special associations imbued with the true spirit of the Church. The work of these teachers, this sacred synod declares, is in the real sense of the word an apostolate most suited to and necessary for our times and at once a true service offered to society. The Council also reminds Catholic parents of the duty of entrusting their children to Catholic schools wherever and whenever it is possible and of supporting these schools to the best of their ability and of cooperating with them for the education of their children.[28]

---

26. Cf. especially the document mentioned in the first note; moreover this law of the Church is proclaimed by many provincial councils and in the most recent declarations of very many of the episcopal conferences.

27. Cf. Pius XI's encyclical letter, *Divini Illius Magistri*, 1 p. 8off.; Pius XII's allocution to the Catholic Association of Italian Teachers in Secondary Schools, Jan. 5, 1954: Discourses and Radio Messages, 15, pp. 551–558; John XXIII's allocution to the 6th Congress of the Associations of Catholic Italian Teachers Sept. 5, 1959: *Discourses, Messages, Conversations*, 1, Rome, 1960, pp. 427–431.

28. Cf. Pius XII's allocution to the Catholic Association of Italian Teachers in Secondary Schools, Jan. 5, 1954, 1, p. 555.

9. *Different Types of Catholic Schools*

To this concept of a Catholic school all schools that are in any way dependent on the Church must conform as far as possible, though the Catholic school is to take on different forms in keeping with local circumstances.[29] Thus the Church considers very dear to her heart those Catholic schools, found especially in the areas of the new churches, which are attended also by students who are not Catholics.

Attention should be paid to the needs of today in establishing and directing Catholic schools. Therefore, though primary and secondary schools, the foundation of education, must still be fostered, great importance is to be attached to those which are required in a particular way by contemporary conditions, such as: professional[30] and technical schools, centers for educating adults and promoting social welfare, or for the retarded in need of special care, and also schools for preparing teachers for religious instruction and other types of education.

This Sacred Council of the Church earnestly entreats pastors and all the faithful to spare no sacrifice in helping Catholic schools fulfill their function in a continually more perfect way, and especially in caring for the needs of those who are poor in the goods of this world or who are deprived of the assistance and affection of a family or who are strangers to the gift of Faith.

10. *Catholic Colleges and Universities*

The Church is concerned also with schools of a higher level, especially colleges and universities. In those schools dependent on her she intends that by their very constitution individual subjects be pursued according to their own principles, method, and liberty of scientific inquiry, in such a way that an ever deeper understanding in these fields may be obtained and that, as questions that are new and current are raised and investigations carefully made according to the example of the doctors of the Church and especially of St. Thomas Aquinas,[31] there may be a deeper realization of the harmony of faith and science. Thus there is accomplished a public, enduring and pervasive influence of the Christian mind in the furtherance of culture and the students of these institutions are molded into men truly outstanding in their training, ready to

---

29. Cf. Paul VI's allocution to the International Office of Catholic Education, Feb. 25, 1964: *Encyclicals and Discourses of Paul VI*, 2, Rome, 1964, p. 232.

30. Cf. Paul VI's allocution to the Christian Association of Italian Workers, Oct. 6, 1963: *Encyclicals and Discourses of Paul VI*, 1, Rome, 1964, p. 229.

31. Cf. Paul VI's allocution to the International Thomistic Congress, Sept. 10, 1965: *L'Osservatore Romano*, Sept. 13–14, 1965.

undertake weighty responsibilities in society and witness to the faith in the world.[32]

In Catholic universities where there is no faculty of sacred theology there should be established an institute or chair of sacred theology in which there should be lectures suited to lay students. Since science advances by means of the investigations peculiar to higher scientific studies, special attention should be given in Catholic universities and colleges to institutes that serve primarily the development of scientific research.

The sacred synod heartily recommends that Catholic colleges and universities be conveniently located in different parts of the world, but in such a way that they are outstanding not for their numbers but for their pursuit of knowledge. Matriculation should be readily available to students of real promise, even though they be of slender means, especially to students from the newly emerging nations.

Since the destiny of society and of the Church itself is intimately linked with the progress of young people pursuing higher studies,[33] the pastors of the Church are to expend their energies not only on the spiritual life of students who attend Catholic universities, but, solicitous for the spiritual formation of all their children, they must see to it, after consultations between bishops, that even at universities that are not Catholic there should be associations and university centers under Catholic auspices in which priests, religious and laity, carefully selected and prepared, should give abiding spiritual and intellectual assistance to the youth of the university. Whether in Catholic universities or others, young people of greater ability who seem suited for teaching or research should be specially helped and encouraged to undertake a teaching career.

11. *Faculties of Sacred Sciences*

The Church expects much from the zealous endeavors of the faculties of the sacred sciences.[34] For to them she entrusts the very serious responsibility of preparing her own students not only for the priestly ministry, but especially for

---

32. Cf. Pius XII's allocution to teachers and students of French Institutes of Higher Catholic Education, Sept. 21, 1950: *Discourses and Radio Messages*, 12, pp. 219–221; letters to the 22nd congress of Pax Romana, Aug. 12, 1952: Discourses and Radio Messages, 14, pp. 567–569; John XXIII's allocution to the Federation of Catholic Universities, April 1, 1959: *Discourses, Messages and Conversations*, 1, Rome, 1960, pp. 226–229; Paul VI's allocution to the Academic Senate of the Catholic University of Milan, April 5, 1964: *Encyclicals and Discourses of Paul VI*, 2, Rome, 1964, pp. 438–443.

33. Cf. Pius XII's allocution to the academic senate and students of the University of Rome, June 15, 1952: *Discourses and Radio Messages*, 14, p. 208: "The direction of today's society principally is placed in the mentality and hearts of the universities of today."

34. Cf. Pius XII's apostolic constitution, *Deus Scientiarum Dominus*, May 24, 1931: *AAS* 23 (1931) pp. 245–247.

teaching in the seats of higher ecclesiastical studies or for promoting learning on their own or for undertaking the work of a more rigorous intellectual apostolate. Likewise it is the role of these very faculties to make more penetrating inquiry into the various aspects of the sacred sciences so that an ever deepening understanding of sacred Revelation is obtained, the legacy of Christian wisdom handed down by our forefathers is more fully developed, the dialogue with our separated brethren and with non-Christians is fostered, and answers are given to questions arising from the development of doctrine.[35]

Therefore ecclesiastical faculties should reappraise their own laws so that they can better promote the sacred sciences and those linked with them and, by employing up-to-date methods and aids, lead their students to more penetrating inquiry.

12. *Coordination to be Fostered in Scholastic Matters*

Cooperation is the order of the day. It increases more and more to supply the demand on a diocesan, national and international level. Since it is altogether necessary in scholastic matters, every means should be employed to foster suitable cooperation between Catholic schools, and between these and other schools that collaboration should be developed which the good of all mankind requires.[36] From greater coordination and cooperative endeavor greater fruits will be derived particularly in the area of academic institutions. Therefore in every university let the various faculties work mutually to this end, insofar as their goal will permit. In addition, let the universities also endeavor to work together by promoting international gatherings, by sharing scientific inquiries with one another, by communicating their discoveries to one another, by having exchange of professors for a time and by promoting all else that is conducive to greater assistance.

Conclusion

The sacred synod earnestly entreats young people themselves to become aware of the importance of the work of education and to prepare themselves to take it up, especially where because of a shortage of teachers the education of youth is in jeopardy. This same sacred synod, while professing its gratitude to priests, Religious men and women, and the laity who by their evangelical self-dedica-

---

35. Cf. Pius XII's encyclical letter, *Humani Generis* Aug. 12, 1950 *AAS* 42 (1950) pp. 568ff. and 578; Paul VI's encyclical letter, *Ecclesiam Suam*, part III Aug. 6, 1964; *AAS* 56 (1964) pp. 637–659; Second Vatican Council's Decree on Ecumenism: *AAS* 57 (1965) pp. 90–107.

36. Cf. John XXIII's encyclical letter, *Pacem in Terris*, April 11, 1963: *AAS* 55 (1963) p. 284 and elsewhere.

tion are devoted to the noble work of education and of schools of every type and level, exhorts them to persevere generously in the work they have undertaken and, imbuing their students with the spirit of Christ, to strive to excel in pedagogy and the pursuit of knowledge in such a way that they not merely advance the internal renewal of the Church but preserve and enhance its beneficent influence upon today's world, especially the intellectual world.

ON EVANGELIZATION IN THE MODERN WORLD
EVANGELII NUNTIANDI

APOSTOLIC EXHORTATION OF HIS HOLINESS POPE PAUL VI
TO THE EPISCOPATE, TO THE CLERGY AND TO ALL THE
FAITHFUL OF THE ENTIRE WORLD

Venerable brothers and dear sons and daughters:
health and the apostolic blessing.

1 There is no doubt that the effort to proclaim the Gospel to the people of today, who are buoyed up by hope but at the same time often oppressed by fear and distress, is a service rendered to the Christian community and also to the whole of humanity.

For this reason the duty of confirming the brethren—a duty which with the office of being the Successor of Peter[1] we have received from the Lord, and which is for us a "daily preoccupation,"[2] a program of life and action, and a fundamental commitment of our Pontificate—seems to us all the more noble and necessary when it is a matter of encouraging our brethren in their mission as evangelizers, in order that, in this time of uncertainty and confusion, they may accomplish this task with ever increasing love, zeal and joy.

2 This is precisely what we wish to do here, at the end of this Holy Year during which the Church, "striving to proclaim the Gospel to all people,"[3] has had the single aim of fulfilling her duty of being the messenger of the Good News of Jesus Christ—the Good News proclaimed through two fundamental commands: "Put on the new self"[4] and "Be reconciled to God."[5]

We wish to do so on this tenth anniversary of the closing of the Second Vatican Council, the objectives of which are definitively summed up in this single one: to make the Church of the twentieth century ever better fitted for proclaiming the Gospel to the people of the twentieth century

We wish to do so one year after the Third General Assembly of the Synod of Bishops, which as is well known, was devoted to evangelization; and we do so all the more willingly because it has been asked of us by the Synod Fathers

---

1. Cf. *Lk* 22:32.
2. *2 Cor* 11:28.
3. Cf. Second Vatican Ecumenical Council, Decree on the Church's Missionary Activity *Ad Gentes*, 1: *AAS* 58 (1966), p. 947.
4. Cf. *Eph* 4:24, 2:15; *Col* 3:10; *Gal* 3:27; *Rom* 13:114; *2 Cor* 5:17.
5. *2 Cor* 5:20.

themselves. In fact, at the end of that memorable Assembly, the Fathers decided to remit to the Pastor of the universal Church, with great trust and simplicity, the fruits of all their labors, stating that they awaited from him a fresh forward impulse, capable of creating within a Church still more firmly rooted in the undying power and strength of Pentecost a new period of evangelization.[6]

3 We have stressed the importance of this theme of evangelization on many occasions, well before the Synod took place. On June 22, 1973, we said to the Sacred College of Cardinals: "The conditions of the society in which we live oblige all of us therefore to revise methods, to seek by every means to study how we can bring the Christian message to modern man. For it is only in the Christian message that modern man can find the answer to his questions and the energy for his commitment of human solidarity."[7] And we added that in order to give a valid answer to the demands of the Council which call for our attention, it is absolutely necessary for us to take into account a heritage of faith that the Church has the duty of preserving in its untouchable purity, and of presenting it to the people of our time, in a way that is as understandable and persuasive as possible.

4 This fidelity both to a message whose servants we are and to the people to whom we must transmit it living and intact is the central axis of evangelization. It poses three burning questions, which the 1974 Synod kept constantly in mind:

• In our day, what has happened to that hidden energy of the Good News, which is able to have a powerful effect on man's conscience?

• To what extent and in what way is that evangelical force capable of really transforming the people of this century?

• What methods should be followed in order that the power of the Gospel may have its effect?

Basically, these inquiries make explicit the fundamental question that the Church is asking herself today and which may be expressed in the following terms: after the Council and thanks to the Council, which was a time given her by God, at this turning-point of history, does the Church or does she not find herself better equipped to proclaim the Gospel and to put it into people's hearts with conviction, freedom of spirit and effectiveness?

---

6. Cf. Paul VI, *Address for the closing of the Third General Assembly of the Synod of Bishops* (26 October 1974): *AAS* 66 (1974), pp. 634–635, 637.

7. Paul VI, *Address to the College of Cardinals* (22 June 1973): *AAS* 65 (1973), p. 383.

5 We can all see the urgency of giving a loyal, humble and courageous answer to this question, and of acting accordingly.

In our "anxiety for all the Churches,"[8] we would like to help our brethren and sons and daughters to reply to these inquiries. Our words come from the wealth of the Synod and are meant to be a meditation on evangelization. May they succeed in inviting the whole People of God assembled in the Church to make the same meditation; and may they give a fresh impulse to everyone, especially those "who are assiduous in preaching and teaching,"[9] so that each one of them may follow "a straight course in the message of the truth,"[10] and may work as a preacher of the Gospel and acquit himself perfectly of his ministry.

Such an exhortation seems to us to be of capital importance, for the presentation of the Gospel message is not an optional contribution for the Church. It is the duty incumbent on her by the command of the Lord Jesus, so that people can believe and be saved. This message is indeed necessary. It is unique. It cannot be replaced. It does not permit either indifference, syncretism or accommodation. It is a question of people's salvation. It is the beauty of the Revelation that it represents. It brings with it a wisdom that is not of this world. It is able to stir up by itself faith—faith that rests on the power of God.[11] It is truth. It merits having the apostle consecrate to it all his time and all his energies, and to sacrifice for it, if necessary, his own life.

6 The witness that the Lord gives of Himself and that Saint Luke gathered together in his Gospel—"I must proclaim the Good News of the kingdom of God"[12]—without doubt has enormous consequences, for it sums up the whole mission of Jesus: "That is what I was sent to do."[13] These words take on their full significance if one links them with the previous verses, in which Christ has just applied to Himself the words of the prophet Isaiah: "The Spirit of the Lord has been given to me, for he has anointed me. He has sent me to bring the good news to the poor."[14]

Going from town to town, preaching to the poorest—and frequently the most receptive—the joyful news of the fulfillment of the promises and of the Covenant offered by God is the mission for which Jesus declares that He is sent by the Father. And all the aspects of His mystery—the Incarnation itself, His miracles, His teaching, the gathering together of the disciples, the sending out

8. *2 Cor* 11:28.
9. *1 Tim* 5:17.
10. *2 Tim* 2:15.
11. Cf. *1 Cor* 2:5.
12. *Lk* 4:43.
13. *Ibid.*
14. *Lk* 4:18; cf. *Is* 61:1.

of the Twelve, the cross and the resurrection, the permanence of His presence in the midst of His own—were components of His evangelizing activity.

7 During the Synod, the bishops very frequently referred to this truth: Jesus Himself, the Good News of God,[15] was the very first and the greatest evangelizer; He was so through and through: to perfection and to the point of the sacrifice of His earthly life.

To evangelize: what meaning did this imperative have for Christ? It is certainly not easy to express in a complete synthesis the meaning, the content and the modes of evangelization as Jesus conceived it and put it into practice. In any case the attempt to make such a synthesis will never end. Let it suffice for us to recall a few essential aspects.

8 As an evangelizer, Christ first of all proclaims a kingdom, the kingdom of God; and this is so important that, by comparison, everything else becomes "the rest," which is "given in addition."[16] Only the kingdom therefore is absolute and it makes everything else relative. The Lord will delight in describing in many ways the happiness of belonging to this kingdom (a paradoxical happiness which is made up of things that the world rejects),[17] the demands of the kingdom and its Magna Charta,[18] the heralds of the kingdom,[19] its mysteries,[20] its children,[21] the vigilance and fidelity demanded of whoever awaits its definitive coming.[22]

9 As the kernel and center of His Good News, Christ proclaims salvation, this great gift of God which is liberation from everything that oppresses man but which is above all liberation from sin and the Evil One, in the joy of knowing God and being known by Him, of seeing Him, and of being given over to Him. All of this is begun during the life of Christ and definitively accomplished by His death and resurrection. But it must be patiently carried on during the course of history, in order to be realized fully on the day of the final coming of Christ, whose date is known to no one except the Father.[23]

---

15. Cf. *Mk* 1:1; *Rom* 1:1–3.
16. Cf. *Mt* 6:33.
17. Cf. *Mt* 5:3–12.
18. Cf. *Mt* 5–7.
19. Cf. *Mt* 10.
20. Cf. *Mt* 13.
21. *Mt* 18.
22. Cf. *Mt* 24–25.
23. Cf. *Mt* 24:36; *Acts* 1:7; *1 Thess* 5:1–2.

10 This kingdom and this salvation, which are the key words of Jesus Christ's evangelization, are available to every human being as grace and mercy, and yet at the same time each individual must gain them by force — they belong to the violent, says the Lord,[24] through toil and suffering, through a life lived according to the Gospel, through abnegation and the cross, through the spirit of the beatitudes. But above all each individual gains them through a total interior renewal which the Gospel calls metanoia; it is a radical conversion, a profound change of mind and heart.[25]

11 Christ accomplished this proclamation of the kingdom of God through the untiring preaching of a word which, it will be said, has no equal elsewhere: "Here is a teaching that is new, and with authority behind it."[26] "And he won the approval of all, and they were astonished by the gracious words that came from his lips.[27] There has never been anybody who has spoken like him."[28] His words reveal the secret of God, His plan and His promise, and thereby change the heart of man and his destiny.

12 But Christ also carries out this proclamation by innumerable signs, which amaze the crowds and at the same time draw them to Him in order to see Him, listen to Him and allow themselves to be transformed by Him: the sick are cured, water is changed into wine, bread is multiplied, the dead come back to life. And among all these signs there is the one to which He attaches great importance: the humble and the poor are evangelized, become His disciples and gather together "in His name" in the great community of those who believe in Him. For this Jesus who declared, "I must preach the Good News of the Kingdom of God"[29] is the same Jesus of whom John the Evangelist said that He had come and was to die "to gather together in unity the scattered children of God."[30] Thus He accomplishes His revelation, completing it and confirming it by the entire revelation that He makes of Himself, by words and deeds, by signs and miracles, and more especially by His death, by His resurrection and by the sending of the Spirit of Truth.[31]

---

24. Cf. *Mt* 11:12; *Lk* 16:16.
25. Cf. *Mt* 4:17.
26. *Mk* 1:27.
27. *Lk* 4:22.
28. *Jn* 7:46.
29. *Lk* 4:43.
30. *Jn* 11:52.
31. Cf. Second Vatican Ecumenical Council, Dogmatic Constitution on Divine Revelation *Dei Verbum*, 4: AAS 58 (1966), pp. 818–819.32. *1 Pt* 2:9.

13 Those who sincerely accept the Good News, through the power of this acceptance and of shared faith therefore gather together in Jesus' name in order to seek together the kingdom, build it up and live it. They make up a community which is in its turn evangelizing. The command to the Twelve to go out and proclaim the Good News is also valid for all Christians, though in a different way. It is precisely for this reason that Peter calls Christians "a people set apart to sing the praises of God,"[32] those marvelous things that each one was able to hear in his own language.[33] Moreover, the Good News of the kingdom which is coming and which has begun is meant for all people of all times. Those who have received the Good News and who have been gathered by it into the community of salvation can and must communicate and spread it.

14 The Church knows this. She has a vivid awareness of the fact that the Savior's words, "I must proclaim the Good News of the kingdom of God,"[34] apply in all truth to herself: She willingly adds with St. Paul: "Not that I boast of preaching the gospel, since it is a duty that has been laid on me; I should be punished if I did not preach it."[35] It is with joy and consolation that at the end of the great Assembly of 1974 we heard these illuminating words: "We wish to confirm once more that the task of evangelizing all people constitutes the essential mission of the Church."[36] It is a task and mission which the vast and profound changes of present-day society make all the more urgent. Evangelizing is in fact the grace and vocation proper to the Church, her deepest identity. She exists in order to evangelize, that is to say, in order to preach and teach, to be the channel of the gift of grace, to reconcile sinners with God, and to perpetuate Christ's sacrifice in the Mass, which is the memorial of His death and glorious resurrection.

15 Anyone who rereads in the New Testament the origins of the Church, follows her history step by step and watches her live and act, sees that she is linked to evangelization in her most intimate being:

• The Church is born of the evangelizing activity of Jesus and the Twelve. She is the normal, desired, most immediate and most visible fruit of this activity: "Go, therefore, make disciples of all the nations."[37] Now, "they accepted what he said and were baptized. That very day about three thou-

---

32. *1 Pt* 2:9.
33. Cf. *Acts* 2:11.
34. *Lk* 4:43.
35. *1 Cor* 9:16.
36. "Declaration of the Synod Fathers," 4: *L'Osservatore Romano* (27 October 1974), p. 6.
37. *Mt* 28:19.

sand were added to their number.... Day by day the Lord added to their community those destined to be saved."[38] — Having been born consequently out of being sent, the Church in her turn is sent by Jesus. The Church remains in the world when the Lord of glory returns to the Father. She remains as a sign — simultaneously obscure and luminous — of a new presence of Jesus, of His departure and of His permanent presence. She prolongs and continues Him. And it is above all His mission and His condition of being an evangelizer that she is called upon to continue.[39] For the Christian community is never closed in upon itself. The intimate life of this community — the life of listening to the Word and the apostles' teaching, charity lived in a fraternal way, the sharing of the bread,[40] this intimate life only acquires its full meaning when it becomes a witness, when it evokes admiration and conversion, and when it becomes the preaching and proclamation of the Good News. Thus it is the whole Church that receives the mission to evangelize, and the work of each individual member is important for the whole.

• The Church is an evangelizer, but she begins by being evangelized herself. She is the community of believers, the community of hope lived and communicated, the community of brotherly love, and she needs to listen unceasingly to what she must believe, to her reasons for hoping, to the new commandment of love. She is the People of God immersed in the world, and often tempted by idols, and she always needs to hear the proclamation of the "mighty works of God"[41] which converted her to the Lord; she always needs to be called together afresh by Him and reunited. In brief, this means that she has a constant need of being evangelized, if she wishes to retain freshness, vigor and strength in order to proclaim the Gospel. The Second Vatican Council recalled[42] and the 1974 Synod vigorously took up again this theme of the Church which is evangelized by constant conversion and renewal, in order to evangelize the world with credibility.

• The Church is the depositary of the Good News to be proclaimed. The promises of the New Alliance in Jesus Christ, the teaching of the Lord and the apostles, the Word of life, the sources of grace and of God's loving

---

38. *Acts* 2:41, 47.

39. Cf. Second Vatican Ecumenical Council, Dogmatic Constitution on the Church *Lumen Gentium*, 8: *AAS* 57 (1965), p. 11; Decree on the Church's Missionary Activity *Ad Gentes*, 5: *AAS* 58 (1966), pp. 951-952.

40. Cf. *Acts* 2:42–46; 4:32–35; 5:12–16.

41. Cf. *Acts* 2:11; *1 Pt* 2:9.

42. Cf. Decree on the Church's Missionary Activity *Ad Gentes*, 5, 11–12: *AAS* 58 (1966), pp. 951–952, 959–961.

kindness, the path of salvation—all these things have been entrusted to her. It is the content of the Gospel, and therefore of evangelization, that she preserves as a precious living heritage, not in order to keep it hidden but to communicate it.

• Having been sent and evangelized, the Church herself sends out evangelizers. She puts on their lips the saving Word, she explains to them the message of which she herself is the depositary, she gives them the mandate which she herself has received and she sends them out to preach. To preach not their own selves or their personal ideas,[43] but a Gospel of which neither she nor they are the absolute masters and owners, to dispose of it as they wish, but a Gospel of which they are the ministers, in order to pass it on with complete fidelity.

16 There is thus a profound link between Christ, the Church and evangelization. During the period of the Church that we are living in, it is she who has the task of evangelizing. This mandate is not accomplished without her, and still less against her.

It is certainly fitting to recall this fact at a moment like the present one when it happens that not without sorrow we can hear people—whom we wish to believe are well-intentioned but who are certainly misguided in their attitude—continually claiming to love Christ but without the Church, to listen to Christ but not the Church, to belong to Christ but outside the Church. The absurdity of this dichotomy is clearly evident in this phrase of the Gospel: "Anyone who rejects you rejects me."[44] And how can one wish to love Christ without loving the Church, if the finest witness to Christ is that of St. Paul: "Christ loved the Church and sacrificed himself for her"?[45]

17 In the Church's evangelizing activity there are of course certain elements and aspects to be specially insisted on. Some of them are so important that there will be a tendency simply to identify them with evangelization. Thus it has been possible to define evangelization in terms of proclaiming Christ to those who do not know Him, of preaching, of catechesis, of conferring Baptism and the other sacraments.

Any partial and fragmentary definition which attempts to render the reality of evangelization in all its richness, complexity and dynamism does so only at the risk of impoverishing it and even of distorting it. It is impossible to grasp

43. Cf. *2 Cor* 4:5; Saint Augustine *Sermo* XLVI, *De Pastoribus:* CCL, XLI, pp. 529–530.

44. *Lk* 10:16; cf. Saint Cyprian, *De Unitate Ecclesiae*, 14: PL 4, 527; Saint Augustine, *Enarrat*, 88, *Sermo*, 2, 14: PL 37, 1140; Saint John Chrysostom, *Hom. de capto Eutropio*, 6: p. 52, 462.

45. *Eph* 5:25.

the concept of evangelization unless one tries to keep in view all its essential elements.

These elements were strongly emphasized at the last Synod, and are still the subject of frequent study, as a result of the Synod's work. We rejoice in the fact that these elements basically follow the lines of those transmitted to us by the Second Vatican Council, especially in *"Lumen gentium," "Gaudium et spes"* and *"Ad gentes."*

18 For the Church, evangelizing means bringing the Good News into all the strata of humanity, and through its influence transforming humanity from within and making it new: "Now I am making the whole of creation new."[46] But there is no new humanity if there are not first of all new persons renewed by Baptism[47] and by lives lived according to the Gospel.[48] The purpose of evangelization is therefore precisely this interior change, and if it had to be expressed in one sentence the best way of stating it would be to say that the Church evangelizes when she seeks to convert,[49] solely through the divine power of the message she proclaims, both the personal and collective consciences of people, the activities in which they engage, and the lives and concrete milieu which are theirs.

19 Strata of humanity which are transformed: for the Church it is a question not only of preaching the Gospel in ever wider geographic areas or to ever greater numbers of people, but also of affecting and as it were upsetting, through the power of the Gospel, mankind's criteria of judgment, determining values, points of interest, lines of thought, sources of inspiration and models of life, which are in contrast with the Word of God and the plan of salvation.

20 All this could he expressed in the following words: what matters is to evangelize man's culture and cultures (not in a purely decorative way, as it were, by applying a thin veneer, but in a vital way, in depth and right to their very roots), in the wide and rich sense which these terms have in *Gaudium et spes*,[50] always taking the person as one's starting-point and always coming back to the relationships of people among themselves and with God.

The Gospel, and therefore evangelization, are certainly not identical with culture, and they are independent in regard to all cultures. Nevertheless, the kingdom which the Gospel proclaims is lived by men who are profoundly

---

46. *Rev.* 21:5; cf. *2 Cor* 5:17; *Gal* 6:15.
47. Cf. *Rom* 6:4.
48. Cf. *Eph* 4:24–25; *Col* 3:9–10.
49. Cf. *Rom* 1:16; *1 Cor* 1:18, 2:4.
50. Cf. 53: *AAS* 58 (1966), p. 1075.

linked to a culture, and the building up of the kingdom cannot avoid borrowing the elements of human culture or cultures. Though independent of cultures, the Gospel and evangelization are not necessarily incompatible with them; rather they are capable of permeating them all without becoming subject to any one of them.

The split between the Gospel and culture is without a doubt the drama of our time, just as it was of other times. Therefore every effort must be made to ensure a full evangelization of culture, or more correctly of cultures. They have to be regenerated by an encounter with the Gospel. But this encounter will not take place if the Gospel is not proclaimed.

21 Above all the Gospel must be proclaimed by witness. Take a Christian or a handful of Christians who, in the midst of their own community, show their capacity for understanding and acceptance, their sharing of life and destiny with other people, their solidarity with the efforts of all for whatever is noble and good. Let us suppose that, in addition, they radiate in an altogether simple and unaffected way their faith in values that go beyond current values, and their hope in something that is not seen and that one would not dare to imagine. Through this wordless witness these Christians stir up irresistible questions in the hearts of those who see how they live: Why are they like this? Why do they live in this way? What or who is it that inspires them? Why are they in our midst? Such a witness is already a silent proclamation of the Good News and a very powerful and effective one. Here we have an initial act of evangelization. The above questions will ask, whether they are people to whom Christ has never been proclaimed, or baptized people who do not practice, or people who live as nominal Christians but according to principles that are in no way Christian, or people who are seeking, and not without suffering, something or someone whom they sense but cannot name. Other questions will arise, deeper and more demanding ones, questions evoked by this witness which involves presence, sharing, solidarity, and which is an essential element, and generally the first one, in evangelization."[51]

All Christians are called to this witness, and in this way they can be real evangelizers. We are thinking especially of the responsibility incumbent on immigrants in the country that receives them.

22 Nevertheless this always remains insufficient, because even the finest witness will prove ineffective in the long run if it is not explained, justified—what Peter called always having "your answer ready for people who ask you the reason

---

51. Cf. Tertullian *Apologeticum*, 39: CCL, I, pp. 150–153; Minucius Felix, *Octavius* 9 and 31: CSLP, Turin (1963), pp. 11–13, 47–48.

for the hope that you all have"[52]—and made explicit by a clear and unequivocal proclamation of the Lord Jesus. The Good News proclaimed by the witness of life sooner or later has to be proclaimed by the word of life. There is no true evangelization if the name, the teaching, the life, the promises, the kingdom and the mystery of Jesus of Nazareth, the Son of God are not proclaimed. The history of the Church, from the discourse of Peter on the morning of Pentecost onwards, has been intermingled and identified with the history of this proclamation. At every new phase of human history, the Church, constantly gripped by the desire to evangelize, has but one preoccupation: whom to send to proclaim the mystery of Jesus? In what way is this mystery to be proclaimed? How can one ensure that it will resound and reach all those who should hear it? This proclamation—kerygma, preaching or catechesis—occupies such an important place in evangelization that it has often become synonymous with it; and yet it is only one aspect of evangelization.

23 In fact the proclamation only reaches full development when it is listened to, accepted and assimilated, and when it arouses a genuine adherence in the one who has thus received it. An adherence to the truths which the Lord in His mercy has revealed; still more, an adherence to a program of life—a life henceforth transformed—which He proposes. In a word, adherence to the kingdom, that is to say, to the "new world," to the new state of things, to the new manner of being, of living, of living in community, which the Gospel inaugurates. Such an adherence, which cannot remain abstract and unincarnated, reveals itself concretely by a visible entry into a community of believers. Thus those whose life has been transformed enter a community which is itself a sign of transformation, a sign of newness of life: it is the Church, the visible sacrament of salvation.[53] Our entry into the ecclesial community will in its turn be expressed through many other signs which prolong and unfold the sign of the Church. In the dynamism of evangelization, a person who accepts the Church as the Word which saves[54] normally translates it into the following sacramental acts: adherence to the Church, and acceptance of the sacraments, which manifest and support this adherence through the grace which they confer.

24 Finally, the person who has been evangelized goes on to evangelize others. Here lies the test of truth, the touchstone of evangelization: it is unthinkable

---

52. *1 Pt* 3:15.

53. Cf. Second Vatican Ecumenical Council, Dogmatic Constitution on the Church *Lumen Gentium*, 1, 9, 48; *AAS* 57 (1965), pp. 5, 12-14, 53-54; Pastoral Constitution on the Church in the Modern World *Gaudium et Spes*, 42, 45, *AAS* 58 (1966), pp. 1060–1061, 1065–1066; Decree on the Church's Missionary Activity *Ad Gentes*, 1, 5: *AAS* 58 (1966), pp. 947, 951–952.

54. Cf. *Rom* 1:16; *1 Cor* 1:18.

that a person should accept the Word and give himself to the kingdom without becoming a person who bears witness to it and proclaims it in his turn.

To complete these considerations on the meaning of evangelization, a final observation must be made, one which we consider will help to clarify the reflections that follow.

Evangelization, as we have said, is a complex process made up of varied elements: the renewal of humanity, witness, explicit proclamation, inner adherence, entry into the community, acceptance of signs, apostolic initiative. These elements may appear to be contradictory, indeed mutually exclusive. In fact they are complementary and mutually enriching. Each one must always be seen in relationship with the others. The value of the last Synod was to have constantly invited us to relate these elements rather than to place them in opposition one to the other, in order to reach a full understanding of the Church's evangelizing activity.

It is this global vision which we now wish to outline, by examining the content of evangelization and the methods of evangelizing and by clarifying to whom the Gospel message is addressed and who today is responsible for it.

25 In the message which the Church proclaims there are certainly many secondary elements. Their presentation depends greatly on changing circumstances. They themselves also change. But there is the essential content, the living substance, which cannot be modified or ignored without seriously diluting the nature of evangelization itself.

26 It is not superfluous to recall the following points: to evangelize is first of all to bear witness, in a simple and direct way, to God revealed by Jesus Christ, in the Holy Spirit, to bear witness that in His Son God has loved the world—that in His Incarnate Word He has given being to all things and has called men to eternal life. Perhaps this attestation of God will be for many people the unknown God[55] whom they adore without giving Him a name, or whom they seek by a secret call of the heart when they experience the emptiness of all idols. But it is fully evangelizing in manifesting the fact that for man the Creator is not an anonymous and remote power; He is the Father: "... that we should be called children of God; and so we are."[56] And thus we are one another's brothers and sisters in God.

27 Evangelization will also always contain—as the foundation, center, and at the same time, summit of its dynamism—a clear proclamation that, in Jesus Christ, the Son of God made man, who died and rose from the dead, salvation

---

55. Cf. Acts 17:22–23.
56. 1 Jn 3:1; cf. Rom 8:14–17.

is offered to all men, as a gift of God's grace and mercy.[57] And not an immanent salvation, meeting material or even spiritual needs, restricted to the framework of temporal existence and completely identified with temporal desires, hopes, affairs and struggles, but a salvation which exceeds all these limits in order to reach fulfillment in a communion with the one and only divine Absolute: a transcendent and eschatological salvation, which indeed has its beginning in this life but which is fulfilled in eternity.

28 Consequently evangelization cannot but include the prophetic proclamation of a hereafter, man's profound and definitive calling, in both continuity and discontinuity with the present situation: beyond time and history, beyond the transient reality of this world, and beyond the things of this world, of which a hidden dimension will one day be revealed—beyond man himself, whose true destiny is not restricted to his temporal aspect but will be revealed in the future life.[58] Evangelization therefore also includes the preaching of hope in the promises made by God in the new Covenant in Jesus Christ; the preaching of God's love for us and of our love for God; the preaching of brotherly love for all men—the capacity of giving and forgiving, of self-denial, of helping one's brother and sister—which, springing from the love of God, is the kernel of the Gospel; the preaching of the mystery of evil and of the active search for good. The preaching likewise—and this is always urgent—of the search for God Himself through prayer which is principally that of adoration and thanksgiving, but also through communion with the visible sign of the encounter with God which is the Church of Jesus Christ; and this communion in its turn is expressed by the application of those other signs of Christ living and acting in the Church which are the sacraments. To live the sacraments in this way, bringing their celebration to a true fullness, is not, as some would claim, to impede or to accept a distortion of evangelization: it is rather to complete it. For in its totality, evangelization—over and above the preaching of a message—consists in the implantation of the Church, which does not exist without the driving force which is the sacramental life culminating in the Eucharist.[59]

29 But evangelization would not be complete if it did not take account of the unceasing interplay of the Gospel and of man's concrete life, both personal and

---

57. Cf. *Eph* 2:8; *Rom* 1:16. Cf. Sacred Congregation for the Doctrine of the Faith, *Declaratio ad fidem tuendam in mysteria Incarnationis et SS. Trinitatis e quibusdam recentibus erroribus* (21 February 1972): *AAS* 64 (1972), pp. 237–241.

58. Cf. *1 Jn* 3:2; *Rom* 8:29; *Phil* 3: 20-21. Cf. Second Vatican Ecumenical Council, Dogmatic Constitution on the Church *Lumen Gentium* 48–51: *AAS* 57 (1965), pp. 53–58.

59. Cf. Sacred Congregation for the Doctrine of the Faith, *Declaratio circa Catholicam Doctrinam de Ecclesia contra nonnullos errores hodiernos tuendam* (24 June 1973): *AAS* 65 (1973), pp. 396–408.

social. This is why evangelization involves an explicit message, adapted to the different situations constantly being realized, about the rights and duties of every human being, about family life without which personal growth and development is hardly possible,[60] about life in society, about international life, peace, justice and development—a message especially energetic today about liberation.

30 It is well known in what terms numerous bishops from all the continents spoke of this at the last Synod, especially the bishops from the Third World, with a pastoral accent resonant with the voice of the millions of sons and daughters of the Church who make up those peoples. Peoples, as we know, engaged with all their energy in the effort and struggle to overcome everything which condemns them to remain on the margin of life: famine, chronic disease, illiteracy, poverty, injustices in international relations and especially in commercial exchanges, situations of economic and cultural neo-colonialism sometimes as cruel as the old political colonialism. The Church, as the bishops repeated, has the duty to proclaim the liberation of millions of human beings, many of whom are her own children—the duty of assisting the birth of this liberation, of giving witness to it, of ensuring that it is complete. This is not foreign to evangelization.

31 Between evangelization and human advancement—development and liberation—there are in fact profound links. These include links of an anthropological order, because the man who is to be evangelized is not an abstract being but is subject to social and economic questions. They also include links in the theological order, since one cannot dissociate the plan of creation from the plan of Redemption. The latter plan touches the very concrete situations of injustice to be combated and of justice to be restored. They include links of the eminently evangelical order, which is that of charity: how in fact can one proclaim the new commandment without promoting in justice and in peace the true, authentic advancement of man? We ourself have taken care to point this out, by recalling that it is impossible to accept "that in evangelization one could or should ignore the importance of the problems so much discussed today, concerning justice, liberation, development and peace in the world. This would be to forget the lesson which comes to us from the Gospel concerning love of our neighbor who is suffering and in need."[61]

---

60. Cf. Second Vatican Ecumenical Council, Pastoral Constitution on the Church in the Modern World *Gaudium et Spes*, 47–52: *AAS* 58 (1966): pp. 1067–1074; Paul VI, Encyclical Letter *Humanae Vitae*: *AAS* 60 (1968), pp. 481–503.

61. Paul VI, *Address for the opening of the Third General Assembly of the Synod of Bishops* (27 September 1974): *AAS* 66 (1974), p. 562.

The same voices which during the Synod touched on this burning theme with zeal, intelligence and courage have, to our great joy, furnished the enlightening principles for a proper understanding of the importance and profound meaning of liberation, such as it was proclaimed and achieved by Jesus of Nazareth and such as it is preached by the Church.

32 We must not ignore the fact that many, even generous Christians who are sensitive to the dramatic questions involved in the problem of liberation, in their wish to commit the Church to the liberation effort are frequently tempted to reduce her mission to the dimensions of a simply temporal project. They would reduce her aims to a man-centered goal; the salvation of which she is the messenger would be reduced to material well-being. Her activity, forgetful of all spiritual and religious preoccupation, would become initiatives of the political or social order. But if this were so, the Church would lose her fundamental meaning. Her message of liberation would no longer have any originality and would easily be open to monopolization and manipulation by ideological systems and political parties. She would have no more authority to proclaim freedom as in the name of God. This is why we have wished to emphasize, in the same address at the opening of the Synod, "the need to restate clearly the specifically religious finality of evangelization. This latter would lose its reason for existence if it were to diverge from the religious axis that guides it: the kingdom of God, before anything else, in its fully theological meaning. . . ."[62]

33 With regard to the liberation which evangelization proclaims and strives to put into practice one should rather say this:

• It cannot be contained in the simple and restricted dimension of economics, politics, social or cultural life; it must envisage the whole man, in all his aspects, right up to and including his openness to the absolute, even the divine Absolute;

• It is therefore attached to a view of man which it can never sacrifice to the needs of any strategy, practice or short-term efficiency.

34 Hence, when preaching liberation and associating herself with those who are working and suffering for it, the Church is certainly not willing to restrict her mission only to the religious field and dissociate herself from man's temporal problems. Nevertheless she reaffirms the primacy of her spiritual vocation and refuses to replace the proclamation of the kingdom by the proclamation of forms of human liberation—she even states that her contribution to liberation is incomplete if she neglects to proclaim salvation in Jesus Christ.

62. *Ibid.*

35 The Church links human liberation and salvation in Jesus Christ, but she never identifies them, because she knows through revelation, historical experience and the reflection of faith that not every notion of liberation is necessarily consistent and compatible with an evangelical vision of man, of things and of events; she knows too that in order that God's kingdom should come it is not enough to establish liberation and to create well-being and development.

And what is more, the Church has the firm conviction that all temporal liberation, all political liberation—even if it endeavors to find its justification in such or such a page of the Old or New Testament, even if it claims for its ideological postulates and its norms of action theological data and conclusions, even if it pretends to be today's theology—carries within itself the germ of its own negation and fails to reach the ideal that it proposes for itself whenever its profound motives are not those of justice in charity, whenever its zeal lacks a truly spiritual dimension and whenever its final goal is not salvation and happiness in God.

36 The Church considers it to be undoubtedly important to build up structures which are more human, more just, more respectful of the rights of the person and less oppressive and less enslaving, but she is conscious that the best structures and the most idealized systems soon become inhuman if the inhuman inclinations of the human heart are not made wholesome, if those who live in these structures or who rule them do not undergo a conversion of heart and of outlook.

37 The Church cannot accept violence, especially the force of arms—which is uncontrollable once it is let loose—and indiscriminate death as the path to liberation, because she knows that violence always provokes violence and irresistibly engenders new forms of oppression and enslavement which are often harder to bear than those from which they claimed to bring freedom. We said this clearly during our journey in Colombia: "We exhort you not to place your trust in violence and revolution: that is contrary to the Christian spirit, and it can also delay instead of advancing that social uplifting to which you lawfully aspire."[63] "We must say and reaffirm that violence is not in accord with the Gospel, that it is not Christian; and that sudden or violent changes of structures would be deceitful, ineffective of themselves, and certainly not in conformity with the dignity of the people."[64]

---

63. Paul VI, *Address to the Campesinos of Colombia* (23 August 1968): *AAS* 60 (1968), p. 623.

64. Paul VI, *Address for the Day of Development at Bogota* (23 August 1968): *AAS* 60 (1968), p. 627; Cf. Saint Augustine, *Epistola* 229, 2: PL 33, 1020.

38 Having said this, we rejoice that the Church is becoming ever more conscious of the proper manner and strictly evangelical means that she possesses in order to collaborate in the liberation of many. And what is she doing? She is trying more and more to encourage large numbers of Christians to devote themselves to the liberation of men. She is providing these Christian "liberators" with the inspiration of faith, the motivation of fraternal love, a social teaching which the true Christian cannot ignore and which he must make the foundation of his wisdom and of his experience in order to translate it concretely into forms of action, participation and commitment. All this must characterize the spirit of a committed Christian, without confusion with tactical attitudes or with the service of a political system. The Church strives always to insert the Christian struggle for liberation into the universal plan of salvation which she herself proclaims.

What we have just recalled comes out more than once in the Synod debates. In fact we devoted to this theme a few clarifying words in our address to the Fathers at the end of the assembly.[65]

It is to be hoped that all these considerations will help to remove the ambiguity which the word "liberation" very often takes on in ideologies, political systems or groups. The liberation which evangelization proclaims and prepares is the one which Christ Himself announced and gave to man by His sacrifice.

39 The necessity of ensuring fundamental human rights cannot be separated from this just liberation which is bound up with evangelization and which endeavors to secure structures safeguarding human freedoms. Among these fundamental human rights, religious liberty occupies a place of primary importance. We recently spoke of the relevance of this matter, emphasizing "how many Christians still today, because they are Christians, because they are Catholics, live oppressed by systematic persecution! The drama of fidelity to Christ and of the freedom of religion continues, even if it is disguised by categorical declarations in favor of the rights of the person and of life in society!"[66]

40 The obvious importance of the content of evangelization must not overshadow the importance of the ways and means.

This question of "how to evangelize" is permanently relevant, because the methods of evangelizing vary according to the different circumstances of time, place and culture, and because they thereby present a certain challenge to our capacity for discovery and adaptation.

---

65. Paul VI, *Address for the closing of the Third General Assembly of the Synod of Bishops* (26 October 1974); *AAS* 66 (1974), p. 637.

66. Paul VI, *Address given on 15 October 1975: L'Osservatore Romano* (17 October 1975).

On us particularly, the pastors of the Church, rests the responsibility for reshaping with boldness and wisdom, but in complete fidelity to the content of evangelization, the means that are most suitable and effective for communicating the Gospel message to the men and women of our times.

Let it suffice, in this meditation, to mention a number of methods which, for one reason or another, have a fundamental importance.

41 Without repeating everything that we have already mentioned, it is appropriate first of all to emphasize the following point: for the Church, the first means of evangelization is the witness of an authentically Christian life, given over to God in a communion that nothing should destroy and at the same time given to one's neighbor with limitless zeal. As we said recently to a group of lay people, "Modern man listens more willingly to witnesses than to teachers, and if he does listen to teachers, it is because they are witnesses."[67] St. Peter expressed this well when he held up the example of a reverent and chaste life that wins over even without a word those who refuse to obey the word.[68] It is therefore primarily by her conduct and by her life that the Church will evangelize the world, in other words, by her living witness of fidelity to the Lord Jesus—the witness of poverty and detachment, of freedom in the face of the powers of this world, in short, the witness of sanctity.

42 Secondly, it is not superfluous to emphasize the importance and necessity of preaching. "And how are they to believe in him of whom they have never heard? And how are they to hear without a preacher? . . . So faith comes from what is heard and what is heard comes by the preaching of Christ."[69] This law once laid down by the Apostle Paul maintains its full force today.

Preaching, the verbal proclamation of a message, is indeed always indispensable. We are well aware that modern man is sated by talk; he is obviously often tired of listening and, what is worse, impervious to words. We are also aware that many psychologists and sociologists express the view that modern man has passed beyond the civilization of the word, which is now ineffective and useless, and that today he lives in the civilization of the image. These facts should certainly impel us to employ, for the purpose of transmitting the Gospel message, the modern means which this civilization has produced. Very positive efforts have in fact already been made in this sphere. We cannot but praise them and encourage their further development. The fatigue produced these days by so

---

67. Pope Paul VI, *Address to the Members of the Consilium de Laicis* (2 October 1974): *AAS* 66 (1974), p. 568.

68. Cf. *1 Pt* 3:1.

69. *Rom* 10:14, 17.

much empty talk and the relevance of many other forms of communication must not however diminish the permanent power of the word, or cause a loss of confidence in it. The word remains ever relevant, especially when it is the bearer of the power of God.[70] This is why St. Paul's axiom, "Faith comes from what is heard,"[71] also retains its relevance: it is the Word that is heard which leads to belief.

43 This evangelizing preaching takes on many forms, and zeal will inspire the reshaping of them almost indefinitely. In fact there are innumerable events in life and human situations which offer the opportunity for a discreet but incisive statement of what the Lord has to say in this or that particular circumstance. It suffices to have true spiritual sensitivity for reading God's message in events. But at a time when the liturgy renewed by the Council has given greatly increased value to the Liturgy of the Word, it would be a mistake not to see in the homily an important and very adaptable instrument of evangelization. Of course it is necessary to know and put to good use the exigencies and the possibilities of the homily, so that it can acquire all its pastoral effectiveness. But above all it is necessary to be convinced of this and to devote oneself to it with love. This preaching, inserted in a unique way into the Eucharistic celebration, from which it receives special force and vigor, certainly has a particular role in evangelization, to the extent that it expresses the profound faith of the sacred minister and is impregnated with love. The faithful assembled as a Paschal Church, celebrating the feast of the Lord present in their midst, expect much from this preaching, and will greatly benefit from it provided that it is simple, clear, direct, well-adapted, profoundly dependent on Gospel teaching and faithful to the magisterium, animated by a balanced apostolic ardor coming from its own characteristic nature, full of hope, fostering belief, and productive of peace and unity. Many parochial or other communities live and are held together thanks to the Sunday homily, when it possesses these qualities.

Let us add that, thanks to the same liturgical renewal, the Eucharistic celebration is not the only appropriate moment for the homily. The homily has a place and must not be neglected in the celebration of all the sacraments, at paraliturgies, and in assemblies of the faithful. It will always be a privileged occasion for communicating the Word of the Lord.

44 A means of evangelization that must not be neglected is that of catechetical instruction. The intelligence, especially that of children and young people,

---

70. Cf. *1 Cor* 2:1–5.
71. *Rom* 10:17.

needs to learn through systematic religious instruction the fundamental teachings, the living content of the truth which God has wished to convey to us and which the Church has sought to express in an ever richer fashion during the course of her long history. No one will deny that this instruction must be given to form patterns of Christian living and not to remain only notional. Truly the effort for evangelization will profit greatly—at the level of catechetical instruction given at church, in the schools, where this is possible, and in every case in Christian homes—if those giving catechetical instruction have suitable texts, updated with wisdom and competence, under the authority of the bishops. The methods must be adapted to the age, culture and aptitude of the persons concerned, they must seek always to fix in the memory, intelligence and heart the essential truths that must impregnate all of life. It is necessary above all to prepare good instructors—parochial catechists, teachers, parents—who are desirous of perfecting themselves in this superior art, which is indispensable and requires religious instruction. Moreover, without neglecting in any way the training of children, one sees that present conditions render ever more urgent catechetical instruction, under the form of the catechumenate, for innumerable young people and adults who, touched by grace, discover little by little the face of Christ and feel the need of giving themselves to Him.

45 Our century is characterized by the mass media or means of social communication, and the first proclamation, catechesis or the further deepening of faith cannot do without these means, as we have already emphasized.

When they are put at the service of the Gospel, they are capable of increasing almost indefinitely the area in which the Word of God is heard; they enable the Good News to reach millions of people. The Church would feel guilty before the Lord if she did not utilize these powerful means that human skill is daily rendering more perfect. It is through them that she proclaims "from the housetops"[72] the message of which she is the depositary. In them she finds a modern and effective version of the pulpit. Thanks to them she succeeds in speaking to the multitudes.

Nevertheless the use of the means of social communication for evangelization presents a challenge: through them the evangelical message should reach vast numbers of people, but with the capacity of piercing the conscience of each individual, of implanting itself in his heart as though he were the only person being addressed, with all his most individual and personal qualities, and evoke an entirely personal adherence and commitment.

---

72. Cf. *Mt* 10:27; *Lk* 12:3.

46 For this reason, side by side with the collective proclamation of the Gospel, the other form of transmission, the person-to-person one, remains valid and important. The Lord often used it (for example, with Nicodemus, Zacchaeus, the Samaritan woman, Simon the Pharisee), and so did the apostles. In the long run, is there any other way of handing on the Gospel than by transmitting to another person one's personal experience of faith? It must not happen that the pressing need to proclaim the Good News to the multitudes should cause us to forget this form of proclamation whereby an individual's personal conscience is reached and touched by an entirely unique word that he receives from someone else. We can never sufficiently praise those priests who through the sacrament of Penance or through pastoral dialogue show their readiness to guide people in the ways of the Gospel, to support them in their efforts, to raise them up if they have fallen, and always to assist them with discernment and availability.

47 Yet, one can never sufficiently stress the fact that evangelization does not consist only of the preaching and teaching of a doctrine. For evangelization must touch life: the natural life to which it gives a new meaning, thanks to the evangelical perspectives that it reveals; and the supernatural life, which is not the negation but the purification and elevation of the natural life.

This supernatural life finds its living expression in the seven sacraments and in the admirable radiation of grace and holiness which they possess.

Evangelization thus exercises its full capacity when it achieves the most intimate relationship, or better still, a permanent and unbroken intercommunication, between the Word and the sacraments. In a certain sense it is a mistake to make a contrast between evangelization and sacramentalization, as is sometimes done. It is indeed true that a certain way of administering the sacraments, without the solid support of catechesis regarding these same sacraments and a global catechesis, could end up by depriving them of their effectiveness to a great extent. The role of evangelization is precisely to educate people in the faith in such a way as to lead each individual Christian to live the sacraments as true sacraments of faith—and not to receive them passively or reluctantly.

48 Here we touch upon an aspect of evangelization which cannot leave us insensitive. We wish to speak about what today is often called popular religiosity.

One finds among the people particular expressions of the search for God and for faith, both in the regions where the Church has been established for centuries and where she is in the course of becoming established. These expressions were for a long time regarded as less pure and were sometimes despised, but today they are almost everywhere being rediscovered. During the last Synod the bishops studied their significance with remarkable pastoral realism and zeal.

Popular religiosity, of course, certainly has its limits. It is often subject to penetration by many distortions of religion and even superstitions. It frequently remains at the level of forms of worship not involving a true acceptance by faith. It can even lead to the creation of sects and endanger the true ecclesial community.

But if it is well oriented, above all by a pedagogy of evangelization, it is rich in values. It manifests a thirst for God which only the simple and poor can know. It makes people capable of generosity and sacrifice even to the point of heroism, when it is a question of manifesting belief. It involves an acute awareness of profound attributes of God: fatherhood, providence, loving and constant presence. It engenders interior attitudes rarely observed to the same degree elsewhere: patience, the sense of the cross in daily life, detachment, openness to others, devotion. By reason of these aspects, we readily call it "popular piety," that is, religion of the people, rather than religiosity.

Pastoral charity must dictate to all those whom the Lord has placed as leaders of the ecclesial communities the proper attitude in regard to this reality, which is at the same time so rich and so vulnerable. Above all one must be sensitive to it, know how to perceive its interior dimensions and undeniable values, be ready to help it to overcome its risks of deviation. When it is well oriented, this popular religiosity can be more and more for multitudes of our people a true encounter with God in Jesus Christ.

49 Jesus' last words in St. Mark's Gospel confer on the evangelization which the Lord entrusts to His apostles a limitless universality: "Go out to the whole world; proclaim the Good News to all creation."[73]

The Twelve and the first generation of Christians understood well the lesson of this text and other similar ones; they made them into a program of action. Even persecution, by scattering the apostles, helped to spread the Word and to establish the Church in ever more distant regions. The admission of Paul to the rank of the apostles and his charism as the preacher to the pagans (the non-Jews) of Jesus' Coming underlined this universality still more.

50 In the course of twenty centuries of history, the generations of Christians have periodically faced various obstacles to this universal mission. On the one hand, on the part of the evangelizers themselves, there has been the temptation for various reasons to narrow down the field of their missionary activity. On the other hand, there has been the often humanly insurmountable resistance of the people being addressed by the evangelizer. Furthermore, we must note with sadness that the evangelizing work of the Church is strongly opposed, if

---

73. *Mk* 16:15.

not prevented, by certain public powers. Even in our own day it happens that preachers of God's Word are deprived of their rights, persecuted, threatened or eliminated solely for preaching Jesus Christ and His Gospel. But we are confident that despite these painful trials the activity of these apostles will never meet final failure in any part of the world.

Despite such adversities, the Church constantly renews her deepest inspiration, that which comes to her directly from the Lord: To the whole world! To all creation! Right to the ends of the earth! She did this once more at the last Synod, as an appeal not to imprison the proclamation of the Gospel by limiting it to one sector of mankind or to one class of people or to a single type of civilization. Some examples are revealing.

51 To reveal Jesus Christ and His Gospel to those who do not know them has been, ever since the morning of Pentecost, the fundamental program which the Church has taken on as received from her Founder. The whole of the New Testament, and in a special way the Acts of the Apostles, bears witness to a privileged and in a sense exemplary moment of this missionary effort which will subsequently leave its mark on the whole history of the Church.

She carries out this first proclamation of Jesus Christ by a complex and diversified activity which is sometimes termed "pre-evangelization" but which is already evangelization in a true sense, although at its initial and still incomplete stage. An almost indefinite range of means can be used for this purpose: explicit preaching, of course, but also art, the scientific approach, philosophical research and legitimate recourse to the sentiments of the human heart.

52 This first proclamation is addressed especially to those who have never heard the Good News of Jesus, or to children. But, as a result of the frequent situations of dechristianization in our day, it also proves equally necessary for innumerable people who have been baptized but who live quite outside Christian life, for simple people who have a certain faith but an imperfect knowledge of the foundations of that faith, for intellectuals who feel the need to know Jesus Christ in a light different from the instruction they received as children, and for many others.

53 This first proclamation is also addressed to the immense sections of mankind who practice non-Christian religions. The Church respects and esteems these non-Christian religions because they are the living expression of the soul of vast groups of people. They carry within them the echo of thousands of years of searching for God, a quest which is incomplete but often made with great sincerity and righteousness of heart. They possess an impressive patrimony of deeply religious texts. They have taught generations of people how to pray.

They are all impregnated with innumerable "seeds of the Word"[74] and can constitute a true "preparation for the Gospel,"[75] to quote a felicitous term used by the Second Vatican Council and borrowed from Eusebius of Caesarea.

Such a situation certainly raises complex and delicate questions that must be studied in the light of Christian Tradition and the Church's magisterium, in order to offer to the missionaries of today and of tomorrow new horizons in their contacts with non-Christian religions. We wish to point out, above all today, that neither respect and esteem for these religions nor the complexity of the questions raised is an invitation to the Church to withhold from these non-Christians the proclamation of Jesus Christ. On the contrary the Church holds that these multitudes have the right to know the riches of the mystery of Christ[76]—riches in which we believe that the whole of humanity can find, in unsuspected fullness, everything that it is gropingly searching for concerning God, man and his destiny, life and death, and truth. Even in the face of natural religious expressions most worthy of esteem, the Church finds support in the fact that the religion of Jesus, which she proclaims through evangelization, objectively places man in relation with the plan of God, with His living presence and with His action; she thus causes an encounter with the mystery of divine paternity that bends over towards humanity. In other words, our religion effectively establishes with God an authentic and living relationship which the other religions do not succeed in doing, even though they have, as it were, their arms stretched out towards heaven.

This is why the Church keeps her missionary spirit alive, and even wishes to intensify it in the moment of history in which we are living. She feels responsible before entire peoples. She has no rest so long as she has not done her best to proclaim the Good News of Jesus the Savior. She is always preparing new generations of apostles. Let us state this fact with joy at a time when there are not lacking those who think and even say that ardor and the apostolic spirit are exhausted, and that the time of the missions is now past. The Synod has replied that the missionary proclamation never ceases and that the Church will always be striving for the fulfillment of this proclamation.

---

74. Cf. Saint Justin, *I Apol.* 46, 1-4: PG 6, *II Apol.* 7 (8) 1–4; 10, 1–3; 13, 3–4; *Florilegium Patristicum II*, Bonn (1911), pp. 81, 125, 129, 133; Clement of Alexandria, *Stromata I*, 19, 91; 94; S. Ch. pp. 117–118; 119–110; Cf. Second Vatican Ecumenical Council, Decree on the Church's Missionary Activity *Ad Gentes*, 11: AAS 58 (1966), p. 960; cf. Second Vatican Ecumenical Council, Dogmatic Constitution on the Church *Lumen Gentium*, 17: AAS 57 (1965), p. 20.

75. Eusebuis of Caesarea, *Praeparatio Evangelica* I, 1: PG 21, 26–28; cf. Second Vatican Ecumenical Council, Dogmatic Constitution on the Church *Lumen Gentium*, 16: AAS 57 (1965), p. 20.

76. Cf. *Eph* 3:8.

54 Nevertheless the Church does not feel dispensed from paying unflagging attention also to those who have received the faith and who have been in contact with the Gospel often for generations. Thus she seeks to deepen, consolidate, nourish and make ever more mature the faith of those who are already called the faithful or believers, in order that they may be so still more.

This faith is nearly always today exposed to secularism, even to militant atheism. It is a faith exposed to trials and threats, and even more, a faith besieged and actively opposed. It runs the risk of perishing from suffocation or starvation if it is not fed and sustained each day. To evangelize must therefore very often be to give this necessary food and sustenance to the faith of believers, especially through a catechesis full of Gospel vitality and in a language suited to people and circumstances.

The Church also has a lively solicitude for the Christians who are not in full communion with her. While preparing with them the unity willed by Christ, and precisely in order to realize unity in truth, she has the consciousness that she would be gravely lacking in her duty if she did not give witness before them of the fullness of the revelation whose deposit she guards.

55 Also significant is the preoccupation of the last Synod in regard to two spheres which are very different from one another but which at the same time are very close by reason of the challenge which they make to evangelization, each in its own way.

The first sphere is the one which can be called the increase of unbelief in the modern world. The Synod endeavored to describe this modern world: how many currents of thought, values and countervalues, latent aspirations or seeds of destruction, old convictions which disappear and new convictions which arise are covered by this generic name!

From the spiritual point of view, the modern world seems to be forever immersed in what a modern author has termed "the drama of atheistic humanism."[77]

On the one hand one is forced to note in the very heart of this contemporary world the phenomenon which is becoming almost its most striking characteristic: secularism. We are not speaking of secularization, which is the effort, in itself just and legitimate and in no way incompatible with faith or religion, to discover in creation, in each thing or each happening in the universe, the laws which regulate them with a certain autonomy, but with the inner conviction that the Creator has placed these laws there. The last Council has in this sense affirmed the legitimate autonomy of culture and particularly of the sciences.[78]

77. Cf. Henri de Lubac, *Le drame de l'humanisme athee*, ed. Spes, Paris, 1945.
78. Cf. Pastoral Constitution on the Church in the Modern World *Gaudium et Spes*, 59: *AAS* 58 (1966), p. 1080.

Here we are thinking of a true secularism: a concept of the world according to which the latter is self-explanatory, without any need for recourse to God, who thus becomes superfluous and an encumbrance. This sort of secularism, in order to recognize the power of man, therefore ends up by doing without God and even by denying Him.

New forms of atheism seem to flow from it: a man centered atheism, no longer abstract and metaphysical but pragmatic, systematic and militant. Hand in hand with this atheistic secularism, we are daily faced, under the most diverse forms, with a consumer society, the pursuit of pleasure set up as the supreme value, a desire for power and domination, and discrimination of every kind: the inhuman tendencies of this "humanism."

In this same modern world, on the other hand, and this is a paradox, one cannot deny the existence of real stepping stones to Christianity, and of evangelical values at least in the form of a sense of emptiness or nostalgia. It would not be an exaggeration to say that there exists a powerful and tragic appeal to be evangelized.

56 The second sphere is that of those who do not practice. Today there is a very large number of baptized people who for the most part have not formally renounced their Baptism but who are entirely indifferent to it and not living in accordance with it. The phenomenon of the non-practicing is a very ancient one in the history of Christianity; it is the result of a natural weakness, a profound inconsistency which we unfortunately bear deep within us. Today however it shows certain new characteristics. It is often the result of the uprooting typical of our time. It also springs from the fact that Christians live in close proximity with non-believers and constantly experience the effects of unbelief. Furthermore, the non-practicing Christians of today, more so than those of previous periods, seek to explain and justify their position in the name of an interior religion, of personal independence or authenticity.

Thus we have atheists and unbelievers on the one side and those who do not practice on the other, and both groups put up a considerable resistance to evangelization. The resistance of the former takes the form of a certain refusal and an inability to grasp the new order of things, the new meaning of the world, of life and of history; such is not possible if one does not start from a divine absolute. The resistance of the second group takes the form of inertia and the slightly hostile attitude of the person who feels that he is one of the homily, who claims to know it all and to have tried it all and who no longer believes it.

Atheistic secularism and the absence of religious practice are found among adults and among the young, among the leaders of society and among the ordinary people, at all levels of education, and in both the old Churches and the young ones. The Church's evangelizing action cannot ignore these two worlds, nor must it come to a standstill when faced with them; it must constantly seek the proper means and language for presenting, or representing, to them God's revelation and faith in Jesus Christ.

57 Like Christ during the time of His preaching, like the Twelve on the morning of Pentecost, the Church too sees before her an immense multitude of people who need the Gospel and have a right to it, for God "wants everyone to be saved and reach full knowledge of the truth."[79]

The Church is deeply aware of her duty to preach salvation to all. Knowing that the Gospel message is not reserved to a small group of the initiated, the privileged or the elect, but is destined for everyone, she shares Christ's anguish at the sight of the wandering and exhausted crowds, "like sheep without a shepherd" and she often repeats His words: "I feel sorry for all these people."[80] But the Church is also conscious of the fact that, if the preaching of the Gospel is to be effective, she must address her message to the heart of the multitudes, to communities of the faithful whose action can and must reach others.

58 The last Synod devoted considerable attention to these "small communities," or *communautés de base*, because they are often talked about in the Church today. What are they, and why should they be the special beneficiaries of evangelization and at the same time evangelizers themselves?

According to the various statements heard in the Synod, such communities flourish more or less throughout the Church. They differ greatly among themselves both within the same region and even more so from one region to another.

In some regions they appear and develop, almost without exception, within the Church, having solidarity with her life, being nourished by her teaching and united with her pastors. In these cases, they spring from the need to live the Church's life more intensely, or from the desire and quest for a more human dimension such as larger ecclesial communities can only offer with difficulty, especially in the big modern cities which lend themselves both to life in the mass and to anonymity. Such communities can quite simply be in their own way an extension on the spiritual and religious level—worship, deepening of faith, fraternal charity, prayer, contact with pastors—of the small sociological community such as the village, etc. Or again their aim may be to bring together, for the purpose of listening to and meditating on the Word, for the sacraments and the bond of the agape, groups of people who are linked by age, culture, civil state or social situation: married couples, young people, professional people, etc.; people who already happen to be united in the struggle for justice,

79. *1 Tim* 2:4.
80. *Mt* 9:36; 15:32.

brotherly aid to the poor, human advancement. In still other cases they bring Christians together in places where the shortage of priests does not favor the normal life of a parish community. This is all presupposed within communities constituted by the Church, especially individual Churches and parishes.

In other regions, on the other hand, *communautés de base* come together in a spirit of bitter criticism of the Church, which they are quick to stigmatize as "institutional" and to which they set themselves up in opposition as charismatic communities, free from structures and inspired only by the Gospel. Thus their obvious characteristic is an attitude of fault-finding and of rejection with regard to the Church's outward manifestations: her hierarchy, her signs. They are radically opposed to the Church. By following these lines their main inspiration very quickly becomes ideological, and it rarely happens that they do not quickly fall victim to some political option or current of thought, and then to a system, even a party, with all the attendant risks of becoming its instrument.

The difference is already notable: the communities which by their spirit of opposition cut themselves off from the Church, and whose unity they wound, can well be called *communautés de base*, but in this case it is a strictly sociological name. They could not, without a misuse of terms, be called ecclesial *communautés de base*, even if while being hostile to the hierarchy, they claim to remain within the unity of the Church. This name belongs to the other groups, those which come together within the Church in order to unite themselves to the Church and to cause the Church to grow.

These latter communities will be a place of evangelization, for the benefit of the bigger communities, especially the individual Churches. And, as we said at the end of the last Synod, they will be a hope for the universal Church to the extent:

- that they seek their nourishment in the Word of God and do not allow themselves to be ensnared by political polarization or fashionable ideologies, which are ready to exploit their immense human potential;

- that they avoid the ever present temptation of systematic protest and a hypercritical attitude, under the pretext of authenticity and a spirit of collaboration;

- that they remain firmly attached to the local Church in which they are inserted, and to the universal Church, thus avoiding the very real danger of becoming isolated within themselves, then of believing themselves to be the only authentic Church of Christ, and hence of condemning the other ecclesial communities;

- that they maintain a sincere communion with the pastors whom the Lord gives to His Church, and with the magisterium which the Spirit of Christ has entrusted to these pastors;

• that they never look on themselves as the sole beneficiaries or sole agents of evangelization—or even the only depositaries of the Gospel—but, being aware that the Church is much more vast and diversified, accept the fact that this Church becomes incarnate in other ways than through themselves;

• that they constantly grow in missionary consciousness, fervor, commitment and zeal;

• that they show themselves to be universal in all things and never sectarian.

On these conditions, which are certainly demanding but also uplifting, the ecclesial *communautés de base* will correspond to their most fundamental vocation: as hearers of the Gospel which is proclaimed to them and privileged beneficiaries of evangelization, they will soon become proclaimers of the Gospel themselves.

59 If people proclaim in the world the Gospel of salvation, they do so by the command of, in the name of and with the grace of Christ the Savior. "They will never have a preacher unless one is sent,"[81] wrote he who was without doubt one of the greatest evangelizers. No one can do it without having been sent.

But who then has the mission of evangelizing?

The Second Vatican Council gave a clear reply to this question: it is upon the Church that "there rests, by divine mandate, the duty of going out into the whole world and preaching the gospel to every creature."[82] And in another text: "... the whole Church is missionary, and the work of evangelization is a basic duty of the People of God."[83]

We have already mentioned this intimate connection between the Church and evangelization. While the Church is proclaiming the kingdom of God and building it up, she is establishing herself in the midst of the world as the sign and instrument of this kingdom which is and which is to come. The Council repeats the following expression of St. Augustine on the missionary activity of the Twelve: "They preached the word of truth and brought forth Churches."[84]

60 The observation that the Church has been sent out and given a mandate to evangelize the world should awaken in us two convictions.

81. *Rom* 10:15.

82. Declaration on Religious Liberty *Dignitatis Humanae*, 13: *AAS* 58 (1966), p. 939; cf. Dogmatic Constitution on the Church *Lumen Gentium*, 5: *AAS* 57 (1965) pp. 7–8; Decree on the Church's Missionary Activity *Ad Gentes*, 1: *AAS* 58 (1966), p. 947.

83. Decree on the Church's Missionary Activity *Ad Gentes*, 35: *AAS* 58 (1966), p. 983.

84. Saint Augustine, *Enarratio in Ps* 44:23: CCL XXXVIII, p. 510; cf. Decree on the Church's Missionary Activity *Ad Gentes*, 1: *AAS* 58 (1966), p. 947.

The first is this: evangelization is for no one an individual and isolated act; it is one that is deeply ecclesial. When the most obscure preacher, catechist or pastor in the most distant land preaches the Gospel, gathers his little community together or administers a sacrament, even alone, he is carrying out an ecclesial act, and his action is certainly attached to the evangelizing activity of the whole Church by institutional relationships, but also by profound invisible links in the order of grace. This presupposes that he acts not in virtue of a mission which he attributes to himself or by a personal inspiration, but in union with the mission of the Church and in her name.

From this flows the second conviction: if each individual evangelizes in the name of the Church, who herself does so by virtue of a mandate from the Lord, no evangelizer is the absolute master of his evangelizing action, with a discretionary power to carry it out in accordance with individualistic criteria and perspectives; he acts in communion with the Church and her pastors.

We have remarked that the Church is entirely and completely evangelizing. This means that, in the whole world and in each part of the world where she is present, the Church feels responsible for the task of spreading the Gospel.

61 Brothers and sons and daughters, at this stage of our reflection, we wish to pause with you at a question which is particularly important at the present time. In the celebration of the liturgy, in their witness before judges and executioners and in their apologetical texts, the first Christians readily expressed their deep faith in the Church by describing her as being spread throughout the universe. They were fully conscious of belonging to a large community which neither space nor time can limit: From the just Abel right to the last of the elect,[85] "indeed to the ends of the earth,[86] "to the end of time."[87]

This is how the Lord wanted His Church to be: universal, a great tree whose branches shelter the birds of the air,[88] a net which catches fish of every kind[89] or which Peter drew in filled with one hundred and fifty-three big fish,[90] a flock which a single shepherd pastures.[91] A universal Church without boundaries or frontiers except, alas, those of the heart and mind of sinful man.

62 Nevertheless this universal Church is in practice incarnate in the individual Churches made up of such or such an actual part of mankind, speaking such

---

85. Saint Gregory the Great, Homily, in *Evangelia* 19, 1: PL 76, 1154.
86. *Acts* 1:8; cf. Didache 9, 1: Fund Patres Apostolici, 1, 22.
87. *Mt* 28:20.
88. Cf. *Mt* 13:32.
89. Cf. *Mt* 13:47.
90. Cf. *Jn* 21:11.
91. Cf. *Jn* 10:1–16.

and such a language, heirs of a cultural patrimony, of a vision of the world, of an historical past, of a particular human substratum. Receptivity to the wealth of the individual Church corresponds to a special sensitivity of modern man.

Let us be very careful not to conceive of the universal Church as the sum, or, if one can say so, the more or less anomalous federation of essentially different individual Churches. In the mind of the Lord the Church is universal by vocation and mission, but when she puts down her roots in a variety of cultural, social and human terrains, she takes on different external expressions and appearances in each part of the world.

Thus each individual Church that would voluntarily cut itself off from the universal Church would lose its relationship to God's plan and would be impoverished in its ecclesial dimension. But, at the same time, a Church *toto orbe diffusa* would become an abstraction if she did not take body and life precisely through the individual Churches. Only continual attention to these two poles of the Church will enable us to perceive the richness of this relationship between the universal Church and the individual Churches.

63 The individual Churches, intimately built up not only of people but also of aspirations, of riches and limitations, of ways of praying, of loving, of looking at life and the world, which distinguish this or that human gathering, have the task of assimilating the essence of the Gospel message and of transposing it, without the slightest betrayal of its essential truth, into the language that these particular people understand, then of proclaiming it in this language.

The transposition has to be done with the discernment, seriousness, respect and competence which the matter calls for in the field of liturgical expression,[92] and in the areas of catechesis, theological formulation, secondary ecclesial structures, and ministries. And the word "language" should be understood here less in the semantic or literary sense than in the sense which one may call anthropological and cultural.

The question is undoubtedly a delicate one. Evangelization loses much of its force and effectiveness if it does not take into consideration the actual people to whom it is addresses, if it does not use their language, their signs and symbols, if it does not answer the questions they ask, and if it does not have an impact on their concrete life. But on the other hand, evangelization risks losing its power and disappearing altogether if one empties or adulterates its content under the

---

92. Cf. Second Vatican Ecumenical Council, Constitution on the Sacred Liturgy *Sacrosanctum Concilium* 37–38: *AAS* 56 (1964), p. 110; cf. also the liturgical books and other documents subsequently issued by the Holy See for the putting into practice of the liturgical reform desired by the same Council.

pretext of translating it; if, in other words, one sacrifices this reality and destroys the unity without which there is no universality, out of a wish to adapt a universal reality to a local situation. Now, only a Church which preserves the awareness of her universality and shows that she is in fact universal is capable of having a message which can be heard by all, regardless of regional frontiers.

Legitimate attention to individual Churches cannot fail to enrich the Church. Such attention is indispensable and urgent. It responds to the very deep aspirations of peoples and human communities to find their own identity ever more clearly.

64 But this enrichment requires that the individual Churches should keep their profound openness towards the universal Church. It is quite remarkable, moreover, that the most simple Christians, the ones who are most faithful to the Gospel and most open to the true meaning of the Church, have a completely spontaneous sensitivity to this universal dimension. They instinctively and very strongly feel the need for it, they easily recognize themselves in such a dimension. They feel with it and suffer very deeply within themselves when, in the name of theories which they do not understand, they are forced to accept a Church deprived of this universality, a regionalist Church, with no horizon.

As history in fact shows, whenever an individual Church has cut itself off from the universal Church and from its living and visible center—sometimes with the best of intentions, with theological, sociological, political or pastoral arguments, or even in the desire for a certain freedom of movement or action—it has escaped only with great difficulty (if indeed it has escaped) from two equally serious dangers. The first danger is that of a withering isolationism, and then, before long, of a crumbling away, with each of its cells breaking away from it just as it itself has broken away from the central nucleus. The second danger is that of losing its freedom when, being cut off from the center and from the other Churches which gave it strength and energy, it finds itself all alone and a prey to the most varied forces of slavery and exploitation.

The more an individual Church is attached to the universal Church by solid bonds of communion, in charity and loyalty, in receptiveness to the Magisterium of Peter, in the unity of the *lex orandi* which is also the *lex credendi*, in the desire for unity with all the other Churches which make up the whole—the more such a Church will be capable of translating the treasure of faith into the legitimate variety of expressions of the profession of faith, of prayer and worship, of Christian life and conduct and of the spiritual influence on the people among which it dwells. The more will it also be truly evangelizing, that is to say, capable of drawing upon the universal patrimony in order to enable its own people to profit from it, and capable too of communicating to the universal Church the experience and the life of this people, for the benefit of all.

65 It was precisely in this sense that at the end of the last Synod we spoke clear words full of paternal affection, insisting on the role of Peter's Successor as a visible, living and dynamic principle of the unity between the Churches and thus of the universality of the one Church.[93] We also insisted on the grave responsibility incumbent upon us, but which we share with our Brothers in the Episcopate, of preserving unaltered the content of the Catholic faith which the Lord entrusted to the apostles. While being translated into all expressions, this content must be neither impaired nor mutilated. While being clothed with the outward forms proper to each people, and made explicit by theological expression which takes account of differing cultural, social and even racial milieu, it must remain the content of the Catholic faith just exactly as the ecclesial magisterium has received it and transmits it.

66 The whole Church therefore is called upon to evangelize, and yet within her we have different evangelizing tasks to accomplish. This diversity of services in the unity of the same mission makes up the richness and beauty of evangelization. We shall briefly recall these tasks.

First, we would point out in the pages of the Gospel the insistence with which the Lord entrusts to the apostles the task of proclaiming the Word. He chose them,[94] trained them during several years of intimate company,[95] constituted[96] and sent them out[97] as authorized witnesses and teachers of the message of salvation. And the Twelve in their turn sent out their successors who, in the apostolic line, continue to preach the Good News.

67 The Successor of Peter is thus, by the will of Christ, entrusted with the preeminent ministry of teaching the revealed truth. The New Testament often shows Peter "filled with the Holy Spirit" speaking in the name of all.[98] It is precisely for this reason that St. Leo the Great describes him as he who has merited the primacy of the apostolate.[99] This is also why the voice of the Church shows the Pope "at the highest point—*in apice, in specula*—of the apostolate."[100] The

---

93. Paul VI, *Address for the closing of the Third General Assembly of the Synod of Bishops* (26 October 1974): *AAS* 66 (1974), p. 636.

94. Cf. *Jn* 15:16; *Mk* 3:13–19; *Lk* 6:13–16.

95. Cf. *Acts* 1:21–22.

96. Cf. *Mk* 3:14.

97. Cf. *Mk* 3:14–15; Lk 9:2.

98. *Acts* 4:8; cf. 2:14; 3:12.

99. Cf. St. Leo the Great, *Sermo* 69, 3; *Sermo* 70, 1–3; *Sermo* 94, 3; *Sermo* 95 2: S.C. 200, pp. 50–52; 58-66; 258–260; 268.

100. Cf. First Ecumenical Council of Lyons, Constitution *Ad apostolicae dignitates: Conciliorum Oecumenicorum Decreta*, ed. Istituto per le Scienze Religiose, Bologna 1973, p. 278; Ecumenical Council of Vienne, Constitution *Ad providam Christi*, ed. cit., p. 343; Fifth Lateran Ecumenical Council,

Second Vatican Council wished to reaffirm this when it declared that "Christ's mandate to preach the Gospel to every creature (cf. *Mk* 16:15) primarily and immediately concerns the bishops with Peter and under Peter."[101]

The full, supreme and universal power"[102] which Christ gives to His Vicar for the pastoral government of His Church is this especially exercised by the Pope in the activity of preaching and causing to be preached the Good News of salvation.

68 In union with the Successor of Peter, the bishops, who are successors of the apostles, receive through the power of their episcopal ordination the authority to teach the revealed truth in the Church. They are teachers of the faith.

Associated with the bishops in the ministry of evangelization and responsible by a special title are those who through priestly ordination "act in the person of Christ."[103] They are educators of the People of God in the faith and preachers, while at the same time being ministers of the Eucharist and of the other sacraments.

We pastors are therefore invited to take note of this duty, more than any other members of the Church. What identifies our priestly service, gives a profound unity to the thousand and one tasks which claim our attention day by day and throughout our lives, and confers a distinct character on our activities, is this aim, ever present in all our action: to proclaim the Gospel of God.[104]

A mark of our identity which no doubts ought to encroach upon and no objection eclipse is this: as pastors, we have been chosen by the mercy of the Supreme Pastor,[105] in spite of our inadequacy, to proclaim with authority the Word of God, to assemble the scattered People of God, to feed this People with the signs of the action of Christ which are the sacraments, to set this People on the road to salvation, to maintain it in that unity of which we are, at different levels, active and living instruments, and unceasingly to keep this community gathered around Christ faithful to its deepest vocation. And when we do all these things, within our human limits and by the grace of God, it is a work of evangelization that we are carrying out. This includes ourself as Pastor of the

---

Constitution *In apostolici culminis*, ed. cit., p. 608; Constitution *Postquam ad universalis*, ed. cit., p. 614; Constitution *Divina disponente clementia*, ed. cit., p. 638.

101. Decree on the Church's Missionary Activity *Ad Gentes*, 38: *AAS* 58 (1966), p. 985.

102. Second Vatican Ecumenical Council, Dogmatic Constitution on the Church *Lumen Gentium*, 22: *AAS* 57 (1965), p. 26.

103. Cf. Second Vatican Ecumenical Council, Dogmatic Constitution on the Church *Lumen Gentium*, 10, 37; *AAS* 57 1965), pp. 14, 43; Decree on the Church's Missionary Activity *Ad Gentes*, 39: *AAS* 58 (1966), p. 986; Decree on the Ministry and Life of Priests *Presbyterorum Ordinis*, 2, 12, 13: *AAS* 58 (1966), pp. 992, 1010, 1011.

104. Cf. *1 Thess* 2:9.

105. Cf. *1 Pt* 5:4.

universal Church, our brother bishops at the head of the individual Churches, priests and deacons united with their bishops and whose assistants they are, by a communion which has its source in the sacrament of Orders and in the charity of the Church.

69 Religious, for their part, find in their consecrated life a privileged means of effective evangelization. At the deepest level of their being they are caught up in the dynamism of the Church's life, which is thirsty for the divine Absolute and called to holiness. It is to this holiness that they bear witness. They embody the Church in her desire to give herself completely to the radical demands of the beatitudes. By their lives they are a sign of total availability to God, the Church and the brethren.

As such they have a special importance in the context of the witness which, as we have said, is of prime importance in evangelization. At the same time as being a challenge to the world and to the Church herself, this silent witness of poverty and abnegation, of purity and sincerity, of self-sacrifice in obedience, can become an eloquent witness capable of touching also non-Christians who have good will and are sensitive to certain values.

In this perspective one perceives the role played in evangelization by religious men and women consecrated to prayer, silence, penance and sacrifice. Other religious, in great numbers, give themselves directly to the proclamation of Christ. Their missionary activity depends clearly on the hierarchy and must be coordinated with the pastoral plan which the latter adopts. But who does not see the immense contribution that these religious have brought and continue to bring to evangelization? Thanks to their consecration they are eminently willing and free to leave everything and to go and proclaim the Gospel even to the ends of the earth. They are enterprising and their apostolate is often marked by an originality, by a genius that demands admiration. They are generous: often they are found at the outposts of the mission, and they take the greatest of risks for their health and their very lives. Truly the Church owes them much.

70 Lay people, whose particular vocation places them in the midst of the world and in charge of the most varied temporal tasks, must for this very reason exercise a very special form of evangelization.

Their primary and immediate task is not to establish and develop the ecclesial community—this is the specific role of the pastors—but to put to use every Christian and evangelical possibility latent but already present and active in the affairs of the world. Their own field of evangelizing activity is the vast and complicated world of politics, society and economics, but also the world of culture, of the sciences and the arts, of international life, of the mass media. It also includes other realities which are open to evangelization, such as human love, the family, the education of children and adolescents, professional work, suffering. The more Gospel-inspired lay people there are engaged in these realities, clearly involved in them, competent to promote them and conscious that they must exercise to the full their Christian powers which are often buried and suffocated, the more these realities will be at the service of the kingdom of God and therefore of salvation in Jesus Christ, without in any way losing or sacrificing their human content but rather pointing to a transcendent dimension which is often disregarded.

71 One cannot fail to stress the evangelizing action of the family in the evangelizing apostolate of the laity.

At different moments in the Church's history and also in the Second Vatican Council, the family has well deserved the beautiful name of "domestic Church."[106] This means that there should be found in every Christian family the various aspects of the entire Church. Furthermore, the family, like the Church, ought to be a place where the Gospel is transmitted and from which the Gospel radiates.

In a family which is conscious of this mission, all the members evangelize and are evangelized. The parents not only communicate the Gospel to their children, but from their children they can themselves receive the same Gospel as deeply lived by them.

And such a family becomes the evangelizer of many other families, and of the neighborhood of which it forms part. Families resulting from a mixed marriage also have the duty of proclaiming Christ to the children in the fullness of the consequences of a common Baptism; they have moreover the difficult task of becoming builders of unity.

72 Circumstances invite us to make special mention of the young. Their increasing number and growing presence in society and likewise the problems assailing them should awaken in every one the desire to offer them with zeal and intelligence the Gospel ideal as something to be known and lived. And on the other hand, young people who are well trained in faith and prayer must become more and more the apostles of youth. The Church counts greatly on their contribution, and we ourself have often manifested our full confidence in them.

---

106. Dogmatic Constitution on the Church *Lumen Gentium*, 11: *AAS* 57 (1965), p. 16; Decree on the Apostolate of the Laity *Apostolicam Actuositatem*, 11, *AAS* 58 (1966), p. 848; Saint John Chrysostom, *In Genesim Serm.* VI, 2; VII, 1: PG 54, pp.607–68.

73 Hence the active presence of the laity in the temporal realities takes on all its importance. One cannot, however, neglect or forget the other dimension: the laity can also feel themselves called, or be called, to work with their pastors in the service of the ecclesial community for its growth and life, by exercising a great variety of ministries according to the grace and charisms which the Lord is pleased to give them.

We cannot but experience a great inner joy when we see so many pastors, religious and lay people, fired with their mission to evangelize, seeking ever more suitable ways of proclaiming the Gospel effectively. We encourage the openness which the Church is showing today in this direction and with this solicitude. It is an openness to meditation first of all, and then to ecclesial ministries capable of renewing and strengthening the evangelizing vigor of the Church.

It is certain that, side by side with the ordained ministries, whereby certain people are appointed pastors and consecrate themselves in a special way to the service of the community, the Church recognizes the place of non-ordained ministries which are able to offer a particular service to the Church.

A glance at the origins of the Church is very illuminating, and gives the benefit of an early experience in the matter of ministries. It was an experience which was all the more valuable in that it enabled the Church to consolidate herself and to grow and spread. Attention to the sources however has to be complemented by attention to the present needs of mankind and of the Church. To drink at these ever inspiring sources without sacrificing anything of their values, and at the same time to know how to adapt oneself to the demands and needs of today—these are the criteria which will make it possible to seek wisely and to discover the ministries which the Church needs and which many of her members will gladly embrace for the sake of ensuring greater vitality in the ecclesial community. These ministries will have a real pastoral value to the extent that they are established with absolute respect for unity and adhering to the directives of the pastors, who are the ones who are responsible for the Church's unity and the builders thereof.

These ministries, apparently new but closely tied up with the Church's living experience down the centuries—such as catechists, directors of prayer and chant, Christians devoted to the service of God's Word or to assisting their brethren in need, the heads of small communities, or other persons charged with the responsibility of apostolic movements—these ministries are valuable for the establishment, life, and growth of the Church, and for her capacity to influence her surroundings and to reach those who are remote from her. We owe also our special esteem to all the lay people who accept to consecrate a part of their time, their energies, and sometimes their entire lives, to the service of the missions.

A serious preparation is needed for all workers for evangelization. Such preparation is all the more necessary for those who devote themselves to the ministry of the Word. Being animated by the conviction, ceaselessly deepened, of the greatness and riches of the Word of God, those who have the mission of transmitting it must give the maximum attention to the dignity, precision and adaptation of their language. Everyone knows that the art of speaking takes on today a very great importance. How would preachers and catechists be able to neglect this?

We earnestly desire that in each individual Church the bishops should be vigilant concerning the adequate formation of all the ministers of the Word. This serious preparation will increase in them the indispensable assurance and also the enthusiasm to proclaim today Jesus Christ.

74 We would not wish to end this encounter with our beloved brethren and sons and daughters without a pressing appeal concerning the interior attitudes which must animate those who work for evangelization.

In the name of the Lord Jesus Christ, and in the name of the Apostles Peter and Paul, we wish to exhort all those who, thanks to the charisms of the Holy Spirit and to the mandate of the Church, are true evangelizers to be worthy of this vocation, to exercise it without the reticence of doubt or fear, and not to neglect the conditions that will make this evangelization not only possible but also active and fruitful. These, among many others, are the fundamental conditions which we consider it important to emphasize.

75 Evangelization will never be possible without the action of the Holy Spirit. The Spirit descends on Jesus of Nazareth at the moment of His baptism when the voice of the Father—"This is my beloved Son with whom I am well pleased"[107]— manifests in an external way the election of Jesus and His mission. Jesus is "led by the Spirit" to experience in the desert the decisive combat and the supreme test before beginning this mission.[108] It is "in the power of the Spirit"[109] that He returns to Galilee and begins His preaching at Nazareth, applying to Himself the passage of Isaiah: "The Spirit of the Lord is upon me." And He proclaims: "Today this Scripture has been fulfilled."[110] To the disciples whom He was about to send forth He says, breathing on them, "Receive the Holy Spirit."[111]

In fact, it is only after the coming of the Holy Spirit on the day of Pentecost that the apostles depart to all the ends of the earth in order to begin the great work of the Church's evangelization. Peter explains this event as the fulfillment

---

107. *Mt* 3:17.
108. *Mt* 4:1.
109. *Lk* 4:14.
110. *Lk* 4:18a, 21; cf. *Is* 61:1.
111. *Jn* 20:22.

of the prophecy of Joel: "I will pour out my spirit."[112] Peter is filled with the Holy Spirit so that he can speak to the people about Jesus, the Son of God.[113] Paul too is filled with the Holy Spirit[114] before dedicating himself to his apostolic ministry, as is Stephen when he is chosen for the ministry of service and later on for the witness of blood.[115] The Spirit, who causes Peter, Paul and the Twelve to speak, and who inspires the words that they are to utter, also comes down "on those who heard the word."[116]

It is in the "consolation of the Holy Spirit" that the Church increases.[117] The Holy Spirit is the soul of the Church. It is He who explains to the faithful the deep meaning of the teaching of Jesus and of His mystery. It is the Holy Spirit who, today just as at the beginning of the Church, acts in every evangelizer who allows himself to be possessed and led by Him. The Holy Spirit places on his lips the words which he could not find by himself, and at the same time the Holy Spirit predisposes the soul of the hearer to be open and receptive to the Good News and to the kingdom being proclaimed.

Techniques of evangelization are good, but even the most advanced ones could not replace the gentle action of the Spirit. The most perfect preparation of the evangelizer has no effect without the Holy Spirit. Without the Holy Spirit the most convincing dialectic has no power over the heart of man. Without Him the most highly developed schemas resting on a sociological or psychological basis are quickly seen to be quite valueless.

We live in the Church at a privileged moment of the Spirit. Everywhere people are trying to know Him better, as the Scripture reveals Him. They are happy to place themselves under His inspiration. They are gathering about Him; they want to let themselves be led by Him. Now if the Spirit of God has a preeminent place in the whole life of the Church, it is in her evangelizing mission that He is most active. It is not by chance that the great inauguration of evangelization took place on the morning of Pentecost, under the inspiration of the Spirit.

It must be said that the Holy Spirit is the principal agent of evangelization: it is He who impels each individual to proclaim the Gospel, and it is He who in the depths of consciences causes the word of salvation to be accepted and understood.[118] But it can equally be said that He is the goal of evangelization: He alone stirs up the new creation, the new humanity of which evangelization

---

112. *Acts* 2:17.
113. Cf. *Acts* 4:8.
114. Cf. *Acts* 9:17.
115. Cf. *Acts* 6:5, 10; 7:55.
116. *Acts* 10:44.
117. *Acts* 9:31.
118. Cf. Second Vatican Ecumenical Council, Decree on the Church's Missionary Activity *Ad Gentes*, 4:AAS 58 (1966), pp. 950–951.

is to be the result, with that unity in variety which evangelization wishes to achieve within the Christian community. Through the Holy Spirit the Gospel penetrates to the heart of the world, for it is He who causes people to discern the signs of the times—signs willed by God—which evangelization reveals and puts to use within history.

The Bishops' Synod of 1974, which insisted strongly on the place of the Holy Spirit in evangelization, also expressed the desire that pastors and theologians—and we would also say the faithful marked by the seal of the Spirit by Baptism—should study more thoroughly the nature and manner of the Holy Spirit's action in evangelization today. This is our desire too, and we exhort all evangelizers, whoever they may be, to pray without ceasing to the Holy Spirit with faith and fervor and to let themselves prudently be guided by Him as the decisive inspirer of their plans, their initiatives and their evangelizing activity.

Let us now consider the very persons of the evangelizers.

76 It is often said nowadays that the present century thirsts for authenticity. Especially in regard to young people it is said that they have a horror of the artificial or false and that they are searching above all for truth and honesty.

These "signs of the times" should find us vigilant. Either tacitly or aloud—but always forcefully—we are being asked: Do you really believe what you are proclaiming? Do you live what you believe? Do you really preach what you live? The witness of life has become more than ever an essential condition for real effectiveness in preaching. Precisely because of this we are, to a certain extent, responsible for the progress of the Gospel that we proclaim.

"What is the state of the Church ten years after the Council?" we asked at the beginning of this meditation. Is she firmly established in the midst of the world and yet free and independent enough to call for the world's attention? Does she testify to solidarity with people and at the same time to the divine Absolute? Is she more ardent in contemplation and adoration and more zealous in missionary, charitable and liberating action? Is she ever more committed to the effort to search for the restoration of the complete unity of Christians, a unity that makes more effective the common witness, "so that the world may believe"[119] We are all responsible for the answers that could be given to these questions.

We therefore address our exhortation to our brethren in the Episcopate, placed by the Holy Spirit to govern the Church.[120] We exhort the priests and deacons, the bishops' collaborators in assembling the People of God and in animating spiritually the local communities. We exhort the religious, witnesses of a Church called to holiness and hence themselves invited to a life that bears

---

119. *Jn* 17:21.
120. Cf. *Acts* 20:28.

testimony to the beatitudes of the Gospel. We exhort the laity: Christian families, youth, adults, all those who exercise a trade or profession, leaders, without
forgetting the poor who are often rich in faith and hope—all lay people who are
conscious of their evangelizing role in the service of their Church or in the midst
of society and the world. We say to all of them: our evangelizing zeal must spring
from true holiness of life, and, as the Second Vatican Council suggests, preaching must in its turn make the preacher grow in holiness, which is nourished by
prayer and above all by love for the Eucharist.[121]

The world which, paradoxically, despite innumerable signs of the denial of
God, is nevertheless searching for Him in unexpected ways and painfully expe-
riencing the need of Him—the world is calling for evangelizers to speak to it of
a God whom the evangelists themselves should know and be familiar with as if
they could see the invisible.[122] The world calls for and expects from us simplicity of life, the spirit of prayer, charity towards all, especially towards the lowly
and the poor, obedience and humility, detachment and self-sacrifice. Without
this mark of holiness, our word will have difficulty in touching the heart of
modern man. It risks being vain and sterile.

77 The power of evangelization will find itself considerably diminished if those
who proclaim the Gospel are divided among themselves in all sorts of ways. Is
this not perhaps one of the great sicknesses of evangelization today? Indeed, if
the Gospel that we proclaim is seen to be rent by doctrinal disputes, ideological
polarizations or mutual condemnations among Christians, at the mercy of the
latter's differing views on Christ and the Church and even because of their different concepts of society and human institutions, how can those to whom we
address our preaching fail to be disturbed, disoriented, even scandalized?

The Lord's spiritual testament tells us that unity among His followers is not
only the proof that we are His but also the proof that He is sent by the Father. It
is the test of the credibility of Christians and of Christ Himself. As evangelizers,
we must offer Christ's faithful not the image of people divided and separated by
unedifying quarrels, but the image of people who are mature in faith and capable of finding a meeting-point beyond the real tensions, thanks to a shared, sincere and disinterested search for truth. Yes, the destiny of evangelization is
certainly bound up with the witness of unity given by the Church. This is a
source of responsibility and also of comfort.

At this point we wish to emphasize the sign of unity among all Christians as
the way and instrument of evangelization. The division among Christians is a

---

121. Cf. Decree on the Ministry and Life of Priests *Presbyterorum Ordinis*, 13: *AAS* 58 (1966),
p. 1011.
122. Cf. *Heb* 11:27.

serious reality which impedes the very work of Christ. The Second Vatican Council states clearly and emphatically that this division "damages the most holy cause of preaching the Gospel to all men, and it impedes many from embracing the faith."[123] For this reason, in proclaiming the Holy Year we considered it necessary to recall to all the faithful of the Catholic world that "before all men can be brought together and restored to the grace of God our Father, communion must be reestablished between those who by faith have acknowledged and accepted Jesus Christ as the Lord of mercy who sets men free and unites them in the Spirit of love and truth."[124]

And it is with a strong feeling of Christian hope that look to the efforts being made in the Christian world for this restoration of the full unity willed by Christ. St. Paul assures us that "hope does not disappoint us."[125] While we still work to obtain full unity from the Lord, we wish to see prayer intensified. Moreover we make our own the desire of the Fathers of the Third General Assembly of the Synod of Bishops, for a collaboration marked by greater commitment with the Christian brethren with whom we are not yet united in perfect unity, taking as a basis the foundation of Baptism and the patrimony of faith which is common to us. By doing this we can already give a greater common witness to Christ before the world in the very work of evangelization. Christ's command urges us to do this; the duty of preaching and of giving witness to the Gospel requires this.

78 The Gospel entrusted to us is also the word of truth. A truth which liberates[126] and which alone gives peace of heart is what people are looking for when we proclaim the Good News to them. The truth about God, about man and his mysterious destiny, about the world; the difficult truth that we seek in the Word of God and of which, we repeat, we are neither the masters nor the owners, but the depositaries, the heralds and the servants.

Every evangelizer is expected to have a reverence for truth, especially since the truth that he studies and communicates is none other than revealed truth and hence, more than any other, a sharing in the first truth which is God Himself. The preacher of the Gospel will therefore be a person who even at the price of personal renunciation and suffering always seeks the truth that he must transmit to others. He never betrays or hides truth out of a desire to please men, in order to astonish or to shock, nor for the sake of originality or a desire

123. Decree on the Church's Missionary Activity *Ad Gentes*, 6: *AAS* 58 (1966), pp. 954–955; cf. Decree on Ecumenism *Unitatis Redintegratio*, 1: *AAS* 57 (1965), pp. 90–91.

124. Bull *Apostolorum Limina*, VII: *AAS* 66 (1974), p. 305.

125. *Rom* 5:5.

126. Cf. *Jn* 8:32.

to make an impression. He does not refuse truth. He does not obscure revealed truth by being too idle to search for it, or for the sake of his own comfort, or out of fear. He does not neglect to study it. He serves it generously, without making it serve him.

We are the pastors of the faithful people, and our pastoral service impels us to preserve, defend, and to communicate the truth regardless of the sacrifices that this involves. So many eminent and holy pastors have left us the example of this love of truth. In many cases it was an heroic love. The God of truth expects us to be the vigilant defenders and devoted preachers of truth.

Men of learning—whether you be theologians, exegetes or historians—the work of evangelization needs your tireless work of research, and also care and tact in transmitting the truth to which your studies lead you but which is always greater than the heart of man, being the very truth of God.

Parents and teachers, your task—and the many conflicts of the present day do not make it an easy one—is to help your children and your students to discover truth, including religious and spiritual truth.

79 The work of evangelization presupposes in the evangelizer an ever increasing love for those whom he is evangelizing. That model evangelizer, the Apostle Paul, wrote these words to the Thessalonians, and they are a program for us all: "With such yearning love we chose to impart to you not only the gospel of God but our very selves, so dear had you become to us."[127] What is this love? It is much more than that of a teacher; it is the love of a father; and again, it is the love of a mother.[128] It is this love that the Lord expects from every preacher of the Gospel, from every builder of the Church. A sign of love will be the concern to give the truth and to bring people into unity. Another sign of love will be a devotion to the proclamation of Jesus Christ, without reservation or turning back. Let us add some other signs of this love.

The first is respect for the religious and spiritual situation of those being evangelized. Respect for their tempo and pace; no one has the right to force them excessively. Respect for their conscience and convictions, which are not to be treated in a harsh manner.

Another sign of this love is concern not to wound the other person, especially if he or she is weak in faith,[129] with statements that may be clear for those who are already initiated but which for the faithful can be a source of bewilderment and scandal, like a wound in the soul.

---

127. *1 Thess* 2:8; cf. *Phil* 1:8.
128. Cf. *1 Thess* 2:7–11; *1 Cor* 4:15; *Gal* 4:19.
129. Cf. *1 Cor* 8:9–13; *Rom* 14:15.

Yet another sign of love will be the effort to transmit to Christians not doubts and uncertainties born of an erudition poorly assimilated but certainties that are solid because they are anchored in the Word of God. The faithful need these certainties for their Christian life; they have a right to them, as children of God who abandon themselves entirely into His arms and to the exigencies of love.

80 Our appeal here is inspired by the fervor of the greatest preachers and evangelizers, whose lives were devoted to the apostolate. Among these we are glad to point out those whom we have proposed to the veneration of the faithful during the course of the Holy Year. They have known how to overcome many obstacles to evangelization.

Such obstacles are also present today, and we shall limit ourself to mentioning the lack of fervor. It is all the more serious because it comes from within. It is manifested in fatigue, disenchantment, compromise, lack of interest and above all lack of joy and hope. We exhort all those who have the task of evangelizing, by whatever title and at whatever level, always to nourish spiritual fervor.[130]

This fervor demands first of all that we should know how to put aside the excuses which would impede evangelization. The most insidious of these excuses are certainly the ones which people claim to find support for in such and such a teaching of the Council.

Thus one too frequently hears it said, in various terms, that to impose a truth, be it that of the Gospel, or to impose a way, be it that of salvation, cannot but be a violation of religious liberty. Besides, it is added, why proclaim the Gospel when the whole world is saved by uprightness of heart? We know likewise that the world and history are filled with "seeds of the Word"; is it not therefore an illusion to claim to bring the Gospel where it already exists in the seeds that the Lord Himself has sown?

Anyone who takes the trouble to study in the Council's documents the questions upon which these excuses draw too superficially will find quite a different view.

It would certainly be an error to impose something on the consciences of our brethren. But to propose to their consciences the truth of the Gospel and salvation in Jesus Christ, with complete clarity and with a total respect for the free options which it presents—"without coercion, or dishonorable or unworthy pressure"[131]—far from being an attack on religious liberty is fully to respect that liberty, which is offered the choice of a way that even non-believers consider noble and uplifting. Is it then a crime against others' freedom to proclaim with

---

130. Cf. *Rom* 12:11.

131. Cf. Second Vatican Council, Declaration on Religious Liberty *Dignitatis Humanae*, 4: *AAS* 58 (1966), p. 933.

joy a Good News which one has come to know through the Lord's mercy?[132] And why should only falsehood and error, debasement and pornography have the right to be put before people and often unfortunately imposed on them by the destructive propaganda of the mass media, by the tolerance of legislation, the timidity of the good and the impudence of the wicked? The respectful presentation of Christ and His kingdom is more than the evangelizer's right; it is his duty. It is likewise the right of his fellow men to receive from him the proclamation of the Good News of salvation. God can accomplish this salvation in whomsoever He wishes by ways which He alone knows.[133] And yet, if His Son came, it was precisely in order to reveal to us, by His word and by His life, the ordinary paths of salvation. And He has commanded us to transmit this revelation to others with His own authority. It would be useful if every Christian and every evangelizer were to pray about the following thought: men can gain salvation also in other ways, by God's mercy, even though we do not preach the Gospel to them; but as for us, can we gain salvation if through negligence or fear or shame—what St. Paul called "blushing for the Gospel"[134]—or as a result of false ideas we fail to preach it? For that would be to betray the call of God, who wishes the seed to bear fruit through the voice of the ministers of the Gospel; and it will depend on us whether this grows into trees and produces its full fruit.

Let us therefore preserve our fervor of spirit. Let us preserve the delightful and comforting joy of evangelizing, even when it is in tears that we must sow. May it mean for us—as it did for John the Baptist, for Peter and Paul, for the other apostles and for a multitude of splendid evangelizers all through the Church's history—an interior enthusiasm that nobody and nothing can quench. May it be the great joy of our consecrated lives. And may the world of our time, which is searching, sometimes with anguish, sometimes with hope, be enabled to receive the Good News not from evangelizers who are dejected, discouraged, impatient or anxious, but from ministers of the Gospel whose lives glow with fervor, who have first received the joy of Christ, and who are willing to risk their lives so that the kingdom may be proclaimed and the Church established in the midst of the world.

81 This then, brothers and sons and daughters, is our heartfelt plea. It echoes the voice of our brethren assembled for the Third General Assembly of the Synod of Bishops. This is the task we have wished to give you at the close of a Holy Year which has enabled us to see better than ever the needs and the

---

132. Cf. *Ibid.*, 9–14: loc. cit., pp. 935–940.

133. Cf. Second Vatican Ecumenical Council, Decree on the Church's Missionary Activity *Ad Gentes*, 7: AAS 58 (1966), p. 955.

134. Cf. *Rom* 1:16.

appeals of a multitude of brethren, both Christians and non-Christians, who await from the Church the Word of salvation.

May the light of the Holy Year, which has shone in the local Churches and in Rome for millions of consciences reconciled with God, continue to shine in the same way after the Jubilee through a program of pastoral action with evangelization as its basic feature, for these years which mark the eve of a new century, the eve also of the third millennium of Christianity.

82 This is the desire that we rejoice to entrust to the hands and the heart of the Immaculate Blessed Virgin Mary, on this day which is especially consecrated to her and which is also the tenth anniversary of the close of the Second Vatican Council. On the morning of Pentecost she watched over with her prayer the beginning of evangelization prompted by the Holy Spirit: may she be the Star of the evangelization ever renewed which the Church, docile to her Lord's command, must promote and accomplish, especially in these times which are difficult but full of hope!

In the name of Christ we bless you, your communities, your families, all those who are dear to you, in the words which Paul addressed to the Philippians: "I give thanks to my God every time I think of you—which is constantly, in every prayer I utter—rejoicing, as I plead on your behalf, at the way you have all continually helped to promote the gospel.... I hold all of you dear—you who ... are sharers of my gracious lot ... to defend the solid grounds on which the gospel rests. God himself can testify how much I long for each of you with the affection of Christ Jesus!"[135]

Given in Rome, at Saint Peter's, on the Solemnity of the Immaculate Conception of the Blessed Virgin Mary, December 8, 1975, the thirteenth year of our Pontificate.

PAULUS PP. VI

135. *Phil* 1:3–4, 7–8.

THE CATHOLIC SCHOOL

THE SACRED CONGREGATION FOR CATHOLIC EDUCATION

Introduction

1 The Catholic school is receiving more and more attention in the Church since the Second Vatican Council, with particular emphasis on the Church as she appears in the Constitutions *Lumen Gentium* and *Gaudium et Spes*. In the Council's Declaration *Gravissimum Educationis* it is discussed in the wider sphere of Christian education. The present document develops the idea of this Declaration, limiting itself to a deeper reflection on the Catholic school.

2 The Sacred Congregation for Catholic Education is aware of the serious problems which are an integral part of Christian education in a pluralistic society. It regards as a prime duty, therefore, the focusing of any attention on the nature and distinctive characteristics of school which would present itself as Catholic. Yet the diverse situations and legal systems in which the Catholic school has to function in Christian and non-Christian countries demand that local problems be faced and solved by each Church within its own social-cultural context.

3 While acknowledging this duty of the local Churches, the Sacred Congregation believes that now is the opportune moment to offer its own contribution by re-emphasizing clearly the educational value of the Catholic school. It is in this value that the Catholic school's fundamental reason for existing and the basis of its genuine apostolate is to be found. This document does not pretend to be an exhaustive treatment of the subject; it merely proposes to state the premises that will lead to further fruitful study and implementation.

4 To Episcopal Conferences, pastorally concerned for all young Catholics whatever school they attend,[1] the Sacred Congregation for Catholic Education entrusts this present document in order that they may seek to achieve an effective system of education at all levels which corresponds to the total educational needs of young people today in Catholic schools. The Sacred Congregation also addresses itself to all who are responsible for education—parents, teachers, young people and school authorities—and urges them to pool all their

---

1. Cf. Second Vatican Council, *Declaration on Christian Education "Gravissimum Educationis,"* 7.

resources and the means at their disposal to enable Catholic schools to provide a service which is truly civic and apostolic.

I. THE CATHOLIC SCHOOL
AND THE SALVIFIC MISSION OF THE CHURCH

The Salvific Mission of the Church

5 In the fullness of time, in His mysterious plan of love, God the Father sent His only Son to begin the Kingdom of God on earth and bring about the spiritual rebirth of mankind. To continue His work of salvation, Jesus Christ founded the Church as a visible organism, living by the power of the Spirit.

6 Moved by the same Spirit, the Church is constantly deepening her awareness of herself and meditating on the mystery of her being and mission.[2] Thus she is ever rediscovering her living relationship with Christ "in order to discover greater light, energy, and joy in fulfilling her mission and determining the best way to ensure that her relationship with humanity is closer and more efficacious"[3]—that humanity of which she is a part and yet so undeniably distinct. Her destiny is to serve humanity until it reaches its fullness in Christ.

7 Evangelization is, therefore, the mission of the Church; that is she must proclaim the good news of salvation to all, generate new creatures in Christ through Baptism, and train them to live knowingly as children of God.

Means Available for the Mission of the Church

8 To carry out her saving mission, the Church uses, above all, the means which Jesus Christ has given her. She also uses other means which at different times and in different cultures have proved effective in achieving and, promoting the development of the human person. The Church adapts these means to the changing conditions and emerging needs of mankind.[4] In her encounter with differing cultures and with man's progressive achievements, the Church proclaims the faith and reveals "to all ages the transcendent goal which alone gives life its full meaning."[5] She establishes her own schools because she considers them as a privileged means of promoting the formation of the whole man,

---

2. Cf. Paul VI, *Encyclical Letter "Ecclesiam Suam,"* 7.

3. *Ibid.,* 13.

4. Cf. Second Vatican Council, *Pastoral Constitution on the Church in the Modern World "Gaudium et Spes,"* 4.

5. Paul VI, *Allocution to Cardinal Gabriel-Marie Garrone,* November 27th, 1972.

since the school is a center in which a specific concept of the world, of man, and of history is developed and conveyed.

Contribution of the Catholic School Towards the Salvific Mission of the Church

9 The Catholic school forms part of the saving mission of the Church, especially for education in the faith. Remembering that "the simultaneous development of man's psychological and moral consciousness is demanded by Christ almost as a pre-condition for the reception of the befitting divine gifts of truth and grace,"[6] the Church fulfills her obligation to foster in her children a full awareness of their rebirth to a new life.[7] It is precisely in the Gospel of Christ, taking root in the minds and lives of the faithful, that the Catholic school finds its definition as it comes to terms with the cultural conditions of the times.

The Church's Educational Involvement and Cultural Pluralism

10 In the course of the centuries "while constantly holding to the fullness of divine truth"[8] the Church has progressively used the sources and the means of culture in order to deepen her understanding of revelation and promote constructive dialogue with the world. Moved by the faith through which she firmly believes herself to be led by the Spirit of the Lord, the Church seeks to discern in the events, needs and hopes of our era[9] the most insistent demands which she must answer if she is to carry out God's plan.

11 One such demand is a pressing need to ensure the presence of a Christian mentality in the society of the present day, marked, among other things, by cultural pluralism. For it is Christian thought which constitutes a sound criterion of judgment in the midst of conflicting concepts and behavior: "Reference to Jesus Christ teaches man to discern the values which ennoble from those which degrade him."[10]

12 Cultural pluralism, therefore, leads the Church to reaffirm her mission of education to insure strong character formation. Her children, then, will be

---

6. Paul VI, *Encyclical Letter "Ecclesiam Suam,"* 15.

7. Cf. Second Vatican Council, *Declaration on Christian Education "Gravissimum Educationis,"* 3.

8. Second Vatican Council, *Dogmatic Constitution on Divine Revelation "Dei Verbum,"* 8.

9. Cf. Second Vatican Council, *Pastoral Constitution on the Church in the Modern World "Gaudium et Spes,"* 11.

10. Paul VI, *Allocution to the Ninth Congress of the Catholic International Education Office* (O.I.E.C.), in *L'Osservatore Romano,* June 9th, 1974.

capable both of resisting the debilitating influence of relativism and of living up to the demands made on them by their Baptism. It also stimulates her to foster truly Christian living and apostolic communities, equipped to make their own positive contribution, in a spirit of cooperation, to the building up of the secular society. For this reason the Church is prompted to mobilize her educational resources in the face of the materialism, pragmatism and technocracy of contemporary society.

13 The Church upholds the principle of a plurality of school systems in order to safeguard her objectives in the face of cultural pluralism. In other words, she encourages the co-existence and, if possible, the cooperation of diverse educational institutions which will allow young people to be formed by value judgments based on a specific view of the world and to be trained to take an active part in the construction of a community through which the building of society itself is promoted.

14 Thus, while policies and opportunities differ from place to place, the Catholic school has its place in any national school system. By offering such an alternative the Church wishes to respond to the obvious need for cooperation in a society characterized by cultural pluralism. Moreover, in this way she helps to promote that freedom of teaching which champions and guarantees freedom of conscience and the parental right to choose the school best suited to parents' educational purpose.[11]

15 Finally, the Church is absolutely convinced that the educational aims of the Catholic school in the world of today perform an essential and unique service for the Church herself. It is, in fact, through the school that she participates in the dialogue of culture with her own positive contribution to the cause of the total formation of man. The absence of the Catholic school would be a great loss[12] for civilization and for the natural and supernatural destiny of man.

II. PRESENT DIFFICULTIES OVER CATHOLIC SCHOOLS

16 In the light of her mission of salvation, the Church considers that the Catholic school provides a privileged environment for the complete formation of her members, and that it also provides a highly important service to mankind. Nevertheless, she is aware of the many problems that exist and objections that

---

11. Cf. Second Vatican Council, *Declaration on Christian Education "Gravissimum Educationis,"* 8.

12. Cf. Paul VI, *Allocution to the Ninth Congress of the O.I.E.C.,* in *L'Osservatore Romano,* June 9th, 1974.

are made against Catholic schools sometimes regarding the very validity of their existence and their functions. The issue is really part of a much wider problem which faces all institutions as such in a society as the present, characterized by rapid and profound change.

Objections Raised Against Catholic Schools

17 In the debate about Catholic schools there are some easily identifiable central objections and difficulties. These need to be borne in mind if discussion is to be relevant to the actual situation and if teachers are to make a serious attempt to adapt their work to the needs of the contemporary world.

18 In the first place many people, both inside and outside the Church, motivated by a mistaken sense of the lay role in secular society, attack Catholic schools as institutions. They do not admit that, apart from the individual witness of her members, the Church also may offer witness by means of her institutions, e.g. those dedicated to the search for truth or to works of charity.

19 Others claim that Catholic schools make use of a human institution for religious and confessional purposes. Christian education can sometimes run into the danger of a so-called proselytism, of imparting a one-sided outlook. This can happen only when Christian educators misunderstand the nature and methods of Christian education. Complete education necessarily includes a religious dimension. Religion is an effective contribution to the development of other aspects of a personality in the measure in which it is integrated into general education.

20 According to others, Catholic schools have outlived their time;—as institutions they were a necessary substitute in the past but have no place at a time when civil authority assumes responsibility for education. In fact, as the State increasingly takes control of education and establishes its own so-called neutral and monolithic system, the survival of those natural communities, based on a shared concept of life, is threatened. Faced with this situation, the Catholic school offers an alternative which is in conformity with the wishes of the members of the community of the Church.

21 In some countries Catholic schools have been obliged to restrict their educational activities to wealthier social classes, thus giving an impression of social and economic discrimination in education. But this occurs only where the State has not weighed the advantages of an alternative presence in their pluralistic society. From such nearsightedness considerable difficulties have arisen for Catholic schools.

22 Allied to these points, objections are raised concerning the educational results of the Catholic school. They are sometimes accused of not knowing how to form convinced, articulate Christians ready to take their place in social and political life. Every educational enterprise, however, involves the risk of failure and one must not be too discouraged by apparent or even real failures, since there are very many formative influences on young people and results often have to be calculated on a long-term basis.

23 Before concluding these comments on the objections raised against Catholic schools, one must remember the context in which contemporary work in the field of education is undertaken, and especially in the Church. The school problem in our rapidly changing society is serious for everyone. The Second Vatican Council has encouraged a more open-minded approach which has sometimes been misrepresented in theory and practice. There are difficulties in the provision of adequate staff and finance. In such a situation should the Church perhaps give up her apostolic mission in Catholic schools, as some people would like her to do, and direct her energy to a more direct work of evangelization in sectors considered to be of higher priority or more suited to her spiritual mission, or should she make State schools the sole object of her pastoral activity? Such a solution would not only be contrary to the directives of the Vatican Council, but would also be opposed to the Church's mission and to what is expected of her by Christian people. What follows emphasizes this fact.

Some Aspects of Schools Today

24 To understand the real nature of the Catholic school one cannot divorce it from wider modern problems concerning schools in general. Apart from the ideas advanced by the promoters of de-schooling—a theory which now seems of minor significance—contemporary society tends to place greater importance than ever on the specific function of the school: its social significance (parental participation, increased democratization, equality of opportunity); its tendency to coordinate and eventually include the educational work of other institutions; the extension of the statutory duration of attendance at school.

III. THE SCHOOL AS A CENTER OF HUMAN FORMATION

25 To understand fully the specific mission of the Catholic school it is essential to keep in mind the basic concept of what a school is; that which does not reproduce the characteristic features of a school cannot be a Catholic school.

The General Purpose of a School

26 A close examination of the various definitions of school and of new educational trends at every level, leads one to formulate the concept of school as a place of integral formation by means of a systematic and critical assimilation of culture. A school is, therefore, a privileged place in which, through a living encounter with a cultural inheritance, integral formation occurs.

27 This vital approach takes place in the school in the form of personal contacts and commitments which consider absolute values in a life-context and seek to insert them into a life-framework. Indeed, culture is only educational when young people can relate their study to real-life situations with which they are familiar. The school must stimulate the pupil to exercise his intelligence through the dynamics of understanding to attain clarity and inventiveness. It must help him spell out the meaning of his experiences and their truths. Any school which neglects this duty and which offers merely pre-cast conclusions hinders the personal development of its pupils.

School and Attitudes of Life

28 From this it is clear that the school has to review its entire program of formation, both its content and the methods used, in the light of that vision of the reality from which it draws its inspiration and on which it depends.

29 Either implicit or explicit reference to a determined attitude to life (Weltanschauung) is unavoidable in education because it comes into every decision that is made. It is, therefore, essential, if for no other reason than for a unity in teaching, that each member of the school community, albeit with differing degrees of awareness, adopts a common vision, a common outlook on life, based on adherence to a scale of values in which he believes. This is what gives teachers and adults authority to educate. It must never be forgotten that the purpose of instruction at school is education, that is, the development of man from within, freeing him from that conditioning which would prevent him from becoming a, fully integrated human being. The school must begin from the principle that its educational program is intentionally directed to the growth of the whole person.

30 It is one of the formal tasks of a school, as an institution for education, to draw out the ethical dimension for the precise purpose of arousing the individual's inner spiritual dynamism and to aid his achieving that moral freedom which complements the psychological. Behind this moral freedom, however, stand those absolute values which alone give meaning and value to human life.

This has to be said because the tendency to adopt present-day values as a yard-stick is not absent even in the educational world. The danger is always to react to passing, superficial ideas and to lose sight of the much deeper needs of the contemporary world.

The School in Today's Society

31 Precisely because the school endeavors to answer the needs of a society characterized by depersonalization and a mass production mentality which so easily result from scientific and technological developments, it must develop into an authentically formational school, reducing such risks to a minimum. It must develop persons who are responsible and inner-directed, capable of choosing freely in conformity with their conscience. This is simply another way of saying that the school is an institution where young people gradually learn to open themselves up to life as it is, and to create in themselves a definite attitude to life as it should be.

32 When seen in this light, a school is not only a place where one is given a choice of intellectual values, but a place where one has presented an array of values which are actively lived. The school must be a community whose values are communicated through the interpersonal and sincere relationships of its members and through both individual and corporative adherence to the outlook on life that permeates the school.

IV. THE EDUCATIONAL WORK OF THE CATHOLIC SCHOOL

Specific Character of the Catholic School

33 Having stated the characteristics of the Catholic school from the point of view of "school" we can now examine its Catholic quality, namely its reference to a Christian concept of life centered on Jesus Christ.

34 Christ is the foundation of the whole educational enterprise in a Catholic school. His revelation gives new meaning to life and helps man to direct his thought, action and will according to the Gospel, making the beatitudes his norm of life. The fact that in their own individual ways all members of the school community share this Christian vision, makes the school "Catholic"; principles of the Gospel in this manner become the educational norms since the school then has them as its internal motivation and final goal.

35 The Catholic school is committed thus to the development of the whole man, since in Christ, the Perfect Man, all human values find their fulfillment and unity. Herein lies the specifically Catholic character of the school. Its duty to cultivate human values in their own legitimate right in accordance with its particular mission to serve all men has its origin in the figure of Christ. He is the One Who ennobles man, gives meaning to human life, and is the Model which the Catholic school offers to its pupils.

36 If, like every other school, the Catholic school has as its aim the critical communication of human culture and the total formation of the individual, it works towards this goal guided by its Christian vision of reality "through which our cultural heritage acquires its special place in the total vocational life of man."[13] Mindful of the fact that man has been redeemed by Christ, the Catholic school aims at forming in the Christian those particular virtues which will enable him to live a new life in Christ and help him to play faithfully his part in building up the Kingdom of God.[14]

37 These premises indicate the duties and the content of the Catholic school. Its task is fundamentally a synthesis of culture and faith, and a synthesis of faith and life: the first is reached by integrating all the different aspects of human knowledge through the subjects taught, in the light of the Gospel; the second in the growth of the virtues characteristic of the Christian.

Integration of Faith and Culture

38 In helping pupils to achieve through the medium of its teaching an integration of faith and culture, the Catholic school sets out with a deep awareness of the value of knowledge as such. Under no circumstances does it wish to divert the imparting of knowledge from its rightful objective.

39 Individual subjects must be taught according to their own particular methods. It would be wrong to consider subjects as mere adjuncts to faith or as a useful means of teaching apologetics. They enable the pupil to assimilate skills, knowledge, intellectual methods and moral and social attitudes, all of which help to develop his personality and lead him to take his place as an active member of the community of man. Their aim is not merely the attainment of knowledge but the acquisition of values and the discovery of truth.

---

13. Second Vatican Council, *Pastoral Constitution on the Church in the Modern World "Gaudium et Spes,"* 57.

14. Cf. Second Vatican Council, *Declaration on Christian Education, "Gravissimum Educationis,"* 2.

40 Since the educative mission of the Catholic school is so wide, the teacher is in an excellent position to guide the pupil to a deepening of his faith and to enrich and enlighten his human knowledge with the data of the faith. While there are many occasions in teaching when pupils can be stimulated by insights of faith, a Christian education acknowledges the valid contribution which can be made by academic subjects towards the development of a mature Christian. The teacher can form the mind and heart of his pupils and guide them to develop a total commitment to Christ, with their whole personality enriched by human culture.

41 The school considers human knowledge as a truth to be discovered. In the measure in which subjects rare taught by someone who knowingly and without restraint seeks the truth, they are to that extent Christian. Discovery and awareness of truth leads man to the discovery of Truth itself. A teacher who is full of Christian wisdom, well prepared in his own subject, does more than convey the sense of what he is teaching to his pupils. Over and above what he says, he guides his pupils beyond his mere words to the heart of total Truth.

42 The cultural heritage of mankind includes other values apart from the specific ambient of truth. When the Christian teacher helps a pupil to grasp, appreciate and assimilate these values, he is guiding him towards eternal realities. This movement towards the Uncreated Source of all knowledge highlights the importance of teaching for the growth of faith.

43 The achievement of this specific aim of the Catholic school depends not so much on subject matter or methodology as on the people who work there. The extent to which the Christian message is transmitted through education depends to a very great extent on the teachers. The integration of culture and faith is mediated by the other integration of faith and life in the person of the teacher. The nobility of the task to which teachers are called demands that, in imitation of Christ, the only Teacher, they reveal the Christian message not only by word but also by every gesture of their behavior. This is what makes the difference between a school whose education is permeated by the Christian spirit and one in which religion is only regarded as an academic subject like any other.

Integration of Faith and Life

44 The fundamental aim of teaching is the assimilation of objective values, and, when this is undertaken for an apostolic purpose, it does not stop at an integration of faith and culture but leads the pupil on to a personal integration of faith and life.

45 The Catholic school has as its specific duty the complete Christian formation of its pupils, and this task is of special significance today because of the inadequacy of the family and society. It knows that this integration of faith and life is part of a life-long process of conversion until the pupil becomes what God wishes him to be. Young people have to be taught to share their personal lives with God. They are to overcome their individualism and discover, in the light of faith, their specific vocation to live responsibly in a community with others. The very pattern of the Christian life draws them to commit themselves to serve God in their brethren and to make the world a better place for man to live in.

46 The Catholic school should teach its pupils to discern in the voice of the universe the Creator Whom it reveals and, in the conquests of science, to know God and man better. In the daily life of the school, the pupil should learn that he is called to be a living witness to God's love for men by the way he acts, and that he is part of that salvation history which has Christ, the Savior of the world, as its goal.

47 Being aware that Baptism by itself does not make a Christian—living and acting in conformity with the Gospel is necessary—the Catholic school tries to create within its walls a climate[15] in which the pupil's faith will gradually mature and enable him to assume the responsibility placed on him by Baptism. It will give pride of place in the education it provides through Christian Doctrine to the gradual formation of conscience in fundamental, permanent virtues—above all the theological virtues, and charity in particular, which is, so to speak, the life-giving spirit which transforms a man of virtue into a man of Christ. Christ, therefore, is the teaching-center, the Model on Whom the Christian shapes his life. In Him the Catholic school differs from all others which limit themselves to forming men. Its task is to form Christian men, and, by its teaching and witness, show non-Christians something of the mystery of Christ Who surpasses all human understanding.[16]

48 The Catholic school will work closely with other Christian bodies (the family, the parish and Christian community, youth associations, etc.). But one must not overlook many other spheres of activity in society which are sources of information and in their various ways have an educational influence. Alongside this so-called "parallel school", the school proper is an active force through the

---

15. Cf. Second Vatican Council, *Declaration on Christian Education*, *"Gravissimum Educationis,"* 8.

16. Cf. *Eph*. 3, 18–19.

systematic formation of the pupils' critical faculties to bring them to a measure of self-control[17] and the ability to choose freely and conscientiously in the face of what is offered by the organs of social communication. They must be taught to subject these things to a critical and personal analysis,[18] take what is good, and integrate it into their Christian human culture.

Religious Teaching

49 The specific mission of the school, then, is a critical, systematic transmission of culture in the light of faith and the bringing forth of the power of Christian virtue by the integration of culture with faith and of faith with living.

Consequently, the Catholic school is aware of the importance of the Gospel-teaching as transmitted through the Catholic Church. It is, indeed, the fundamental element in the educative process as it helps the pupil towards his conscious choice of living a responsible and coherent way of life.

50 Without entering into the whole problem of teaching religion in schools, it must be emphasized that, while such teaching is not merely confined to "religious classes" within the school curriculum, it must, nevertheless, also be imparted explicitly and in a systematic manner to prevent a distortion in the child's mind between general and religious culture. The fundamental difference between religious and other forms of education is that its aim is not simply intellectual assent to religious truths but also a total commitment of one's whole being to the Person of Christ.

51 It is recognized that the proper place for catechesis is the family helped by other Christian communities, especially the local parish. But the importance and need for catechetical instruction in Catholic schools cannot be sufficiently emphasized. Here young people are helped to grow towards maturity in faith.

52 The Catholic school must be alert at all times to developments in the fields of child psychology, pedagogy and particularly catechetics, and should especially keep abreast of directives from competent ecclesiastical authorities. The school must do everything in its power to aid the Church to fulfill its catechetical mission and so must have the best possible qualified teachers of religion.

17. Cf. Pastoral Instruction "Communio et Progressio," 67.
18. Cf. Ibid.

The Catholic School as the Center of the Educative Christian Community

53 For all these reasons, Catholic schools must be seen as "meeting places for those who wish to express Christian values in education."[19] The Catholic school, far more than any other, must be a community whose aim is the transmission of values for living. Its work is seen as promoting a faith-relationship with Christ in Whom all values find fulfillment. But faith is principally assimilated through contact with people whose daily life bears witness to it. Christian faith, in fact, is born and grows inside a community.

54 The community aspect of the Catholic school is necessary because of the nature of the faith and not simply because of the nature of man and the nature of the educational process which is common to every school. No Catholic school can adequately fulfill its educational role on its own. It must continually be fed and stimulated by its Source of life, the Saving Word of Christ as it is expressed in Sacred Scripture, in Tradition, especially liturgical and sacramental tradition, and in the lives of people, past and present, who bear witness to that Word.

55 The Catholic school loses its purpose without constant reference to the Gospel and a frequent encounter with Christ. It derives all the energy necessary for its educational work from Him and thus "creates in the school community an atmosphere permeated with the Gospel spirit of freedom and love."[20] In this setting the pupil experiences his dignity as a person before he knows its definition. Faithful, therefore, to the claims of man and of God, the Catholic school makes its own contribution towards man's liberation, making him, in other words, what his destiny implies, one who talks consciously with God, one who is there for God to love.

56 "This simple religious doctrine is the cornerstone of the existential, Christian metaphysic."[21] This is the basis of a Catholic school's educational work. Education is not given for the purpose of gaining power but as an aid towards a fuller understanding of, and communion with man, events and things. Knowledge is not to be considered as a means of material prosperity and success, but as a call to serve and to be responsible for others.

---

19. Paul VI, *Allocution to the Ninth Congress of the O.I.E.C.*, in *L'Osservatore Romano*, June 9th, 1974.

20. Second Vatican Council, *Declaration on Christian Education "Gravissimum Educationis,"* 8.

21. Paul VI, *Valore dell'oblazione nella vita*, in *The Teaching of Pope Paul VI*, vol. 8 (1970), p. 97.

Other Aspects of the Educational Process in Catholic Schools

57 Whether or not the Catholic community forms its young people in the faith by means of a Catholic school, a Catholic school in itself is far from being divisive or presumptuous. It does not exacerbate differences, but rather aids cooperation and contact with others. It opens itself to others and respects their way of thinking and of living. It wants to share their anxieties and their hopes as it, indeed, shares their present and future lot in this world.

58 Since it is motivated by the Christian ideal, the Catholic school is particularly sensitive to the call from every part of the world for a more just society, and it tries to make its own contribution towards it. It does not stop at the courageous teaching of the demands of justice even in the face of local opposition, but tries to put these demands into practice in its own community in the daily life of the school. In some countries, because of local laws and economic conditions, the Catholic school runs the risk of giving counter-witness by admitting a majority of children from wealthier families. Schools may have done this because of their need to be financially self-supporting. This situation is of great concern to those responsible for Catholic education, because first and foremost the Church offers its educational service to "the poor or those who are deprived of family help and affection or those who are far from the faith."[22] Since education is an important means of improving the social and economic condition of the individual and of peoples, if the Catholic school were to turn its attention exclusively or predominantly to those from the wealthier social classes, it could be contributing towards maintaining their privileged position, and could thereby continue to favor a society which is unjust.

59 It is obvious that in such a demanding educational policy all participants must be committed to it freely. It cannot be imposed, but is offered as a possibility, as good news, and as such can be refused. However, in order to bring it into being and to maintain it, the school must be able to count on the unity of purpose and conviction of all its members.

The Participation of the Christian Community in the Catholic School's Work

60 From the outset the Catholic school declares its program and its determination to uphold it. It is a genuine community bent on imparting, over and above an academic education, all the help it can to its members to adopt a

---

22. Second Vatican Council, *Declaration on Christian Education "Gravissimum Educationis,"* 9.

Christian way of life. For the Catholic school mutual respect means service to the Person of Christ. Cooperation is between brothers and sisters in Christ. A policy of working for the common good is undertaken seriously as working for the building up of the Kingdom of God.

61 The cooperation required for the realization of this aim is a duty in conscience for all the members of the community teachers, parents, pupils, administrative personnel. Each has his or her own part to play. Cooperation of all, given in the spirit of the Gospel, is by its very nature a witness not only to Christ as the corner-stone of the community, but also as the light Who shines far beyond it.

The Catholic School as a Service to the Church and to Society

62 The Catholic school community, therefore, is an irreplaceable source of service, not only to the pupils and its other members, but also to society. Today especially one sees a world which clamors for solidarity and yet experiences the rise of new forms of individualism. Society can take note from the Catholic school that it is possible to create true communities out of a common effort for the common good. In the pluralistic society of today the Catholic school, moreover, by maintaining an institutional Christian presence in the academic world, proclaims by its very existence the enriching power of the faith as the answer to the enormous problems which afflict mankind. Above all, it is called to render a humble loving service to the Church by ensuring that she is present in the scholastic field for the benefit of the human family.

63 In this way the Catholic school performs "an authentic apostolate."[23] To work, therefore, in this apostolate "means apostolate performing a unique and invaluable work for the Church."[24]

V. THE RESPONSIBILITY OF THE CATHOLIC SCHOOL TODAY

64 The real problem facing the Catholic school is to identify and lay down the conditions necessary for it to fulfill its mission. It is, therefore, a problem requiring clear and positive thinking, courage, perseverance and cooperation to tackle the necessary measures without being overawed by the size of the

---

23. Second Vatican Council, *Declaration on Christian Education, "Gravissimum Educationis,"* 8.
24. Paul VI, to Prof. Giuseppe Lazzati, Rector of the University of the Sacred Heart (Milano), in *The Teaching of Pope Paul VI,* vol. 9, p. 1082.

difficulties from within and without, nor "by persistent and outdated slogans,"[25] which in the last analysis aim to abolish Catholic schools.[26] To give into them would be suicidal. To favor in a more or less radical form a merely non-institutional presence of the Church in the scholastic field, is a dangerous illusion.[27]

65 At great cost and sacrifice our forebears were inspired by the teaching of the Church to establish schools which enriched mankind and responded to the needs of time and place. While it recognizes its own inadequacies, the Catholic school is conscious of its responsibility to continue this service. Today, as in the past, some scholastic institutions which bear the name Catholic do not appear to correspond fully to the principles of education which should be their distinguishing feature and, therefore, do not fulfill the duties which the Church and the society has every right to expect of them. Without pretending to make an exhaustive enquiry into the factors which may explain the difficulties under which the Catholic school labors, here are a few points in the hope of encouraging some thought as a stimulus to courageous reform.

66 Often what is perhaps fundamentally lacking among Catholics who work in a school is a clear realization of the identity of a Catholic school and the courage to follow all the consequences of its uniqueness. One must recognize that, more than ever before, a Catholic school's job is infinitely more difficult, more complex, since this is a time when Christianity demands to be clothed in fresh garments, when all manner of changes have been introduced in the Church and in secular life, and, particularly, when a pluralist mentality dominates and the Christian Gospel is increasingly pushed to the side-lines.

67 It is because of this that loyalty to the educational aims of the Catholic school demands constant self-criticism and return to basic principles, to the motives which inspire the Church's involvement in education. They do not provide a quick answer to contemporary problems, but they give a direction which can begin to solve them. Account has to be taken of new pedagogical insights and collaboration with others, irrespective of religious allegiance, who work honestly for the true development of mankind—first and foremost with schools of other Christians—in the interests, even in this field, of Christian unity but also with State schools. In addition to meetings of teachers and

---

25. Paul VI, *Allocution to the Ninth Congress of the O.I.E.C.*, in *L'Osservatore Romano*, June 9th, 1974.

26. Cf. *above*, nn. 18, 20, 23.

27. Cf. Paul VI, *Allocution to the Ninth Congress of the O.I.E.C.*,. in *L'Osservatore Romano*, June 9th, 1974.

mutual research, this collaboration can be extended to the pupils themselves and their families.

68 In conclusion it is only right to repeat what has been said above[28] about the considerable difficulties arising from legal and economic systems operating in different countries which hinder the activities of the Catholic school, difficulties which prevent them from extending their service to all social and economic classes and compel them to give the false impression of providing schools simply for the rich.

VI. PRACTICAL DIRECTIONS

69 After reflecting on the difficulties which the Catholic school encounters, we turn now to the practical possibilities open to those who work in, or are responsible for, these schools. The following more serious questions have been selected for special comment: organization and planning, ensuring the distinctive Catholic character of the school, the involvement of religious in the school apostolate, the Catholic school in mission countries, pastoral care of teachers, professional associations, the economic question.

The Organization and Planning of the Catholic School

70 Catholic education is inspired by the general principles enunciated by the Second Vatican Council concerning collaboration between the hierarchy and those who work in the apostolate. In consequence of the principle of participation and co-responsibility, the various groupings which constitute the educational community are, according to their several competencies, to be associated in decision-making concerning the Catholic school and in the application of decisions once taken.[29] It is first and foremost at the stage of planning and of putting into operation an educational project that this principle of the Council is to be applied. The assigning of various responsibilities is governed by the principle of subsidiarity, and, with reference to this principle, ecclesiastical authority respects the competence of the professionals in teaching and education. Indeed, "the right and duty of exercising the apostolate is common to all the faithful, clerical and lay, and lay people have their own proper competence in the building up of the Church."[30]

28. Cf. *above*, n. 58.
29. Cf. Second Vatican Council, *Pastoral Constitution on the Church in the Modern World "Gaudium et Spes,"* 43.
30. Second Vatican Council, *Decree on the Apostolate of the Laity "Apostolicam Actuositatem,"* 25.

71 This principle enunciated by the Second Vatican Council is particularly applicable to the apostolate of the Catholic school which so closely unites teaching and religious education to a well-defined professional activity. It is here, above all, that the particular mission of the lay person is put into effect, a mission which has become "all the more imperative in view of the fact that many areas of human life have become very largely autonomous. This is as it should be, but it sometimes involves a certain withdrawal from ethical and religious influences and thereby creates a serious danger to Christian life."[31] Moreover, lay involvement in Catholic schools is an invitation "to cooperate more closely with the apostolate of the Bishops,"[32] both in the field of religious instruction[33] and in more general religious education which they endeavor to promote by assisting the pupils to a personal integration of culture and faith and of faith and living. The Catholic school in this sense, therefore, receives from the Bishops in some manner the "mandate" of an apostolic undertaking.[34]

72 The essential element of such a mandate is "union with those whom the Holy Spirit has assigned to rule God's Church"[35] and this link is expressed especially in overall pastoral strategy. "In the whole diocese or in given areas of it the coordination and close interconnection of all apostolic works should be fostered under the direction of the Bishop. In this way all undertakings and organization, whether catechetical, missionary, charitable, social, family, educational, or any other program serving a pastoral goal will be coordinated. Moreover, the unity of the diocese will thereby be made more evident."[36] This is something which is obviously indispensable for the Catholic school, inasmuch as it involves "apostolic cooperation on the part of both branches of the clergy, as well as of the religious and the laity."[37]

Ensuring the Distinctive Catholic Character of the School

73 This is the framework which guarantees the distinctive Catholic character of the school. While the Bishop's authority is to watch over the orthodoxy of

---

31. Second Vatican Council, *Decree on the Apostolate of the Laity "Apostolicam Actuositatem,"* 1.

32. Second Vatican Council, *Dogmatic Constitution on the Church, "Lumen Gentium,"* 33.

33. Cf. Second Vatican Council, *Decree on the Apostolate of the Laity "Apostolicam Actuositatem,"* 10.

34. *Ibid.,* 24.

35. *Ibid.,* 23.

36. Second Vatican Council, *Decree on the Bishop's Pastoral Office in the Church "Christus Dominus,"* 17.

37. Second Vatican Council, *Decree on the Apostolate of the Laity "Apostolicam Actuositatem,"* 23.

religious instruction and the observance of Christian morals in the Catholic schools, it is the task of the whole educative community to ensure that a distinctive Christian educational environment is maintained in practice. This responsibility applies chiefly to Christian parents who confide their children to the school. Having chosen it does not relieve them of a personal duty to give their children a Christian upbringing. They are bound to cooperate actively with the school—which means supporting the educational efforts of the school and utilizing the structures offered for parental involvement, in order to make certain that the school remains faithful to Christian principles of education. An equally important role belongs to the teachers in safeguarding and developing the distinctive mission of the Catholic school, particularly with regard to the Christian atmosphere which should characterize its life and teaching. Where difficulties and conflicts arise about the authentic Christian character of the Catholic school, hierarchical authority can and must intervene.

Involvement of Religious in the School Apostolate

74 Some problems arise from the fact that certain Religious Institutes, founded for the school apostolate, have subsequently abandoned school work because of social or political changes and have involved themselves in other activities. In some cases they have given up their schools as a result of their efforts to adapt their lives and mission to the recommendations of the Second Vatican Council and to the spirit of their original foundation.

75 It is necessary, however, to re-assess certain arguments adopted against the teaching apostolate. Some would say they have chosen a "more direct" apostolate,[38] forgetting the excellence and the apostolic value of educational work in the school.[39] Others would appeal to the greater importance of individual over community involvement, of personal over institutional work. The advantages, however, of a community apostolate in the educational field are self-evident. Sometimes the abandonment of Catholic schools is justified on the grounds of an apparent failure to gain perceptible results in pursuing certain objectives. If this were true, it would surely be an invitation to undertake a fundamental revision of the whole conduct of the school, reminding everyone who ventures into education of the need for humility and hope and the conviction that his work cannot be assessed by the same rationalistic criteria which apply to other professions.[40]

---

38. Cf. *above*, 23.
39. Cf. *above*, nn. 38–48.
40. Cf. *above*, n. 22.

76 It is the responsibility of competent local ecclesiastical authority to evaluate the advisability and necessity of any change to other forms of apostolic work whenever particular circumstances dictate the need for a re-assessment of the school apostolate, keeping in mind the observations above on overall pastoral strategy.[41]

The Catholic School in Mission Countries

77 The importance of the Catholic school apostolate is much greater when it is a question of the foreign missions. Where the young Churches still rely on the presence of foreign missionaries, the effectiveness of the Catholic school will largely depend on its ability to adapt to local needs. It must ensure that it is a true expression of the local and national Catholic community and that it contributes to the community's willingness to cooperate. In countries where the Christian community is still at its beginning and incapable of assuming responsibility for its own schools, the Bishops will have to undertake this responsibility themselves for the time being, but must endeavor little by little to fulfill the aims outlined above in connection with the organization of the Catholic schools.[42]

Pastoral Care of Teachers

78 By their witness and their behavior teachers are of the first importance to impart a distinctive character to Catholic schools. It is, therefore, indispensable to ensure their continuing formation through some form of suitable pastoral provision. This must aim to animate them as witnesses of Christ in the classroom and tackle the problems of their particular apostolate, especially regarding a Christian vision of the world and of education, problems also connected with the art of teaching in accordance with the principles of the Gospel. A huge field is thus opened up for national and international organizations which bring together Catholic teachers and educational institutions at all levels.

79 Professional organizations whose aim is to protect the interests of those who work in the educational field cannot themselves be divorced from the specific mission of the Catholic school. The rights of the people who are involved in the school must be safeguarded in strict justice. But, no matter what material interests may be at stake, or what social and moral conditions affect their professional development, the principle of the Second Vatican Council has a special application in this context: "The faithful should learn how to distinguish

41. Cf. *above*, nn. 70–72.
42. *Ibid.*

carefully between those rights and duties which are theirs as members of the Church, and those which they have as members of society. Let them strive to harmonize the two, remembering that in every temporal affair they must be guided by a Christian conscience."[43] Moreover, "even when preoccupied with temporal cares, the laity can and must perform valuable work for the evangelization of the world."[44] Therefore, the special organizations set up to protect the rights of teachers, parents and pupils must not forget the special mission of the Catholic school to be of service in the Christian education of youth. "The layman is at the same time a believer and a citizen and should be constantly led by Christian conscience alone."[45]

80 In the light of what has been said, these associations, while being concerned for the rights of their members, must also be alive to the responsibilities which are part and parcel of the specific apostolate of the Catholic school. Catholic teachers who freely accept posts in schools, which have a distinctive character, are obliged to respect that character and give their active support to it under the direction of those responsible.

Economic Situation of Catholic Schools

81 From the economic point of view the position of very many Catholic schools has improved and in some countries is perfectly acceptable. This is the case where governments have appreciated the advantages and the necessity of a plurality of school systems which offer alternatives to a single State system. While at first Catholic schools received various public grants, often merely conceded, they later began to enter into agreements, conventions, contracts, etc. which guarantee both the preservation of the special status of the Catholic school and its ability to perform its function adequately. Catholic schools are thereby more or less closely associated with the national system and are assured of an economic and juridical status similar to State schools.

82 Such agreements have been reached through the good offices of the respective governments, which have recognized the public service provided by Catholic schools, and through the determination of the Bishops and the Catholic community at the national level. These solutions are an encouragement to those responsible for Catholic schools in countries where the Catholic community must still shoulder a very heavy burden of cost to maintain an often highly

---

43. Second Vatican Council, *Dogmatic Constitution on the Church "Lumen Gentium,"* 36.
44. *Ibid.,* 35.
45. Second Vatican Council, *Decree on the Apostolate of the Laity "Apostolicam Actuositatem,"* 5.

important network of Catholic schools. These Catholics need to be assured, as they strive to regularize the frequent injustices in their school situation, that they are not only helping to provide every child with an education that respects his complete development, but they are also defending freedom of teaching and the right of parents to choose an education for their children which conforms to their legitimate requirements.[46]

VII. COURAGEOUS AND UNIFIED COMMITMENT

83 To commit oneself to working in accordance with the aims of a Catholic School is to make a great act of faith in the necessity and influence of this apostolate. Only one who has this conviction and accepts Christ's message, who has a love for and understands today's young people, who appreciates what people's real problems and difficulties are, will be led to contribute with courage and even audacity to the progress of this apostolate in building up a Catholic school, which puts its theory into practice, which renews itself according to its ideals and to present needs.

84 The validity of the educational results of a Catholic school, however, cannot be measured by immediate efficiency. In the field of Christian education, not only is the freedom-factor of teacher and pupil relationship with each other to be considered, but also the factor of grace. Freedom and grace come to fruition in the spiritual order which defies any merely temporal assessment. When grace infuses human liberty, it makes freedom fully free and raises it to its highest perfection in the freedom of the Spirit. It is when the Catholic school adds its weight, consciously and overtly, to the liberating power of grace, that it becomes the Christian leaven in the world.

85 In the certainty that the Spirit is at work in every person, the Catholic school offers itself to all, non-Christians included, with all its distinctive aims and means, acknowledging, preserving and promoting the spiritual and moral qualities, the social and cultural values, which characterize different civilizations.[47]

86 Such an outlook overrides any question of the disproportion between resources available and the number of children reached directly by the Catholic school; nothing can stop it from continuing to render its service. The only condition it would make, as is its right, for its continued existence would be

---

46. Cf. Second Vatican Council, *Declaration on Christian Education "Gravissimum Educationis,"* 6.

47. Cf. Second Vatican Council, *Declaration on the Relationship of the Church to Non-Christian Religions "Nostra Aetate,"* 2.

remaining faithful to the educational aims of the Catholic school. Loyalty to these aims is, moreover, the basic motive which must inspire any needed reorganization of the Catholic school institution.

87 If all who are responsible for the Catholic school would never lose sight of their mission and the apostolic value of their teaching, the school would enjoy better conditions in which to function in the present and would faithfully hand on its mission to future generations. They themselves, moreover, would most surely be filled with a deep conviction, joy and spirit of sacrifice in the knowledge that they are offering innumerable young people the opportunity of growing in faith, of accepting and living its precious principles of truth, charity and hope.

88 The Sacred Congregation for Catholic Education, to foster the full realization of the aims of the Catholic school, extends once more its warmest and heartfelt encouragement to all who work in these schools. There can be no doubt whatever of the importance of the apostolate of teaching in the total saving mission of the Church.

89 The Church herself in particular looks with confidence and trust to Religious Institutes which have received a special charism of the Holy Spirit and have been most active in the education of the young. May they be faithful to the inspiration of their founders and give their whole-hearted support to the apostolic work of education in Catholic schools and not allow themselves to be diverted from this by attractive invitations to undertake other, often seemingly more effective, apostolates.

90 A little more than ten years after the end of the Second Vatican Council the Sacred Congregation for Catholic Education repeats the final exhortation of the Declaration on Christian Education to the priests, religious and lay people who fulfill their mission in the Catholic school. It reads. "They are urged to persevere generously in their chosen duty, continuing to instill into their pupils the spirit of Christ; let them endeavor to excel in the art of teaching and in the advancement of knowledge. Thus they will not only foster the internal renewal of the Church, but will safeguard and intensify her beneficial presence in the modern world, and above all, in the world of the intellect."[48]

---

48. Second Vatican Council, *Declaration on Christian Education "Gravissimum Educationis,"* Conclusion.

Conclusion

91 This document in no way wishes to minimize the value of the witness and work of the many Catholics who teach in State schools throughout the world. In describing the task confided to the Catholic school it is intended to encourage every effort to promote the cause of Catholic education, since in the pluralistic world in which we live, the Catholic school is in a unique position to offer, more than ever before, a most valuable and necessary service. With the principles of the Gospel as its abiding point of reference, it offers its collaboration to those who are building a new world—one which is freed from a hedonistic mentality and from the efficiency syndrome of modern consumer society.

92 We appeal to each Episcopal Conference to consider and to develop these principles which should inspire the Catholic school and to translate them into concrete programs which will meet the real needs of the educational systems operating in their countries.

93 Realizing that the problems are both delicate and highly complex, the Sacred Congregation for Catholic Education also addresses itself to the whole People of God. In the economy of salvation we poor humans must confront problems, suffer their consequences and work might and main to solve them. We are certain that in the last analysis success in any venture does not come from trust in our own solutions but from trust in Jesus Who allowed Himself to be called Teacher. May He inspire, guide, support and bring to a safe conclusion all that is undertaken in His name.

Rome, March 19th, 1977, the Feast of St. Joseph
GABRIEL-MARIE Cardinal GARRONE, *Prefect*
Antonio M. Javierre, *Secretary*
Titular Archbishop of Meta

LAY CATHOLICS IN SCHOOLS: WITNESSES TO FAITH

THE SACRED CONGREGATION FOR CATHOLIC EDUCATION

Introduction

1 Lay Catholics, both men and women, who devote their lives to teaching in primary and secondary schools, have become more and more vitally important in recent years.[1] Whether we look at schools in general or Catholic schools in particular, the importance is deserved.

For it is the lay teachers, and indeed all lay persons, believers or not, who will substantially determine whether or not a school realizes its aims and accomplishes its objectives.[2] In the Second Vatican Council, and specifically in the Declaration on Christian Education, the Church recognized the role and the responsibility that this situation confers on all those lay Catholics who work in any type of elementary and secondary schools, whether as teachers, directors, administrators, or auxiliary staff. The Declaration invites us to expand on its contents and deepen them; in doing this, it is not our intention to ignore or minimize the significant accomplishments of Christians who belong to other Churches, or of non-Christians, in the field of education.

2 The most basic reason for this new role for Catholic laity, a role which the Church regards as positive and enriching, is theological. Especially in the course of the last century, the authentic image of the laity within the People of God has become increasingly clear; it has now been set down in two documents of the Second Vatican Council, which give profound expression to the richness and uniqueness of the lay vocation: The Dogmatic Constitution on the Church, and the Decree on the Apostolate of the Laity.

3 Theological development has been reinforced by the social, economic, and political developments of recent years. The cultural level has progressively risen; because this is closely tied to advances in science and technology, every profession requires a more extensive preparation. To this must be added a more general awareness of the fact that every person has a right to an integral education, an education which responds to all of the needs of the human person. These two advances in human life have required, and in part have created, an

---

1. Second Vatican Council: Const. *Lumen Gentium*, n. 31: "The term laity is here understood to mean all the faithful except those in holy orders and those in a religious state sanctioned by the Church."

2. Cf. Second Vatican Council: Decl. *Gravissimum Educationis*, n. 8.

extensive development of school systems everywhere in the world, together with an extraordinary increase in the number of people who are professionally trained in education. As a result, there is a corresponding growth in the number of Catholic laity who work in the field.

This process has coincided with a notable decrease in the number of priests and Religious, both men and women, dedicated to teaching. The decrease is due to a lack of vocations, to the urgent call of other apostolic needs, and—at times—to the erroneous opinion that a school is no longer an appropriate place for the Church's pastoral activity.[3] The efficacious work that so many different Religious Congregations have traditionally accomplished through teaching activities is greatly esteemed by the Church; and so she can do no less than regret the decline in Religious personnel which has had such a profound effect on Catholic schools, especially in some countries. The Church believes that, for an integral education of children and young people, both Religious and lay Catholics are needed in the schools.

4 This Sacred Congregation sees a genuine "sign of the times" for schools in the various facts and causes described above; it is an invitation to give special attention to the role of lay Catholics, as witnesses to the faith in what can only be described as a privileged environment for human formation. Without claiming to be exhaustive, but after serious and prolonged reflection on the importance of the theme, it desires to offer some considerations which will complete what has already been said in the document *The Catholic School*, and which will be of help to all those interested in the problem, inspiring them to undertake further and more extended developments of the same.

I. THE IDENTITY OF THE LAY CATHOLIC IN A SCHOOL

5 It seems necessary to begin by trying to delineate the identity of the lay Catholics who work in a school; the way in which they bear witness to the faith will depend on this specific identity, in the Church and in this particular field of labor. In trying to contribute to the investigation, it is the intention of this Sacred Congregation to offer a service to lay Catholics who work in schools (and who should have a clear idea of the specific character of their vocation), and also to the People of God (who need to have a true picture of the laity as an active element, accomplishing an important task for the entire Church through their labor).

---

3. Cf. Sacred Congregation for Catholic Education: *The Catholic School*, March 19, 1979, nn. 18–22.

THE LAITY IN THE CHURCH

6 The lay Catholic working in a school is, along with every Christian, a member of the People of God. As such, united to Christ through Baptism, he or she shares in the basic dignity that is common to all members. For, "they share a common dignity from their rebirth in Christ. They have the same filial grace and the same vocation to perfection. They possess in common one salvation, one hope, and one undivided charity."[4] Although it is true that, in the Church, "by the will of Christ, some are made teachers, dispensers of mysteries and shepherds on behalf of others, yet all share a true equality with regard to the dignity and to the activity common to all the faithful for the building up of the Body of Christ."[5]

Every Christian, and therefore also every lay person, has been made a sharer in "the priestly, prophetic, and kingly functions of Christ,"[6] and their apostolate "is a participation in the saving mission of the Church itself. . . . All are commissioned to that apostolate by the Lord Himself."[7]

7 This call to personal holiness and to apostolic mission is common to all believers; but there are many cases in which the life of a lay person takes on specific characteristics which transform this life into a specific "wonderful" vocation within the Church. The laity "seeks the kingdom of God by engaging in temporal affairs and by ordering them according to the plan of God."[8] They live in the midst of the world's activities and professions, and in the ordinary circumstances of family and social life; and there they are called by God so that by exercising their proper function and being led by the spirit of the Gospel they can work for the sanctification of the world from within, in the manner of leaven. In this way they can make Christ known to others, especially by the testimony of a life resplendent in faith, hope, and charity.[9]

8 The renewal of the temporal order, giving it a Christian inspiration, is the special role of the laity; this should encourage them to heal "the institutions and conditions of the world"[10] when it is seen that these can be inducements to sin. In this way, human reality is raised up, and conformed to the Gospel as far as this is possible; and "the world is permeated by the Spirit of Christ, and more

---

4. Second Vatican Council: Const. *Lumen Gentium*, n. 32.
5. *Ibid.*
6. *Ibid.*, n. 31.
7. *Ibid.*, n. 33.
8. *Ibid.*, n. 31.
9. *Ibid.*
10. Second Vatican Council: Const. *Lumen Gentium*, n. 36; Cf. Decl. *Apostolicam actuositatem*, n. 7.

effectively achieves its purpose in justice, charity, and peace."[11] "Therefore, by their competence in secular fields, and by their personal activity, elevated from within by the grace of Christ, let them labor vigorously so that, by human labor, technical skill, and civic culture, created goods may be perfected for the benefit of every last person . . . and be more suitably distributed among them."[12]

9 The evangelization of the world involves an encounter with such a wide variety and complexity of different situations that very frequently, in concrete circumstances and for most people, only the laity can be effective witnesses of the Gospel. Therefore, "the laity are called in a special way to make the Church present and operative in those places and circumstances where only through them can she become the salt of the earth."[13] In order to achieve this presence of the whole Church, and of the Savior whom she proclaims, lay people must be ready to proclaim the message through their words, and witness to it in what they do.

10 Because of the experiences that lay people acquire in their lives, and through their presence in all of the various spheres of human activity, they will be especially capable of recognizing and clarifying the signs of the times that characterize the present historical period of the People of God. Therefore, as a proper part of their vocation, they should contribute their initiative, their creativity, and their competent, conscious, and enthusiastic labor to this task. In this way, the whole People of God will be able to distinguish more precisely those elements of the signs that are Gospel values, or values contrary to the Gospel.

LAY CATHOLICS IN THE SCHOOLS

11 All those elements proper to the lay vocation in the Church are, surely, also true of those lay people who live their vocation in a school. But the fact that lay people can concretize their specific vocation in a variety of different sectors and areas of human life would seem to imply that the one common vocation will receive different specific characteristics from the different situations and states of life in which it is lived.

If, then, we are to have a better understanding of the school vocation of the lay Catholic, we must first look more precisely at the school.

---

11. Second Vatican Council: Const. *Lumen Gentium*, n. 36.
12. *Ibid.*
13. *Ibid.*, n. 33.

The School

12 While it is true that parents are the first and foremost educators of their children[14] and that the rights and duties that they have in this regard are "original and primary with respect to the educational role of others,"[15] it is also true that among the means which will assist and complement the exercise of the educational rights and duties of the family, the school has a value and an importance that are fundamental. In virtue of its mission, then, the school must be concerned with constant and careful attention to cultivating in students the intellectual, creative, and aesthetic faculties of the human person; to develop in them the ability to make correct use of their judgment, will, and affectivity; to promote in them a sense of values; to encourage just attitudes and prudent behavior; to introduce them to the cultural patrimony handed down from previous generations; to prepare them for professional life, and to encourage the friendly interchange among students of diverse cultures and backgrounds that will lead to mutual understanding.[16] For all of these reasons, the school enters into the specific mission of the Church.

13 The function exercised by the school in society has no substitute; it is the most important institution that society has so far developed to respond to the right of each individual to an education and, therefore, to full personal development; it is one of the decisive elements in the structuring and the life of society itself. In today's world, social interchange and mass media grow in importance (and their influence is sometimes harmful or counter-productive); the cultural milieu continues to expand; preparation for professional life is becoming ever more complex, more varied, and more specialized. The family, on its own, is less and less able to confront all of these serious problems; the presence of the school, then, becomes more and more necessary.

14 If the school is such an important educational instrument, then the individual being educated has the right to choose the system of education—and therefore the type of school—that he or she prefers.[17] (When a person does not yet have the capacity to do this, then the parents, who have the primary rights in the education of their children,[18] have the right to make this choice). From this it clearly follows that, in principle, a State monopoly of education is not

---

14. Cf. Second Vatican Council: Decl. *Gravissimum Educationis*, n. 3.
15. John Paul II, Apostolic Exhortation *Familiaris Consortio*, Nov. 22, 1981, *AAS*, 74 (1982) n. 36. p.126.
16. Cf. Second Vatican Council: Decl. *Gravissimum Educationis*, n. 5.
17. *Ibid.*, n. 3.
18. *Ibid.*, n. 6; Universal Declaration on Human Rights, art. 26, 3.

permissible,[19] and that only a pluralism of school systems will respect the fundamental right and the freedom of individuals—although the exercise of this right may be conditioned by a multiplicity of factors, according to the social realities of each country. The Church offers the Catholic school as a specific and enriching contribution to this variety of school possibilities. The lay Catholic, however, exercises the role of evangelization in all the different schools, not only in the Catholic school, to the extent that this is possible in the diverse socio-political contexts of the present world.

The Lay Catholic as an Educator

15 The Second Vatican Council gives specific attention to the vocation of an educator, a vocation which is as proper to the laity[20] as to those who follow other states of life in the Church.

Every person who contributes to integral human formation is an educator; but teachers have made integral human formation their very profession. When, then, we discuss the school, teachers deserve special consideration: because of their number, but also because of the institutional purpose of the school. But everyone who has a share in this formation is also to be included in the discussion: especially those who are responsible for the direction of the school, or are counselors, tutors or coordinators; also those who complement and complete the educational activities of the teacher or help in administrative and auxiliary positions. While the present analysis of the lay Catholic as an educator will concentrate on the role of the teacher, the analysis is applicable to all of the other roles, each according to their own proper activity. The material can be a basis for deep personal reflection.

16 The teacher under discussion here is not simply a professional person who systematically transmits a body of knowledge in the context of a school; "teacher" is to be understood as "educator"—one who helps to form human persons. The task of a teacher goes well beyond transmission of knowledge, although that is not excluded. Therefore, if adequate professional preparation is required in order to transmit knowledge, then adequate professional preparation is even more necessary in order to fulfill the role of a genuine teacher. It is an indispensable human formation, and without it, it would be foolish to undertake any educational work.

One specific characteristic of the educational profession assumes its most profound significance in the Catholic educator: the communication of truth.

19. Cf. Second Vatican Council: Decl. *Gravissimum Educationis*, n. 6.

20. *Ibid.*, n. 5; Cf. Paul VI, Apostolic Exhortation *Evangelii Nuntiandi*, December 8, 1975, *AAS* 68 (1976) n. 70, pp. 59–60.

For the Catholic educator, whatever is true is a participation in Him who is the Truth; the communication of truth, therefore, as a professional activity, is thus fundamentally transformed into a unique participation in the prophetic mission of Christ, carried on through one's teaching.

17 The integral formation of the human person, which is the purpose of education, includes the development of all the human faculties of the students, together with preparation for professional life, formation of ethical and social awareness, becoming aware of the transcendental, and religious education. Every school, and every educator in the school, ought to be striving "to form strong and responsible individuals, who are capable of making free and correct choices," thus preparing young people "to open themselves more and more to reality, and to form in themselves a clear idea of the meaning of life."[21]

18 Each type of education, moreover, is influenced by a particular concept of what it means to be a human person. In today's pluralistic world, the Catholic educator must consciously inspire his or her activity with the Christian concept of the person, in communion with the Magisterium of the Church. It is a concept which includes a defense of human rights, but also attributes to the human person the dignity of a child of God; it attributes the fullest liberty, freed from sin itself by Christ, the most exalted destiny, which is the definitive and total possession of God Himself, through love. It establishes the strictest possible relationship of solidarity among all persons; through mutual love and an ecclesial community. It calls for the fullest development of all that is human, because we have been made masters of the world by its Creator. Finally, it proposes Christ, Incarnate Son of God and perfect Man, as both model and means; to imitate Him, is, for all men and women, the inexhaustible source of personal and communal perfection. Thus, Catholic educators can be certain that they make human beings more human.[22] Moreover, the special task of those educators who are lay persons is to offer to their students a concrete example of the fact that people deeply immersed in the world, living fully the same secular life as the vast majority of the human family, possess this same exalted dignity.

19 The vocation of every Catholic educator includes the work of ongoing social development: to form men and women who will be ready to take their place in society, preparing them in such a way that they will make the kind of social commitment which will enable them to work for the improvement of

---

21. Sacred Congregation for Catholic Education: *The Catholic School*, n. 31.

22. Cf. Paul VI, Encyclical Letter *Populorum Progressio*; March 26, 1967, *AAS* 59 (1967), n. 19, pp. 267–268; cf. John Paul II, *Discourse to UNESCO*, June 2, 1980, *AAS* 72 (1980) n. 11, p. 742.

social structures, making these structures more conformed to the principles of the Gospel. Thus, they will form human beings who will make human society more peaceful, fraternal, and communitarian. Today's world has tremendous problems: hunger, illiteracy and human exploitation; sharp contrasts in the standard of living of individuals and of countries; aggression and violence, a growing drug problem, legalization of abortion, along with many other examples of the degradation of human life. All of this demands that Catholic educators develop in themselves, and cultivate in their students, a keen social awareness and a profound sense of civic and political responsibility. The Catholic educator, in other words, must be committed to the task of forming men and women who will make the "civilization of love"[23] a reality.

But lay educators must bring the experience of their own lives to this social development and social awareness, so that students can be prepared to take their place in society with an appreciation of the specific role of the lay person—for this is the life that nearly all of the students will be called to live.

20 A school uses its own specific means for the integral formation of the human person: the communication of culture. It is extremely important, then, that the Catholic educator reflect on the profound relationship that exists between culture and the Church. For the Church not only influences culture and is, in turn, conditioned by culture; the Church embraces everything in human culture which is compatible with Revelation and which it needs in order to proclaim the message of Christ and express it more adequately according to the cultural characteristics of each people and each age. The close relationship between culture and the life of the Church is an especially clear manifestation of the unity that exists between creation and redemption.

For this reason, if the communication of culture is to be a genuine educational activity, it must not only be organic, but also critical and evaluative, historical and dynamic. Faith will provide Catholic educators with some essential principles for critique and evaluation; faith will help them to see all of human history as a history of salvation which culminates in the fullness of the Kingdom. This puts culture into a creative context, constantly being perfected.

Here too, in the communication of culture, lay educators have a special role to play. They are the authors of, and the sharers in, the more lay aspects of culture; their mission, then, is to help the students come to understand, from a lay point of view, the global character that is proper to culture, the synthesis which will join together the lay and the religious aspects of culture, and the personal contribution which those in the lay state can be expected to make to culture.

---

23. Paul VI, *Discourse on Christmas Night*, December 25, 1976, *AAS* 68 (1976) p. 145.

21 The communication of culture in an educational context involves a methodology, whose principles and techniques are collected together into a consistent pedagogy. A variety of pedagogical theories exist; the choice of the Catholic educator, based on a Christian concept of the human person, should be the practice of a pedagogy which gives special emphasis to direct and personal contact with the students. If the teacher undertakes this contact with the conviction that students are already in possession of fundamentally positive values, the relationship will allow for an openness and a dialogue which will facilitate an understanding of the witness to faith that is revealed through the behavior of the teacher.

22 Everything that the Catholic educator does in a school takes place within the structure of an educational community, made up of the contacts and the collaboration among all of the various groups—students, parents, teachers, directors, non-teaching staff—that together are responsible for making the school an instrument for integral formation. Although it is not exhaustive, this concept of the scholarly institution as an educational community, together with a more widespread awareness of this concept, is one of the most enriching developments for the contemporary school. The Catholic educator exercises his or her profession as a member of one of the constitutive elements of this community. The professional structure itself offers an excellent opportunity to live—and bring to life in the students the communitarian dimension of the human person. Every human being is called to live in a community, as a social being, and as a member of the People of God.

Therefore, the educational community of a school is itself a "school." It teaches one how to be a member of the wider social communities; and when the educational community is at the same time a Christian community—and this is what the educational community of a Catholic school must always be striving toward—then it offers a great opportunity for the teachers to provide the students with a living example of what it means to be a member of that great community which is the Church.

23 The communitarian structure of the school brings the Catholic educator into contact with a wide and rich assortment of people; not only the students, who are the reason why the school and the teaching profession exist, but also with one's colleagues in the work of education, with parents, with other personnel in the school, with the school directors. The Catholic educator must be a source of spiritual inspiration for each of these groups, as well as for each of the scholastic and cultural organizations that the school comes in contact with, for the local Church and the parishes, for the entire human ambience in which he or she is inserted and, in a variety of ways, should have an effect on. In this way, the Catholic educator is called to display that kind of spiritual inspiration which will manifest different forms of evangelization.

24 To summarize: The Lay Catholic educator is a person who exercises a specific mission within the Church by living, in faith, a secular vocation in the communitarian structure of the school: with the best possible professional qualifications, with an apostolic intention inspired by faith, for the integral formation of the human person, in a communication of culture, in an exercise of that pedagogy which will give emphasis to direct and personal contact with students, giving spiritual inspiration to the educational community of which he or she is a member, as well as to all the different persons related to the educational community. To this lay person, as a member of this community, the family and the Church entrust the school's educational endeavor. Lay teachers must be profoundly convinced that they share in the sanctifying, and therefore educational mission of the Church; they cannot regard themselves as cut off from the ecclesial complex.

II. HOW TO LIVE ONE'S PERSONAL IDENTITY

25 The human person is called to be a worker; work is one of the characteristics which distinguish human beings from the rest of creatures.[24] From this it is evident that it is not enough to possess a vocational identity, an identity which involves the whole person; it must be lived. More concretely, if, through their work, human beings must contribute "above all to elevating unceasingly the cultural and moral level of society,"[25] then the educator who does not educate can no longer truly be called an educator. And if there is no trace of Catholic identity in the education, the educator can hardly be called a Catholic educator. Some of the aspects of this living out of one's identity are common and essential; they must be present no matter what the school is in which the lay educator exercises his or her vocation. Others will differ according to the diverse nature of various types of schools.

COMMON ELEMENTS OF AN IDENTITY THAT IS BEING LIVED

Realism Combined with Hope

26 The identity of the lay Catholic educator is, of necessity, an ideal; innumerable obstacles stand in the way of its accomplishment. Some are the result of

---

24. Cf. John Paul II, Encyclical Letter *Laborem Exercens*, 14. Sept. 1981, *AAS* 73 (1981), Foreword, p. 578.

25. John Paul II, Encyclical Letter *Laborem Exercens, ibid.*, p. 577.

one's own personal situation; others are due to deficiencies in the school and in society; all of them have their strongest effect on children and young people. Identity crisis, loss of trust in social structures, the resulting insecurity and loss of any personal convictions, the contagion of a progressive secularization of society, loss of the proper concept of authority and lack of a proper use of freedom—these are only a few of the multitude of difficulties which, in varying degrees, according to the diverse cultures and the different countries, the adolescents and young people of today bring to the Catholic educator. Moreover, the lay state in which the teacher lives is itself seriously threatened by crises in the family and in the world of labor.

These present difficulties should be realistically recognized. But they should, at the same time, be viewed and confronted with a healthy optimism, and with the forceful courage that Christian hope and a sharing in the mystery of the Cross demand of all believers. Therefore, the first indispensable necessity in one who is going to live the identity of a lay Catholic educator is to sincerely share in, and make one's own, the statements that the Church, illuminated by Divine Revelation, has made about the identity of an educator. The strength needed to do this should be found through a personal identification with Christ.

Professionalism. A Christian Concept of Humanity and of Life

27 Professionalism is one of the most important characteristics in the identity of every lay Catholic. The first requirement, then, for a lay educator who wishes to live out his or her ecclesial vocation, is the acquisition of a solid professional formation. In the case of an educator, this includes competency in a wide range of cultural, psychological, and pedagogical areas.[26] However, it is not enough that the initial training be at a good level; this must be maintained and deepened, always bringing it up to date. This can be very difficult for a lay teacher, and to ignore this fact is to ignore reality: salaries are often inadequate, and supplementary employment is often a necessity. Such a situation is incompatible with professional development, either because of the time required for other work, or because of the fatigue that results. In many countries, especially in those less developed, the problem is insoluble at the present time.

Even so, educators must realize that poor teaching, resulting from insufficient preparation of classes or outdated pedagogical methods, is going to hinder them severely in their call to contribute to an integral formation of the students; it will also obscure the life witness that they must present.

---

26. Cf. above, n. 16.

28 The entire effort of the Catholic teacher is oriented toward an integral formation of each student. New horizons will be opened to students through the responses that Christian revelation brings to questions about the ultimate meaning of the human person, of human life, of history, and of the world. These must be offered to the students as responses which flow out of the profound faith of the educator, but at the same time with the greatest sensitive respect for the conscience of each student. Students will surely have many different levels of faith response; the Christian vision of existence must be presented in such a way that it meets all of these levels, ranging from the most elementary evangelization all the way to communion in the same faith. And whatever the situation, the presentation must always be in the nature of a gift: though offered insistently and urgently, it cannot be imposed.

On the other hand, the gift cannot be offered coldly and abstractly. It must be seen as a vital reality, one which deserves the commitment of the entire person, something which is to become a part of one's own life.

Synthesis of Faith, Culture and Life

29 For the accomplishment of this vast undertaking, many different educational elements must converge; in each of them, the lay Catholic must appear as a witness to faith. An organic, critical, and value-oriented communication of culture[27] clearly includes the communication of truth and knowledge; while doing this, a Catholic teacher should always be alert for opportunities to initiate the appropriate dialogue between culture and faith—two things which are intimately related—in order to bring the interior synthesis of the student to this deeper level. It is, of course, a synthesis which should already exist in the teacher.

30 Critical transmission also involves the presentation of a set of values and counter-values. These must be judged within the context of an appropriate concept of life and of the human person. The Catholic teacher, therefore, cannot be content simply to present Christian values as a set of abstract objectives to be admired, even if this be done positively and with imagination; they must be presented as values which generate human attitudes, and these attitudes must be encouraged in the students. Examples of such attitudes would be these: a freedom which includes respect for others; conscientious responsibility; a sincere and constant search for truth; a calm and peaceful critical spirit; a spirit of solidarity with and service toward all other persons; a sensitivity for justice; a special awareness of being called to be positive agents of change in a society that is undergoing continuous transformation.

27. Cf. above, n. 20.

Since Catholic teachers frequently have to exercise their mission within a general atmosphere of secularization and unbelief, it is important that they not be limited to a mentality that is merely experimental and critical; thus, they will be able to bring the students to an awareness of the transcendental, and dispose them to welcome revealed truth.

31 In the process of developing attitudes such as these, the teacher can more easily show the positive nature of the behavior that flows from such attitudes. Ideally, attitudes and behavior will gradually be motivated by, and flow out of, the interior faith of the individual student. In this way, the fullness of faith will be achieved; it will then extend to such things as filial prayer, sacramental life, love for one another, and a following of Jesus Christ—all of the elements that form a part of the specific heritage of the faithful. Knowledge, values, attitudes, and behavior fully integrated, with faith will result in the student's personal synthesis of life and faith. Very few Catholics, then, have the opportunity that the educator has to accomplish the very purpose of evangelization: the incarnation of the Christian message in the lives of men and women.

Personal Life Witness. Direct and Personal Contact with Students

32 Conduct is always much more important than speech; this fact becomes especially important in the formation period of students. The more completely an educator can give concrete witness to the model of the ideal person that is being presented to the students, the more this ideal will be believed and imitated. For it will then be seen as something reasonable and worthy of being lived, something concrete and realizable. It is in this context that the faith witness of the lay teacher becomes especially important. Students should see in their teachers the Christian attitude and behavior that is often so conspicuously absent from the secular atmosphere in which they live. Without this witness, living in such an atmosphere, they may begin to regard Christian behavior as an impossible ideal. It must never be forgotten that, in the crises "which have their greatest effect on the younger generations," the most important element in the educational endeavor is "always the individual person: the person, and the moral dignity of that person which is the result of his or her principles, and the conformity of actions with those principles."[28]

33 In this context, what was said above about direct and personal contact between teachers and students[29] becomes especially significant: it is a privileged

---

28. John Paul II, *Discourse to UNESCO*, June 2, 1980, *AAS* 72 (1980) n. 11, p. 742.
29. Cf. above, n. 21.

opportunity for giving witness. A personal relationship is always a dialogue rather than a monologue, and the teacher must be convinced that the enrichment in the relationship is mutual. But the mission must never be lost sight of: the educator can never forget that students need a companion and guide during their period of growth; they need help from others in order to overcome doubts and disorientation. Also, rapport with the students ought to be a prudent combination of familiarity and distance; and this must be adapted to the need of each individual student. Familiarity will make a personal relationship easier, but a certain distance is also needed: students need to learn how to express their own personality without being pre-conditioned; they need to be freed from inhibitions in the responsible exercise of their freedom.

It is good to remember here that a responsible use of freedom also involves the choice of one's own state of life. In contacts with those students who are believers, Catholic teachers should not be hesitant to discuss the question of one's personal vocation in the Church. They should try to discover and cultivate vocations to the priesthood or to Religious life, or the call to live a private commitment in a Secular Institute or Catholic apostolic organization; these latter possibilities are areas which are often neglected. And they should also help students to discern a vocation to marriage or to celibacy, including consecrated celibacy, within the lay state.

This direct and personal contact is not just a methodology by which the teacher can help in the formation of the students; it is also the means by which teachers learn what they need to know about the students in order to guide them adequately. The difference in generation is deeper, and the time between generations is shorter, today more than ever before; direct contact, then, is more necessary than ever.

Communitarian Aspects

34 Along with a proper development of their individual personalities, and as an integral part of this process, students should be guided by their Catholic teachers toward the development of an attitude of sociability: toward others in the educational community, in the other communities that they may belong to, and with the entire human community. Lay Catholic educators are also members of the educational community; they influence, and are influenced by, the social ambience of the school. Therefore, close relationship should be established with one's colleagues; they should work together as a team. And teachers should establish close relationships with the other groups that make up the educational community, and be willing to contribute their share to all of the diverse activities that make up the common educational endeavor of a scholastic institution.

The family is "the first and fundamental school of social living"[30] therefore, there is a special duty to accept willingly and even to encourage opportunities for contact with the parents of students. These contacts are very necessary, because the educational task of the family and that of the school complement one another in many concrete areas; and they will facilitate the "serious duty" that parents have "to commit themselves totally to a cordial and active relationship with the teachers and the school authorities."[31] Finally, such contacts will offer to many families the assistance they need in order to educate their own children properly; and thus fulfill the "irreplaceable and inalienable"[32] function that is theirs.

35 A teacher must also be constantly attentive to the socio-cultural, economic, and political environment of the school: in the immediate area that the school is located in, and also in the region and the nation. Given today's means of communication, the national scene exerts a great influence on the local situation. Only close attention to the global reality—local, national, and international—will provide the data needed to give the kind of formation that students need now, and to prepare them for the future that can now be predicted.

36 While it is only natural to expect lay Catholic educators to give preference to Catholic professional associations, it is not foreign to their educational role to participate in and collaborate with all educational groups and associations, along with other groups that are connected with education. They should also lend support to the struggle for an adequate national educational policy, in whatever ways such support is possible. Their involvement may also include Trade Union activity, though always mindful of human rights and Christian educational principles.[33] Lay teachers should be reminded that professional life can sometimes be very remote from the activities of associations; they should realize that if they are never involved in or even aware of these activities, this absence could be seriously harmful to important educational issues.

It is true that there is often no reward for such activities; success or failure depends on the generosity of those who participate. But when there are issues at stake so vital that the Catholic teacher cannot ignore them, then generosity is urgently needed.

---

30. John Paul II, Apostolic Exhortation *Familiaris Consortio, AAS* 74 (1982) n. 37, p. 127.

31. *Ibid.*, n. 40.

32. *Ibid.*, n. 36.

33. Cf. John Paul II, Encyclical Letter *Laborem Exercens*, September 14, 1981, *AAS* 73 (1981) n. 20, pp. 629–632.

A Vocation, Rather than a Profession

37 The work of a lay educator has an undeniably professional aspect; but it cannot be reduced to professionalism alone. Professionalism is marked by, and raised to, a super-natural Christian vocation. The life of the Catholic teacher must be marked by the exercise of a personal vocation in the Church, and not simply by the exercise of a profession. In a lay vocation, detachment and generosity are joined to legitimate defense of personal rights; but it is still a vocation, with the fullness of life and the personal commitment that the word implies. It offers ample opportunity for a life filled with enthusiasm.

It is, therefore, very desirable that every lay Catholic educator become fully aware of the importance, the richness, and the responsibility of this vocation. They should fully respond to all of its demands, secure in the knowledge that their response is vital for the construction and ongoing renewal of the earthly city, and for the evangelization of the world.

ELEMENTS OF THE CATHOLIC EDUCATIONAL VOCATION WHICH ARE SPECIFIC TO DIFFERENT TYPES OF SCHOOLS

In the Catholic School

38 The distinctive feature of the Catholic school is "to create for the school community an atmosphere enlivened by the gospel spirit of freedom and charity. It aims to help the adolescent in such a way that the development of his or her own personality will be matched by the growth of that new creation which he or she becomes by baptism. It strives to relate all human culture eventually to the news of salvation, so that the light of faith will illumine the knowledge which students gradually gain of the world, of life and of the human race."[34] From all this, it is obvious that the Catholic school "fully enters into the salvific mission of the Church, especially in the need for education in the faith,"[35] and involves a sincere adherence to the Magisterium of the Church, a presentation of Christ as the supreme model of the human person, and a special care for the quality of the religious education in the school.

The lay Catholic who works in a Catholic school should be aware of the ideals and specific objectives which constitute the general educational philosophy of the institution, and realize that it is because of this educational philosophy that the Catholic school is the school in which the vocation of a lay Catholic

---

34. Second Vatican Council: Decl. *Gravissimum Educationis*, n. 8; cf. Sacred Congregation for Catholic Education: *The Catholic School*, n. 34.

35. Sacred Congregation for Catholic Education: *The Catholic School*, n. 9.

teacher can be lived most freely and most completely. It is the model for the apostolic activity of lay Catholics in all other schools, according to the possibilities that each one of them offers. This realization will inspire lay Catholics in Catholic schools to commit themselves sincerely and personally to share in the responsibility for the attainment of these ideals and objectives. This is not to deny that difficulties exist; among them we mention, because of the great consequences that it has, the great heterogeneity of both students and teachers within the Catholic schools of many countries today.

39 Certain elements will be characteristic of all Catholic schools. But these can be expressed in a variety of ways; often enough, the concrete expression will correspond to the specific charism of the Religious Institute that founded the school and continues to direct it. Whatever be its origin—diocesan, Religious, or lay—each Catholic school can preserve its own specific character, spelled out in an educational philosophy, rationale, or in its own pedagogy. Lay Catholics should try to understand the special characteristics of the school they are working in, and the reasons that have inspired them. They should try to so identify themselves with these characteristics that their own work will help toward realizing the specific nature of the school.

40 As a visible manifestation of the faith they profess and the life witness they are supposed to manifest,[36] it is important that lay Catholics who work in a Catholic school participate simply and actively in the liturgical and sacramental life of the school. Students will share in this life more readily when they have concrete examples: when they see the importance that this life has for believers. In today's secularized world, students will see many lay people who call themselves Catholics, but who never take part in liturgy or sacraments. It is very important that they also have the example of lay adults who take such things seriously, who find in them a source and nourishment for Christian living.

41 The educational community of a Catholic school should be trying to become a Christian community: a genuine community of faith. This will not take place, it will not even begin to happen, unless there is a sharing of the Christian commitment among at least a portion of each of the principal groups that make up the educational community: parents, teachers, and students. It is highly desirable that every lay Catholic, especially the educator, be ready to participate actively in groups of pastoral inspiration, or in other groups capable of nourishing a life lived according to the Gospel.

---

36. Cf. above, n. 29 and n. 32.

42 At times there are students in Catholic schools who do not profess the Catholic faith, or perhaps are without any religious faith at all. Faith does not admit of violence; it is a free response of the human person to God as He reveals Himself. Therefore, while Catholic educators will teach doctrine in conformity with their own religious convictions and in accord with the identity of the school, they must at the same time have the greatest respect for those students who are not Catholics. They should be open at all times to authentic dialogue, convinced that in these circumstances the best testimony that they can give of their own faith is a warm and sincere appreciation for anyone who is honestly seeking God according to his or her own conscience.[37]

43 Education in the faith is a part of the finality of a Catholic school. The more fully the educational community represents the richness of the ecclesial community, the more capable it will be of fulfilling this mission. When priests, men and women Religious, and lay people are all present together in a school, they will present students with a living image of this richness, which can lead to a better understanding of the reality of the Church. Lay Catholics should reflect on the importance of their presence, from this point of view, alongside the priests and Religious. For each of these types of ecclesial vocation presents to the students its own distinct incarnational model: lay Catholics, the intimate dependence of earthly realities on God in Christ, the lay professional as one who disposes the world toward God; the priest, the multiple sources of grace offered by Christ to all believers through the sacraments, the revealing light of the Word, and the character of service which clothes the hierarchical structure of the Church; Religious, the radical spirit of Beatitudes, the continuous call of the Kingdom as the single definitive reality, the love of Christ, and the love of all men and women in Christ.

44 If each vocation has its own distinct characteristics, then all should be aware of the fact that a mutual and complementary presence will be a great help in ensuring the character of the Catholic school. This means that each one should be dedicated to the search for unity and coordination. Furthermore, the attitude of the lay people should be one which will help to insert the Catholic school into pastoral activities, in union with the local Church—a perspective which must never be forgotten—in ways that are complementary to the activities of parish ministry. The initiatives and experiences of lay people should also help to bring about more effective relationships and closer collaboration among Catholic schools, as well as between Catholic schools and other schools—especially those which share a Christian orientation—and with society as a whole.

---

37. Cf. Second Vatican Council: Decl. *Dignitatis Humanae*, n. 3.

45 Lay Catholic educators must be very aware of the real impoverishment which will result if priests and Religious disappear from the Catholic schools, or noticeably decline in number. This is to be avoided as far as is possible; and yet, the laity must prepare themselves in such a way that they will be able to maintain Catholic schools on their own whenever this becomes necessary or at least more desirable, in the present or in the future. Historical forces at work in the schools of today lead to the conclusion that, at least for the immediate future, continued existence of Catholic schools in many traditionally Catholic countries is going to depend largely on the laity, just as that existence has depended and does depend, with great fruit, on lay people—in so many of the young Churches. This responsibility cannot be assumed with passive attitudes of fear and regret; it is a responsibility that offers a challenge to firm and effective action. And this action should even now look to and plan for the future with the help of the Religious Institutes who see their possibilities diminishing in the days immediately ahead.

46 There are times in which the Bishops will take advantage of the availability of competent lay persons who wish to give clear Christian witness in the field of education, and will entrust them with complete direction of Catholic schools, thus incorporating them more closely into the apostolic mission of the Church.[38]

Given the ever greater expansion of the field of education, the Church needs to take advantage of every available resource for the Christian education of youth. To increase the participation of lay Catholic educators is not meant to diminish the importance of those schools directed by Religious Congregations in any way. The unique kind of witness that men and women Religious give in their own teaching centers, whether as individuals or as a community, surely implies that these schools are more necessary than ever in a secularized world.

Few situations are as apt as their own schools for the members of a Religious community to give this kind of witness. For in the schools, Religious men and women establish an immediate and lasting contact with young people, in a context in which the truths of faith frequently come up spontaneously as a means to illuminate the varied dimensions of existence. This contact has a special importance at a time of life in which ideas and experiences leave such a lasting impression on the personality of the students.

However, the call of the Church to lay Catholic educators, to commit themselves to an active apostolate in education, is not a call limited to the Church's own schools. It is a call that extends to the entire vast teaching field, to the extent in which it may be possible to give Christian witness in teaching.

---

38. Cf. Second Vatican Council: Decree *Apostolicam Actuositatem*, n. 2.

In Schools That Have Different Educational Philosophies

47 We now consider all those schools, public or private, whose educational philosophy is different from that of the Catholic school, but is not essentially incompatible with the Christian concept of the human person and of life. Schools of this type form the vast majority of the schools that exist in the world. Their educational philosophy may be developed by means of a well-defined concept of the human person and of life; more simply and narrowly, they may have a determined ideology;[39] or the school may admit the coexistence of a variety of philosophies and ideologies among the teachers, within the framework of some general principles. "Coexistence" should be understood here as a manifestation of pluralism: in such schools, each of the educators gives lessons, explains principles, and promotes values according to his or her own concept of the human person, and specific ideology. We do not speak here about the so-called neutral school because, in practice, such a school does not exist.

48 In today's pluralistic and secularized world, it will frequently happen that the presence of lay Catholics in these schools is the only way in which the Church is present. This is a concrete example of what was said above: that the Church can only reach out to certain situations or institutions through the laity.[40] A clear awareness of this fact will be a great help to encourage lay Catholics to assume the responsibility that is theirs.

49 Lay Catholic teachers should be influenced by a Christian faith vision in the way they teach their course, to the extent that this is consistent with the subject matter, and the circumstances of the student body and the school. In doing this, they will help students to discover true human values; and even though they must work within the limitations proper to a school that makes no attempt to educate in the faith, in which many factors will actually work directly against faith education, they will still be able to contribute to the beginnings of a dialogue between faith and culture. It is a dialogue which may, one day, lead to the students' genuine synthesis of the two. This effort can be especially fruitful for those students who are Catholics; it can be a form of evangelization for those who are not.

50 In a pluralistic school, living according to one's faith must be joined to careful respect for the ideological convictions and the work of the other educators, assuming always that they do not violate the human rights of the students.

---

39. The concept here is a more ample one: a system of ideas joined to social, economic, and/or political structures.

40. Cf. above n. 9.

Mutual respect should lead to constructive dialogue, especially with other Christians, but with all men and women of good will. In this way it can become clearly evident that religious and human freedom, the logical fruit of a pluralistic society, is not only defended in theory by Christian faith, but also concretely practiced.

51 Active participation in the activities of colleagues, in relationships with other members of the educational community; and especially in relationships with parents of the students, is extremely important. In this way the objectives, programs, and teaching methods of the school in which the lay Catholic is working can be gradually impregnated with the spirit of the Gospel.

52 Professional commitment; support of truth, justice and freedom; openness to the point of view of others, combined with an habitual attitude of service; personal commitment to the students, and fraternal solidarity with everyone; a life that is integrally moral in all its aspects. The lay Catholic who brings all of this to his or her work in a pluralist school becomes a living mirror, in whom every individual in the educational community will see reflected an image of one inspired by the Gospel.

In Other Schools

53 Here we consider more specifically the situation in schools of what are called mission countries, or countries where the practice of Christianity has almost totally disappeared. The lay Catholic may be the only presence of the Church, not only in the school, but also in the place in which he or she is living. The call of faith makes this situation especially compelling: the lay Catholic teacher may be the only voice that proclaims the message of the Gospel: to students, to other members of the educational community, to everyone that he or she comes in contact with, as an educator or simply as a person.[41] Everything that has been said above about awareness of responsibility, a Christian perspective in teaching (and in education more generally), respect for the convictions of others, constructive dialogue with other Christians as well as with those who do not believe in Christianity, active participation in various school groups, and, most important of all, personal life witness all of these things become crucially important in this type of school situation.

54 Finally, we cannot forget those lay Catholics who work in schools in countries where the Church is persecuted, where one who is known to be a Christian

---

41. Cf. Second Vatican Council: Decl. *Ad Gentes*, n. 21.

is forbidden to function as an educator. The orientation of the school is atheist; laity who work in them must conceal the fact that they are believers. In this difficult situation simple presence, if it is the silent but vital presence of a person inspired by the Gospel, is already an efficacious proclamation of the message of Christ. It is a counterbalance to the pernicious intentions of those who promote an atheistic education in the school. And this witness, when joined to personal contact with the students, can, in spite of the difficulties, lead to opportunities for more explicit evangelization. Although forced to live his or her Catholicism anonymously, the lay educator can still be (because of regrettable human and religious motives) the only way that many of the young people in these countries can come to some genuine knowledge of the Gospel and of the Church, which are distorted and attacked in the school.

55 In every kind of school, the Catholic educator will not infrequently come in contact with non-Catholic students, especially in some countries. The attitude should not only be one of respect, but also welcoming, and open to dialogue motivated by a universal Christian love. Furthermore, they should always remember that true education is not limited to the imparting of knowledge; it promotes human dignity and genuine human relationships, and prepares the way for opening oneself to the Truth that is Christ.

The Lay Catholic Educator as a Teacher of Religion

56 Religious instruction is appropriate in every school, for the purpose of the school is human formation in all of its fundamental dimensions, and the religious dimension is an integral part of this formation. Religious education is actually a right—with the corresponding duties—of the student and of the parents. It is also, at least in the case of the Catholic religion, an extremely important instrument for attaining the adequate synthesis of faith and culture that has been insisted on so often.

Therefore, the teaching of the Catholic religion, distinct from and at the same time complementary to catechesis properly so-called,[42] ought to form a part of the curriculum of every school.

57 The teaching of religion is, along with catechesis, "an eminent form of the lay apostolate."[43] Because of this, and because of the number of religion teachers needed for today's vast school systems, lay people will have the respon-

---

42. Cf. John Paul II, *Discourse to the Clerics of Rome Concerning the Teaching of Religion and Catechesis*, March 5, 1981, *Insegnamenti di Giovanni Paolo II*, 1981, IV, I, n. 3, p. 630.

43. John Paul II, Apostolic Exhortation *Catechesi Tradendae*, October 16, 1979, *AAS* 71 n. 66, p. 1331.

sibility for religious education in the majority of cases, especially at the level of basic education.

58 Lay Catholics, therefore, in different places and according to different circumstances, should become aware of the great role that is offered to them in this field of religious education. Without their generous collaboration, the number of religious teachers will not be adequate to meet the need that exists; this is already the situation in some countries. In this respect, as in so many others, the Church depends on lay collaboration. The need can be especially urgent in young Churches.

59 The role of the religion teacher is of first importance; for "what is asked for is not that one impart one's own doctrine, or that of some other teacher, but the teaching of Jesus Christ Himself."[44] In their teaching, therefore, taking into account the nature of the group being taught, teachers of religion (and also catechists) "should take advantage of every opportunity to profit from the fruits of theological research, which can shed light on their own reflections and also on their teaching, always taking care ... to be faithful to the genuine sources, and to the light of the Magisterium," on which they depend for the proper fulfillment of their role; and "they should refrain from upsetting the minds of children and young people ... with outlandish theories."[45] The norms of the local bishop should be faithfully followed in everything that has to do with their own theological and pedagogical formation, and also in the course syllabi; and they should remember that, in this area above all, life witness and an intensely lived spirituality have an especially great importance.

III. THE FORMATION THAT IS NEEDED IF LAY CATHOLICS ARE TO GIVE WITNESS TO THE FAITH IN A SCHOOL

60 The concrete living out of a vocation as rich and profound as that of the lay Catholic in a school requires an appropriate formation, both on the professional plane and on the religious plane. Most especially, it requires the educator to have a mature spiritual personality, expressed in a profound Christian life. "This calling," says the Second Vatican Council, speaking about educators, requires "extremely careful preparation."[46] "[Teachers] should therefore be trained with particular care, so that they may be enriched with both secular and religious knowledge, appropriately certified, and may be equipped with an edu-

---

44. *Ibid.*, n. 6.
45. *Ibid.*, n. 61.
46. Second Vatican Council: Decl. *Gravissimum Educationis*, n. 5.

cational skill which reflects modern day findings."[47] The need for an adequate formation is often felt most acutely in religious and spiritual areas; all too frequently, lay Catholics have not had a religious formation that is equal to their general, cultural, and, most especially, professional formation.

AWARENESS AND STIMULATION

61 Generally speaking, lay Catholics preparing themselves for work in a school have a genuine human vocation; they are very aware of the good professional formation that they need in order to become educators. But an awareness that is limited only to the professional level is not what ought to characterize a lay Catholic, whose educational work is the basic instrument for personal sanctification and the exercise of an apostolic mission. What is being asked of lay Catholics who work in schools is precisely an awareness that what they are doing is exercising a vocation. To what extent they actually do have such an awareness is something that these lay people should be asking themselves.

62 The need for religious formation is related to this specific awareness that is being asked of lay Catholics; religious formation must be broadened and be kept up to date, on the same level as, and in harmony with, human formation as a whole. Lay Catholics need to be keenly aware of the need for this kind of religious formation; it is not only the exercise of an apostolate that depends on it, but even an appropriate professional competence, especially when the competence is in the field of education.

63 The purpose of these reflections is to help awaken such a consciousness, and to help each individual to consider his or her own personal situation in an area which is so fundamental for the full exercise of the lay vocation of a Catholic educator. What is at stake is so essential that simply to become aware of it should be a major stimulus toward putting forth the effort needed: to acquire whatever may have been lacking in formation, and to maintain at an adequate level all that has been already acquired. Lay Catholic educators also have a right to expect that, within the ecclesial community, bishops, priests, and Religious, especially those dedicated to the apostolate of education, and also various groups and associations of lay Catholic educators, will help to awaken them to their personal needs in the area of formation, and will find the means to stimulate them so that they can give themselves more totally to the social commitment that such a formation requires.

47. *Ibid.*, n. 8.

PROFESSIONAL AND RELIGIOUS FORMATION

64 It may be worth noting that centers of teacher formation will differ in their ability to provide the kind of professional training that will best help Catholic educators to fulfill their educational mission. The reason for this is the close relationship that exists between the way a discipline (especially in the humanities) is taught, and the teacher's basic concept of the human person, of life, and of the world. If the ideological orientation of a center for teacher formation is pluralist, it can easily happen that the future Catholic educator will have to do supplementary work in order to make a personal synthesis of faith and culture in the different disciplines that are being studied. It must never be forgotten, during the days of formation, that the role of a teacher is to present the class materials in such a way that students can easily discover a dialogue between faith and culture, and gradually be led to a personal synthesis of these. If we take all of this into account, it follows that it would be better to attend a center for teacher formation under the direction of the Church where one exists, and to create such centers, if possible, where they do not yet exist.

65 For the Catholic educator, religious formation does not come to an end with the completion of basic education; it must be a part of and a complement to one's professional formation, and so be proportionate to adult faith, human culture, and the specific lay vocation. This means that religious formation must be oriented toward both personal sanctification and apostolic mission, for these are two inseparable elements in a Christian vocation. "Formation for apostolic mission means a certain human and well-rounded formation, adapted to the natural abilities and circumstances of each person" and requires "in addition to spiritual formation . . . solid doctrinal instruction . . . in theology, ethics and philosophy."[48] Nor can we forget, in the case of an educator, adequate formation in the social teachings of the Church, which are "an integral part of the Christian concept of life,"[49] and help to keep intensely alive the kind of social sensitivity that is needed.[50]

With regard to the doctrinal plane, and speaking more specifically of teachers, it may be worth recalling that the Second Vatican Council speaks of the need for religious knowledge guaranteed by appropriate certification.[51] It is highly recommended, therefore, that all Catholics who work in schools, and most especially those who are educators, obtain the necessary qualifications by pur-

48. Second Vatican Council: Decree *Apostolicam Actuositatem*, n. 29.

49. John Paul II, *Discourse on the Occasion of the 90th Anniversary of Rerum Novarum*, May 13, 1981 (not delivered), *L'Osservatore Romano*, May 15, 1981.

50. Cf. *Ibid.*

51. Cf. Second Vatican Council: Decl. *Gravissimum Educationis*, n. 8.

suing programs of religious formation in Ecclesiastical Faculties or in Institutes of Religious Science that are suitable for this purpose, wherever this is possible.

66 With appropriate degrees, and with an adequate preparation in religious pedagogy, they will have the basic training needed for the teaching of religion. Bishops will promote and provide for the necessary training, both for teachers of religion and for catechists; at the same time, they will not neglect the kind of dialogue with the corps of teachers being formed that can be mutually enlightening.

UPDATING PERMANENT FORMATION

67 Recent years have witnessed an extraordinary growth in science and technology; every object, situation, or value is subjected to a constant critical analysis. One effect is that our age is characterized by change; change that is constant and accelerated, that affects every last aspect of the human person and the society that he or she lives in. Because of change, knowledge that has been acquired, and structures that have been established, are quickly outdated; the need for new attitudes and new methods is constant.

68 Faced with this reality, which lay people are the first to experience, the Catholic educator has an obvious and constant need for updating: in personal attitudes, in the content of the subjects, that are taught, in the pedagogical methods that are used. Recall that the vocation of an educator requires "a constant readiness to begin anew and to adapt."[52] If the need for updating is constant, then the formation must be permanent. This need is not limited to professional formation; it includes religious formation and, in general, the enrichment of the whole person. In this way, the Church will constantly adapt its pastoral mission to the circumstances of the men and women of each age, so that the message of Jesus Christ can be brought to them in a way that is understandable and adapted to their condition.

69 Permanent formation involves a wide variety of different elements; a constant search for ways to bring it about is therefore required of both individuals and the community. Among the variety of means for permanent formation, some have become ordinary and virtually indispensable instruments: reading periodicals and pertinent books, attending conferences and seminars, participating in workshops, assemblies and congresses, making appropriate use of periods of free time for formation. All lay Catholics who work in schools

---

52. Second Vatican Council: Decl. *Gravissimum Educationis*, n. 5.

should make these a habitual part of their own human, professional, and religious life.

70 No one can deny that permanent formation, as the name itself suggests, is a difficult task; not everyone succeeds in doing it. This becomes especially true in the face of the growing complexity of contemporary life and the difficult nature of the educational mission, combined with the economic insecurity that so often accompanies it. But in spite of all these factors, no lay Catholic who works in a school can ignore this present-day need. To do so would be to remain locked up in outdated knowledge, criteria, and attitudes. To reject a formation that is permanent and that involves the whole person—human, professional, and religious—is to isolate oneself from that very world that has to be brought closer to the Gospel.

IV. THE SUPPORT THAT THE CHURCH OFFERS TO LAY CATHOLICS WORKING IN SCHOOLS

71 The different circumstances in which lay Catholics have to carry out their work in schools can often create feelings of isolation or misunderstanding, and as a result lead to depression, or even to the giving up of teaching responsibilities. In order to find help in overcoming such difficulties; in order, more generally, to be helped to fulfill the vocation to which they are called, lay Catholics who work in schools should always be able to count on the support and aid of the entire Church.

SUPPORT IN THE FAITH, IN THE WORD, AND IN SACRAMENTAL LIFE

72 Above all else, lay Catholics will find support in their own faith. Faith is the unfailing source of the humility, the hope, and the charity needed for perseverance in their vocation.[53] For every educator is in need of humility in order to recognize one's own limitations, one's mistakes, along with the need for constant growth, and the realization that the ideal being pursued is always beyond one's grasp. Every educator needs a firm hope, because the teacher is never the one who truly reaps the fruits of the labor expended on the students. And, finally, every educator is in need of a permanent and growing charity, in order to love each of the students as an individual created in the image and likeness of God, raised to the status of a child of God by the redemption of Jesus Christ.

---

53. Cf. Sacred Congregation for Catholic Education, *The Catholic School*, n. 75.

This humble faith, this hope, and this charity are supported by the Church through the Word, the life of the Sacraments, and the prayer of the entire People of God.

For the Word will speak to educators, and remind them of the tremendous greatness of their identity and of their task; Sacramental life will give them the strength they need to live this career, and bring support when they fail; the prayer of the whole Church will present to God, with them and for them, with the assured response that Jesus Christ has promised, all that the human heart desires and pleads for, and even the things that it does not dare to desire or plead for.

COMMUNITY SUPPORT

73 The work of education is arduous, and very important; for that reason, its realization is delicate and complex. It requires calm, interior peace, freedom from an excessive amount of work, continuous cultural and religious enrichment. In today's society, it is seldom that conditions can all be met simultaneously. The nature of the educational vocation of lay Catholics should be publicized more frequently and more profoundly among the People of God by those in the Church most capable of doing it. The theme of education, with all that is implied in this term, should be developed more insistently; for education is one of the great opportunities for the salvific mission of the Church.

74 From this knowledge will logically flow understanding and proper esteem. All of the faithful should be conscious of the fact that, without lay Catholics as educators, the Church's education in the faith would lack one of its important basic elements. As far as they can, therefore, all believers should actively collaborate in the work of helping educators to reach the social status and the economic level that is their due, together with the stability and the security that they must have if they are to accomplish their task. No members of the Church can be considered exempt from the struggle to ensure that, in each of their countries, both the legislation of educational policy and the practical carrying out of this legislation reflect, as far as possible, Christian educational principles.

75 Contemporary world conditions should be an inducement for the hierarchy, along with those Religious Institutes that have a commitment to education, to give their support to existing groups, movements, and Catholic Associations of lay believers engaged in education; and also to create other, new groups, always searching for the type of association that will best respond to the needs of the times and the different situations in different countries. The vocation of the lay Catholic educator requires the fulfillment of many educational objectives, along with the social and religious objectives that flow from them. These will be virtually impossible to bring into reality without the united strength of strong associations.

THE SUPPORT OF THE EDUCATIONAL INSTITUTIONS THEMSELVES: THE CATHOLIC SCHOOL AND THE LAITY

76 The importance of the Catholic school suggests that we reflect specifically on this case; it can serve as a concrete example of how other Catholic institutions should support the lay people who work in them. In speaking about lay people, this Sacred Congregation has declared without hesitation that "by their witness and behavior, teachers are of the first importance to impart a distinctive character to Catholic schools."[54]

77 Before all else, lay people should find in a Catholic school an atmosphere of sincere respect and cordiality; it should be a place in which authentic human relationships can be formed among all of the educators. Priests, men and women Religious, and lay persons, each preserving their specific vocational identity,[55] should be integrated fully into one educational community; and each one should be treated as a fully equal member of that community.

78 If the directors of the school and the lay people who work in the school are to live according to the same ideals, two things are essential. First, lay people must receive an adequate salary, guaranteed by a well defined contract, for the work they do in the school: a salary that will permit them to live in dignity, without excessive work or a need for additional employment that will interfere with the duties of an educator. This may not be immediately possible without putting an enormous financial burden on the families, or making the school so expensive that it becomes a school for a small elite group; but so long as a truly adequate salary is not being paid, the laity should see in the school directors a genuine preoccupation to find the resources necessary to achieve this end. Secondly, laity should participate authentically in the responsibility for the school; this assumes that they have the ability that is needed in all areas, and are sincerely committed to the educational objectives which characterize a Catholic school. And the school should use every means possible to encourage this kind of commitment; without it, the objectives of the school can never be fully realized. It must never be forgotten that the school itself is always in the process of being created, due to the labor brought to fruition by all those who have a role

---

54. Sacred Congregation for Catholic Education, *The Catholic School*, n. 78.
55. Cf. above, n. 43

to play in it, and most especially by those who are teachers.[56] To achieve the kind of participation that is desirable, several conditions are indispensable: genuine esteem of the lay vocation, sharing the information that is necessary, deep confidence, and, finally, when it should become necessary, turning over the distinct responsibilities for teaching, administration, and government of the school, to the laity.

79 As a part of its mission, an element proper to the school is solicitous care for the permanent professional and religious formation of its lay members. Lay people should be able to look to the school for the orientation and the assistance that they need, including the willingness to make time available when this is needed. Formation is indispensable; without it, the school will wander further and further away from its objectives. Often enough, if it will join forces with other educational centers and with Catholic professional organizations, a Catholic school will not find it too difficult to organize conferences, seminars, and other meetings which will provide the needed formation. According to circumstances, these could be expanded to include other lay Catholic educators who do not work in Catholic schools; these people would thus be offered an opportunity they are frequently in need of, and do not easily find elsewhere.

80 The ongoing improvement of the Catholic school, and the assistance which the school, joined to other educational institutions of the Church, can offer to lay Catholic educators, depend heavily on the support that Catholic families offer to the school—families in general, and most especially those that send their children to these schools. Families should recognize the level of their responsibility for a support that extends to all aspects of the school: interest, esteem, collaboration, and economic assistance. Not everyone can collaborate to the same degree or in the same way; nonetheless, each one should be ready to be as generous as possible, according to the resources that are available. Collaboration of the families should extend to a share in accomplishing the objectives of the school, and also sharing in responsibility for the school. And the school should keep the families informed about the ways in which the educational philosophy is being applied or improved on, about formation, about administration, and, in certain cases, about the management.

Conclusion

81 Lay Catholic educators in schools, whether teachers, directors, administrators, or auxiliary staff, must never have any doubts about the fact that they con-

---

56. Cf. John Paul II, Encyclical Letter *Laborem Exercens*, AAS 73, (1981) n. 14, p. 614.

stitute an element of great hope for the Church. The Church puts its trust in them entrusting them with the task of gradually bringing about an integration of temporal reality with the Gospel, so that the Gospel can thus reach into the lives of all men and women. More particularly, it has entrusted them with the integral human formation and the faith education of young people. These young people are the ones who will determine whether the world of tomorrow is more closely or more loosely bound to Christ.

82 This Sacred Congregation for Catholic Education echoes the same hope. When it considers the tremendous evangelical resource embodied in the millions of lay Catholics who devote their lives to schools, it recalls the words with which the Second Vatican Council ended its Decree on the Apostolate of the Laity, and "earnestly entreats in the Lord that all lay persons give a glad, generous, and prompt response to the voice of Christ, who is giving them an especially urgent invitation at this moment; . . . they should respond to it eagerly and magnanimously . . . and, recognizing that what is His is also their own (*Phil* 2, 5), to associate themselves with Him in His saving mission. . . . Thus they can show that they are His co-workers in the various forms and methods of the Church's one apostolate, which must be constantly adapted to the new needs of the times. May they always abound in the works of God, knowing that they will not labor in vain when their labor is for Him (Cf. *1 Cor* 15, 58)."[57]

Rome, October 15, 1982, Feast of St. Teresa of Jesus, in the Fourth Centenary of her death.

WILLIAM Cardinal BAUM, *Prefect*
Antonio M. Javierre, *Secretary*
Titular Archbishop of Meta

---

57. Second Vatican Council: Decree *Apostolicam Actuositatem,* n. 33.

THE RELIGIOUS DIMENSION
OF EDUCATION IN A CATHOLIC SCHOOL
GUIDELINES FOR REFLECTION AND RENEWAL

CONGREGATION FOR CATHOLIC EDUCATION

Introduction

1 On October 28, 1965, the Second Vatican Council promulgated the Declaration on Christian Education *Gravissimum Educationis*. The document describes the distinguishing characteristic of a Catholic school in this way: "The Catholic school pursues cultural goals and the natural development of youth to the same degree as any other school. What makes the Catholic school distinctive is its attempt to generate a community climate in the school that is permeated by the Gospel spirit of freedom and love. It tries to guide the adolescents in such a way that personality development goes hand in hand with the development of the 'new creature' that each one has become through baptism. It tries to relate all of human culture to the good news of salvation so that the light of faith will illumine everything that the students will gradually come to learn about the world, about life, and about the human person."[1]

The Council, therefore, declared that what makes the Catholic school distinctive is its religious dimension, and that this is to be found in *a*) the educational climate, *b*) the personal development of each student, *c*) the relationship established between culture and the Gospel, *d*) the illumination of all knowledge with the light of faith.

2 More than twenty years have passed since this declaration of the Council. In response to suggestions received from many parts of the world, the Congregation for Catholic Education warmly invites local ordinaries and the superiors of Religious Congregations dedicated to the education of young people to examine whether or not the words of the Council have become a reality. The Second Extraordinary General Assembly of the Synod of Bishops of 1985 said that this opportunity should not be missed! The reflection should lead to concrete decisions about what can and should be done to make Catholic schools more effective in meeting the expectations of the Church, expectations shared by many families and students.

---

1. *Gravissimum Educationis*, 8.

3 In order to be of assistance in implementing the Council's declaration, the Congregation for Catholic Education has already published several papers dealing with questions of concern to Catholic schools. *The Catholic School*[2] develops a basic outline of the specific identity and mission of the school in today's world. *Lay Catholics in Schools: Witnesses to the Faith*[3] emphasizes the contributions of lay people, who complement the valuable service offered in the past and still offered today by so many Religious Congregations of men and women. This present document is closely linked to the preceding ones; it is based on the same sources, appropriately applied to the world of today.[4]

4 The present document restricts its attention to Catholic schools: that is, educational institutions of whatever type, devoted to the formation of young people at all preuniversity levels, dependent on ecclesiastical authority, and therefore falling within the competence of this Dicastery. This clearly leaves many other questions untouched, but it is better to concentrate our attention on one area rather than try to deal with several different issues at once. We are confident that attention will be given to the other questions at some appropriate time.[5]

5 The pages which follow contain guidelines which are rather general. Different regions, different schools, and even different classes within the same school will have their own distinct history, ambience, and personal characteristics. The Congregation asks bishops, Religious superiors and those in charge of the schools to study these general guidelines and adapt them to their own local situations.

---

2. March 19, 1977.

3. October 15, 1982.

4. From Vatican Council II: Declaration on Christian Education *Gravissimum Educationis*; Dogmatic Constitution on the Church *Lumen Gentium*; Pastoral Constitution on the Church in the Modern World *Gaudium et Spes*; Dogmatic Constitution on Divine Revelation *Dei Verbum*; Constitution on the Liturgy *Sacrosanctum Concilium*; Decree on the Apostolate of the Laity *Apostolicam Actuositatem*; Decree on Missionary Activity *Ad Gentes Divinitus*; Declaration on Non-Christian Religions *Nostra Aetate*; Decree on Ecumenism *Unitatis Redintegratio*; Declaration on Religious Liberty *Dignitatis Humanae*. From Paul VI, the Apostolic Exhortation *Evangelii Nuntiandi* of December 8, 1975. From John Paul II, the Apostolic Exhortation *Catechesi Tradendae* of October 16, 1979; in addition, a number of his talks given to educators and to young people will be cited below. From the Congregation for Clergy, the *Directorium Catechisticum Generale* of April 11, 1971. All of these documents will be cited by their Latin titles in the notes which follow. In a few places, pastoral letters of bishops will be quoted.

5. Note that the Congregation has also published *Educational Guidance in Human Love: Outlines for Sex Education*, November 1, 1983. This theme, therefore, will receive only brief and passing mention in the present document.

6 Not all students in Catholic schools are members of the Catholic Church; not all are Christians. There are, in fact, countries in which the vast majority of the students are not Catholics—a reality which the Council called attention to.[6] The religious freedom and the personal conscience of individual students and their families must be respected, and this freedom is explicitly recognized by the Church.[7] On the other hand, a Catholic school cannot relinquish its own freedom to proclaim the Gospel and to offer a formation based on the values to be found in a Christian education; this is its right and its duty. To proclaim or to offer is not to impose, however; the latter suggests a moral violence which is strictly forbidden, both by the Gospel and by Church law.[8]

I. THE RELIGIOUS DIMENSION IN THE LIVES OF TODAY'S YOUTH

Youth in a Changing World

7 The Council provided a realistic analysis of the religious condition in the world today,[9] and paid explicit attention to the special situation of young people;[10] educators must do the same. Whatever methods they employ to do this, they should be attentive to the results of research with youth done at the local level, and they should be mindful of the fact that the young today are, in some respects, different from those that the Council had in mind.

8 Many Catholic schools are located in countries which are undergoing radical changes in outlook and in life-style: these countries are becoming urbanized and industrialized, and are moving into the so-called "tertiary" economy, characterized by a high standard of living, a wide choice of educational opportunities, and complex communication systems. Young people in these countries are familiar with the media from their infancy; they have been exposed to a wide variety of opinions on every possible topic, and are surprisingly well-informed even when they are still very young.

9 These young people absorb a wide and varied assortment of knowledge from all kinds of sources, including the school. But they are not yet capable of order-

---

6. *Gravissimum Educationis*, 9: "It is clear that the Church has a deep respect for those Catholic schools, especially in countries where the Church is young, which have large numbers of students who are not Catholics."

7. Cf. *Dignitatis Humanae*, 2; 9; 10; 12 *et passim*.

8. C.I.C., canon 748 § 2: "Homines ad amplectendam fidem catholicam contra ipsorum conscientiam per coactionem adducere nemini umquam fas est."

9. Cf. *Gaudium et Spes*, 4–10.

10. *Ibid.*, 7: "The change of mentality and of structures often call into question traditional values, especially among the young. . . ."

ing or prioritizing what they have learned. Often enough, they do not yet have the critical ability needed to distinguish the true and good from their opposites; they have not yet acquired the necessary religious and moral criteria that will enable them to remain objective and independent when faced with the prevailing attitudes and habits of society. Concepts such as truth, beauty and goodness have become so vague today that young people do not know where to turn to find help; even when they are able to hold on to certain values, they do not yet have the capacity to develop these values into a way of life; all too often they are more inclined simply to go their own way, accepting whatever is popular at the moment.

Changes occur in different ways and at different rates. Each school will have to look carefully at the religious behavior of the young people "in loco" in order to discover their thought processes, their life-style, their reaction to change. Depending on the situation, the change may be profound, it may be only beginning, or the local culture may be resistant to change. Even a culture resistant to change is being influenced by the all-pervasive mass media!

Some Common Characteristics of the Young

10 Although local situations create great diversity, there are characteristics that today's young people have in common, and educators need to be aware of them.

Many young people find themselves in a condition of radical instability. On the one hand they live in a one-dimensional universe in which the only criterion is practical utility and the only value is economic and technological progress. On the other hand, these same young people seem to be progressing to a stage beyond this narrow universe; nearly everywhere, evidence can be found of a desire to be released from it.

11 Others live in an environment devoid of truly human relationships; as a result, they suffer from loneliness and a lack of affection. This is a widespread phenomenon that seems to be independent of life-style: it is found in oppressive regimes, among the homeless, and in the cold and impersonal dwellings of the rich. Young people today are notably more depressed than in the past; this is surely a sign of the poverty of human relationships in families and in society today.

12 Large numbers of today's youth are very worried about an uncertain future. They have been influenced by a world in which human values are in chaos because these values are no longer rooted in God; the result is that these young people are very much afraid when they think about the appalling problems in the world: the threat of nuclear annihilation, vast unemployment, the high number of marriages that end in separation or divorce, widespread poverty, etc. Their worry and insecurity become an almost irresistible urge to focus in on themselves, and this can lead to violence when young people are together—a violence that is not always limited to words.

13 Not a few young people, unable to find any meaning in life or trying to find an escape from loneliness, turn to alcohol, drugs, the erotic, the exotic, etc. Christian education is faced with the huge challenge of helping these young people discover something of value in their lives.

14 The normal instability of youth is accentuated by the times they are living in. Their decisions are not solidly based: today's "yes" easily becomes tomorrow's "no."

Finally, a vague sort of generosity is characteristic of many young people. Filled with enthusiasm, they are eager to join in popular causes. Too often, however, these movements are without any specific orientation or inner coherence. It is important to channel this potential for good and, when possible, give it the orientation that comes from the light of faith.

15 In some parts of the world it might be profitable to pay particular attention to the reasons why young people abandon their faith. Often enough, this begins by giving up religious practices. As time goes on, it can develop into a hostility toward Church structures and a crisis of conscience regarding the truths of faith and their accompanying moral values. This can be especially true in those countries where education in general is secular or even imbued with atheism. The crisis seems to occur more frequently in places where there is high economic development and rapid social and cultural change. Sometimes the phenomenon is not recent; it is something that the parents went through, and they are now passing their own attitudes along to the new generation. When this is the case, it is no longer a personal crisis, but one that has become religious and social. It has been called a "split between the Gospel and culture."[11]

16 A break with the faith often takes the form of total religious indifference. Experts suggest that certain patterns of behavior found among young people are actually attempts to fill the religious void with some sort of a substitute: the pagan cult of the body, drug escape, or even those massive "youth events" which sometimes deteriorate into fanaticism and total alienation from reality.

---

11. Cf. *Evangelii Nuntiandi*, 20.

17 Educators cannot be content with merely observing these behavior patterns; they have to search for the causes. It may be some lack at the start, some problem in the family background. Or it may be that parish and Church organizations are deficient. Christian formation given in childhood and early adolescence is not always proof against the influence of the environment. Perhaps there are cases in which the fault lies with the Catholic school itself.

18 There are also a number of positive signs, which give grounds for encouragement. In a Catholic school, as in any school, one can find young people who are outstanding in every way—in religious attitude, moral behavior, and academic achievement. When we look for the cause, we often discover an excellent family background reinforced by both Church and school. There is always a combination of factors, open to the interior workings of grace.

Some young people are searching for a deeper understanding of their religion; as they reflect on the real meaning of life they begin to find answers to their questions in the Gospel. Others have already passed through the crisis of indifference and doubt, and are now ready to commit themselves—or recommit themselves—to a Christian way of life. These positive signs give us reason to hope that a sense of religion can develop in more of today's young people, and that it can be more deeply rooted in them.

19 For some of today's youth, the years spent in a Catholic school seem to have scarcely any effect. They seem to have a negative attitude toward all the various ways in which a Christian life is expressed—prayer, participation in the Mass, or frequenting of the Sacraments. Some even reject these expressions outright, especially those associated with an institutional Church. If a school is excellent as an academic institution, but does not witness to authentic values, then both good pedagogy and a concern for pastoral care make it obvious that renewal is called for—not only in the content and methodology of religious instruction, but in the overall school planning which governs the whole process of formation of the students.

20 The religious questioning of young people today needs to be better understood. Many of them are asking about the value of science and technology when everything could end in a nuclear holocaust; they look at how modern civilization floods the world with material goods, beautiful and useful as these may be, and they wonder whether the purpose of life is really to possess many "things" or whether there may not be something far more valuable; they are deeply disturbed by the injustice which divides the free and the rich from the poor and the oppressed.

21 For many young people, a critical look at the world they are living in leads to crucial questions on the religious plane. They ask whether religion can provide any answers to the pressing problems afflicting humanity. Large numbers of them sincerely want to know how to deepen their faith and live a meaningful life. Then there is the further practical question of how to translate responsible commitment into effective action. Future historians will have to evaluate the "youth group" phenomenon, along with the movements founded for spiritual growth, apostolic work, or service of others. But these are signs that words are not enough for the young people of today. They want to be active—to do something worthwhile for themselves and for others.

22 Catholic schools are spread throughout the world and enroll literally millions of students.[12] These students are children of their own race, nationality, traditions, and family. They are also the children of our age. Each student has a distinct origin and is a unique individual. A Catholic school is not simply a place where lessons are taught; it is a center that has an operative educational philosophy, attentive to the needs of today's youth and illumined by the Gospel message. A thorough and exact knowledge of the real situation will suggest the best educational methods.

23 We must be ready to repeat the basic essentials over and over again, so long as the need is present. We need to integrate what has already been learned, and respond to the questions which come from the restless and critical minds of the young. We need to break through the wall of indifference, and at the same time be ready to help those who are doing well to discover a "better way," offering them a knowledge that also embraces Christian wisdom.[13] The specific methods and the steps used to accomplish the educational philosophy of the school will, therefore, be conditioned and guided by an intimate knowledge of each student's unique situation.[14]

---

12. Cf. the *Annuario Statistico della Chiesa* published by the Central Statistical Office of the Church, an office within the Secretariate of State for Vatican City. By way of example, on December 31, 1985, there were 154,126 Catholic schools with 38,243,304 students.

13. Cf. *1 Cor* 12:31.

14. Various aspects of the religious attitudes of young people developed in this section have been the object of recent statements of the Holy Father. A handy compilation of these numerous talks can be found in a book edited by the Pontifical Council for the Laity, *The Holy Father Speaks to Youth: 1980–1985*. The book is published in several languages.

II. THE RELIGIOUS DIMENSION OF THE SCHOOL CLIMATE

What is a Christian School Climate?

24 In pedagogical circles, today as in the past, great stress is put on the climate of a school: the sum total of the different components at work in the school which interact with one another in such a way as to create favorable conditions for a formation process. Education always takes place within certain specific conditions of space and time, through the activities of a group of individuals who are active and also interactive among themselves. They follow a program of studies which is logically ordered and freely accepted. Therefore, the elements to be considered in developing an organic vision of a school climate are: persons, space, time, relationships, teaching, study, and various other activities.

25 From the first moment that a student sets foot in a Catholic school, he or she ought to have the impression of entering a new environment, one illumined by the light of faith, and having its own unique characteristics. The Council summed this up by speaking of an environment permeated with the Gospel spirit of love and freedom.[15] In a Catholic school, everyone should be aware of the living presence of Jesus the "Master" who, today as always, is with us in our journey through life as the one genuine "Teacher," the perfect Man in whom all human values find their fullest perfection. The inspiration of Jesus must be translated from the ideal into the real. The Gospel spirit should be evident in a Christian way of thought and life which permeates all facets of the educational climate. Having crucifixes in the school will remind everyone, teachers and students alike, of this familiar and moving presence of Jesus, the "Master" who gave his most complete and sublime teaching from the cross.

26 Prime responsibility for creating this unique Christian school climate rests with the teachers, as individuals and as a community. The religious dimension of the school climate is expressed through the celebration of Christian values in Word and Sacrament, in individual behavior, in friendly and harmonious interpersonal relationships, and in a ready availability. Through this daily witness, the students will come to appreciate the uniqueness of the environment to which their youth has been entrusted. If it is not present, then there is little left which can make the school Catholic.

---

15. Cf. *Gravissimum Educationis*, 8. For the Gospel spirit of love and freedom, cf. *Gaudium et Spes*, 38: "[The Lord Jesus] reveals to us that God is love (*1 Jn* 4:8), and at the same time teaches us that the fundamental rule for human perfection, and therefore also for the transformation of the world, is the new commandment of love." See also *2 Cor* 3:17: "Where the Spirit of the Lord is present, there is freedom."

The Physical Environment of a Catholic School

27 Many of the students will attend a Catholic school—often the same school—from the time they are very young children until they are nearly adults. It is only natural that they should come to think of the school as an extension of their own homes, and therefore a "school-home" ought to have some of the amenities which can create a pleasant and happy family atmosphere. When this is missing from the home, the school can often do a great deal to make up for it.

28 The first thing that will help to create a pleasant environment is an adequate physical facility: one that includes sufficient space for classrooms, sports and recreation, and also such things as a staff room and rooms for parent-teacher meetings, group work, etc. The possibilities for this vary from place to place; we have to be honest enough to admit that some school buildings are unsuitable and unpleasant. But students can be made to feel "at home" even when the surroundings are modest, if the climate is humanly and spiritually rich.

29 A Catholic school should be an example of simplicity and evangelical poverty, but this is not inconsistent with having the materials needed to educate properly. Because of rapid technological progress, a school today must have access to equipment that, at times, is complex and expensive. This is not a luxury; it is simply what a school needs to carry out its role as an educational institution. Catholic schools, therefore, have a right to expect the help from others that will make the purchase of modern educational materials possible.[16] Both individuals and public bodies have a duty to provide this support.

Students should feel a responsibility for their "school-home;" they should take care of it and help to keep it as clean and neat as possible. Concern for the environment is part of a formation in ecological awareness, the need for which is becoming increasingly apparent.

An awareness of Mary's presence can be a great help toward making the school into a "home." Mary, Mother and Teacher of the Church, accompanied her Son as he grew in wisdom and grace; from its earliest days, she has accompanied the Church in its mission of salvation.

30 The physical proximity of the school to a church can contribute a great deal toward achieving the educational aims. A church should not be seen as something extraneous, but as a familiar and place where those young people who are believers can find the presence of the Lord: "Behold, I am with you all days."[17]

---

16. This question was treated in *The Catholic School*, 81–82.
17. *Mt* 28:20.

Liturgy planning should be especially careful to bring the school community and the local Church together.

The Ecclesial and Educational Climate of the School

31 The declaration *Gravissimum Educationis*[18] notes an important advance in the way a Catholic school is thought of: the transition from the school as an institution to the school as a community. This community dimension is, perhaps, one result of the new awareness of the Church's nature as developed by the Council. In the Council texts, the community dimension is primarily a theological concept rather than a sociological category; this is the sense in which it is used in the second chapter of *Lumen gentium*, where the Church is described as the People of God.

As it reflects on the mission entrusted to it by the Lord, the Church gradually develops its pastoral instruments so that they may become ever more effective in proclaiming the Gospel and promoting total human formation. The Catholic school is one of these pastoral instruments; its specific pastoral service consists in mediating between faith and culture: being faithful to the newness of the Gospel while at the same time respecting the autonomy and the methods proper to human knowledge.

32 Everyone directly involved in the school is a part of the school community: teachers, directors, administrative and auxiliary staff. Parents are central figures, since they are the natural and irreplaceable agents in the education of their children. And the community also includes the students, since they must be active agents in their own education.[19]

33 At least since the time of the Council, therefore, the Catholic school has had a clear identity, not only as a presence of the Church in society, but also as a genuine and proper instrument of the Church. It is a place of evangelization, of authentic apostolate and of pastoral action—not through complementary or parallel or extracurricular activity, but of its very nature: its work of educating the Christian person. The words of the present Holy Father make this abundantly clear: "the Catholic school is not a marginal or secondary element in the pastoral mission of the bishop. Its function is not merely to be an instrument with which to combat the education given in a State school." [20]

18. *Gravissimum Educationis*, 6.

19. Cf. the address of John Paul II to the parents, teachers and students from the Catholic schools of the Italian Province of Lazio, March 9, 1985, *Insegnamenti*, VIII/1, p. 620.

20. Address of John Paul II to the bishops of Lombardy, Italy, on the occasion of their "Ad limina" visit, January 15, 1982, *Insegnamenti*, V/1, 1982, p. 105.

34 The Catholic school finds its true justification in the mission of the Church; it is based on an educational philosophy in which faith, culture and life are brought into harmony. Through it, the local Church evangelizes, educates, and contributes to the formation of a healthy and morally sound life-style among its members. The Holy Father affirms that "the need for the Catholic school becomes evidently clear when we consider what it contributes to the development of the mission of the People of God, to the dialogue between Church and the human community, to the safeguarding of freedom of conscience...." Above all, according to the Holy Father, the Catholic school helps in achieving a double objective: "of its nature it guides men and women to human and Christian perfection, and at the same time helps them to become mature in their faith. For those who believe in Christ, these are two facets of a single reality."[21]

35 Most Catholic schools are under the direction of Religious Congregations, whose consecrated members enrich the educational climate by bringing to it the values of their own Religious communities. These men and women have dedicated themselves to the service of the students without thought of personal gain, because they are convinced that it is really the Lord whom they are serving.[22]

Through the prayer, work and love that make up their life in community, they express in a visible way the life of the Church. Each Congregation brings the richness of its own educational tradition to the school, found in its original charism; its members each bring the careful professional preparation that is required by the call to be an educator. The strength and gentleness of their total dedication to God enlightens their work, and students gradually come to appreciate the value of this witness. They come to love these educators who seem to have the gift of eternal spiritual youth, and it is an affection which endures long after students leave the school.

36 The Church offers encouragement to these men and women who have dedicated their lives to the fulfillment of an educational charism.[23] It urges those in education not to give up this work, even in situations where it involves suffering and persecution. In fact, the Church hopes that many others will be called to this special vocation. When afflicted by doubts and uncertainty, when difficulties are multiplied, these Religious men and women should recall the nature

---

21. *Insegnamenti*, VIII/1, pp. 618ff.

22. *Mt* 25:40: "For indeed I tell you, as often as you have done these things to one of these least of my brothers, you have done it to me."

23. Cf. *Perfectae Caritatis*, 8: "There are in the Church a great number of institutes, clerical or lay, dedicated to various aspects of the apostolate, which have different gifts according to the grace that has been given to each: 'some exercise a ministry of service; some teach' (cf. *Rom* 12:5–8)." Also see *Ad Gentes Divinitus*, 40.

of their consecration, which is a type of holocaust[24]—a holocaust which is offered "in the perfection of love, which is the scope of the consecrated life."[25] Their merit is the greater because their offering is made on behalf of young people, who are the hope of the Church.

37 At the side of the priests and Religious, lay teachers contribute their competence and their faith witness to the Catholic school. Ideally, this lay witness is a concrete example of the lay vocation that most of the students will be called to. The Congregation has devoted a specific document to lay teachers,[26] meant to remind lay people of their apostolic responsibility in the field of education and to summon them to participate in a common mission, whose point of convergence is found in the unity of the Church. For all are active members of one Church and cooperate in its one mission, even though the fields of labor and the states of life are different because of the personal call each one receives from God.

38 The Church, therefore, is willing to give lay people charge of the schools that it has established, and the laity themselves establish schools. The recognition of the school as a Catholic school is, however, always reserved to the competent ecclesiastical authority.[27] When lay people do establish schools, they should be especially concerned with the creation of a community climate permeated by the Gospel spirit of freedom and love, and they should witness to this in their own lives.

39 The more the members of the educational community develop a real willingness to collaborate among themselves, the more fruitful their work will be. Achieving the educational aims of the school should be an equal priority for teachers, students and families alike, each one according to his or her own role, always in the Gospel spirit of freedom and love. Therefore channels of communication should be open among all those concerned with the school. Frequent meetings will help to make this possible, and a willingness to discuss common problems candidly will enrich this communication.

The daily problems of school life are sometimes aggravated by misunderstandings and various tensions. A determination to collaborate in achieving common educational goals can help to overcome these difficulties and reconcile

24. *Summa Theol.* II–II, q. 186, a. 1: "By antonomasis those are called 'religious' who dedicate themselves to the service of God as if they were offering themselves as a holocaust to the Lord."

25. *Ibid.*, a. 2.

26. Lay Catholics in Schools: *Witnesses to the Faith*.

27. The norms of the Church in this respect are to be found in canons 800–803 of the Code of Canon Law.

different points of view. A willingness to collaborate helps to facilitate decisions that need to be made about the ways to achieve these goals and, while preserving proper respect for school authorities, even makes it possible to conduct a critical evaluation of the school—a process in which teachers, students and families can all take part because of their common concern to work for the good of all.

40 Considering the special age group they are working with, primary schools should try to create a community school climate that reproduces, as far as possible, the warm and intimate atmosphere of family life. Those responsible for these schools will, therefore, do everything they can to promote a common spirit of trust and spontaneity. In addition, they will take great care to promote close and constant collaboration with the parents of these pupils. An integration of school and home is an essential condition for the birth and development of all of the potential which these children manifest in one or the other of these two situations—including their openness to religion with all that this implies.

41 The Congregation wishes to express its appreciation to all those dioceses which have worked to establish primary schools in their parishes; these deserve the strong support of all Catholics. It also wishes to thank the Religious Congregations helping to sustain these primary schools, often at great sacrifice. Moreover, the Congregation offers enthusiastic encouragement to those dioceses and Religious Congregations who wish to establish new schools. Such things as film clubs and sports groups are not enough; not even classes in catechism instruction are sufficient. What is needed is a school. This is a goal which, in some countries, was the starting point. There are countries in which the Church began with schools and only later was able to construct Churches and to establish a new Christian community.[28]

The Catholic School as an Open Community

42 Partnership between a Catholic school and the families of the students must continue and be strengthened: not simply to be able to deal with academic problems that may arise, but rather so that the educational goals of the school can be achieved. Close cooperation with the family is especially important when treating sensitive issues such as religious, moral, or sexual education, orientation toward a profession, or a choice of one's vocation in life. It is not a question of convenience, but a partnership based on faith. Catholic tradition

---

28. Cf. the address of Pope Paul VI to the National Congress of Diocesan Directors of the Teachers' Organizations of Catholic Action, *Insegnamenti*, I, 1963, p. 594.

teaches that God has bestowed on the family its own specific and unique educational mission.

43 The first and primary educators of children are their parents.[29] The school is aware of this fact but, unfortunately, the same is not always true of the families themselves; it is the school's responsibility to give them this awareness. Every school should initiate meetings and other programs which will make the parents more conscious of their role, and help to establish a partnership; it is impossible to do too much along these lines. It often happens that a meeting called to talk about the children becomes an opportunity to raise the consciousness of the parents. In addition, the school should try to involve the family as much as possible in the educational aims of the school—both in helping to plan these goals and in helping to achieve them. Experience shows that parents who were once totally unaware of their role can be transformed into excellent partners.

44 "The involvement of the Church in the field of education is demonstrated especially by the Catholic school."[30] This affirmation of the Council has both historical and practical importance. Church schools first appeared centuries ago, growing up alongside monasteries, cathedrals and parish churches. The Church has always had a love for its schools, because this is where its children receive their formation. These schools have continued to flourish with the help of bishops, countless Religious Congregations, and laity; the Church has never ceased to support the schools in their difficulties and to defend them against governments seeking to close or confiscate them.

Just as the Church is present in the school, so the school is present in the Church; this is a logical consequence of their reciprocal commitment. The Church, through which the Redemption of Christ is revealed and made operative, is where the Catholic school receives its spirit. It recognizes the Holy Father as the center and the measure of unity in the entire Christian community. Love for and fidelity to the Church is the organizing principle and the source of strength of a Catholic school.

Teachers find the light and the courage for authentic Religious education in their unity among themselves and their generous and humble communion with the Holy Father. Concretely, the educational goals of the school include a concern for the life and the problems of the Church, both local and universal. These goals are attentive to the Magisterium, and include cooperation with Church authorities. Catholic students are helped to become active members of the parish and diocesan communities. They have opportunities to join Church

29. Cf. *Gravissimum Educationis*, 3.
30. *Ibid.*, 8.

associations and Church youth groups, and they are taught to collaborate in local Church projects.

Mutual esteem and reciprocal collaboration will be established between the Catholic school and the bishop and other Church authorities through direct contacts. We are pleased to note that a concern for Catholic schools is becoming more of a priority of local Churches in many parts of the world.[31]

45 A Christian education must promote respect for the State and its representatives, the observance of just laws, and a search for the common good. Therefore, traditional civic values such as freedom, justice, the nobility of work and the need to pursue social progress are all included among the school goals, and the life of the school gives witness to them. The national anniversaries and other important civic events are commemorated and celebrated in appropriate ways in the schools of each country.

The school life should also reflect an awareness of international society. Christian education sees all of humanity as one large family, divided perhaps by historical and political events, but always one in God who is Father of all. Therefore a Catholic school should be sensitive to and help to promulgate Church appeals for peace, justice, freedom, progress for all peoples and assistance for countries in need. And it should not ignore similar appeals coming from recognized international organizations such as UNESCO and the United Nations.

46 That Catholic schools help to form good citizens is a fact apparent to everyone. Both government policy and public opinion should, therefore, recognize the work these schools do as a real service to society. It is unjust to accept the service and ignore or fight against its source. Fortunately, a good number of countries seem to have a growing understanding of and sympathy for the Catholic school.[32] A recent survey conducted by the Congregation demonstrates that a new age may be dawning.

III. THE RELIGIOUS DIMENSION OF SCHOOL LIFE AND WORK

The Religious Dimension of School Life

47 Students spend a large share of each day and the greater part of their youth either at school or doing activities that are related to school. "School" is often

---

31. A number of recent documents from national Episcopal Conferences and from individual local ordinaries have had the Catholic school as their theme. These documents should be known and put into practice.

32. See, for example, the *Resolution of the European Parliament* on freedom of education in the European Community, approved by a large majority on March 14, 1984.

identified with "teaching;" actually, classes and lessons are only a small part of school life. Along with the lessons that a teacher gives, there is the active participation of the students individually or as a group: study, research, exercises, para-curricular activities, examinations, relationships with teachers and with one another, group activities, class meetings, school assemblies. While the Catholic school is like any other school in this complex variety of events that make up the life of the school, there is one essential difference: it draws its inspiration and its strength from the Gospel in which it is rooted. The principle that no human act is morally indifferent to one's conscience or before God has clear applications to school life: examples of it are school work accepted as a duty and done with good will; courage and perseverance when difficulties come; respect for teachers; loyalty toward and love for fellow students; sincerity, tolerance, and goodness in all relationships.

48 The educational process is not simply a human activity; it is a genuine Christian journey toward perfection. Students who are sensitive to the religious dimension of life realize that the will of God is found in the work and the human relationships of each day. They learn to follow the example of the Master, who spent his youth working and who did good to all.[33] Those students who are unaware of this religious dimension are deprived of its benefits and they run the risk of living the best years of their lives at a shallow level.

49 Within the overall process of education, special mention must be made of the intellectual work done by students. Although Christian life consists in loving God and doing his will, intellectual work is intimately involved. The light of Christian faith stimulates a desire to know the universe as God's creation. It enkindles a love for the truth that will not be satisfied with superficiality in knowledge or judgment. It awakens a critical sense which examines statements rather than accepting them blindly. It impels the mind to learn with careful order and precise methods, and to work with a sense of responsibility. It provides the strength needed to accept the sacrifices and the perseverance required by intellectual labor. When fatigued, the Christian student remembers the command of Genesis[34] and the invitation of the Lord.[35]

---

33. Cf. *Mk* 6:3; *Acts* 10:35. Useful applications of the ethics of work to the work done in school can be found in the September 14, 1981 Encyclical *Laborem Exercens* of John Paul II, especially in Part Five.
34. *Gen* 3:19: "By the sweat on your face shall you get bread to eat."
35. *Lk* 9:23: "... let him take up his cross each day."

50 The religious dimension enhances intellectual efforts in a variety of ways: interest in academic work is stimulated by the presence of new perspectives; Christian formation is strengthened; supernatural grace is given. How sad it would be if the young people in Catholic schools were to have no knowledge of this reality in the midst of all the difficult and tiring work they have to do!

The Religious Dimension of the School Culture

51 Intellectual development and growth as a Christian go forward hand in hand. As students move up from one class into the next it becomes increasingly imperative that a Catholic school help them become aware that a relationship exists between faith and human culture.[36] Human culture remains human, and must be taught with scientific objectivity. But the lessons of the teacher and the reception of those students who are believers will not divorce faith from this culture;[37] this would be a major spiritual loss. The world of human culture and the world of religion are not like two parallel lines that never meet; points of contact are established within the human person. For a believer is both human and a person of faith, the protagonist of culture and the subject of religion. Anyone who searches for the contact points will be able to find them.[38] Helping in the search is not solely the task of religion teachers; their time is quite limited, while other teachers have many hours at their disposal every day. Everyone should work together, each one developing his or her own subject area with professional competence, but sensitive to those opportunities in which they can help students to see beyond the limited horizon of human reality. In a Catholic school, and analogously in every school, God cannot be the Great Absent One or the unwelcome intruder. The Creator does not put obstacles in the path of someone trying to learn more about the universe he created, a universe which is given new significance when seen with the eyes of faith.

52 A Catholic secondary school will give special attention to the "challenges" that human culture poses for faith. Students will be helped to attain that synthesis of faith and culture which is necessary for faith to be mature. But a mature faith is also able to recognize and reject cultural counter-values which

---

36. *Gravissimum Educationis*, 8: among the elements characteristic of the Catholic school, there is that of "developing the relationship between human culture and the message of salvation, so that the knowledge of the world, of life and of the human person which the students are gradually acquiring is illuminated by faith."

37. For a description of culture and of the relationship between culture and faith, see *Gaudium et Spes*, 54ff.

38. Cf. Denz: Schön. 3016–3017 for the traditional doctrine on the rapport between reason and faith, as defined by Vatican Council I.

threaten human dignity and are therefore contrary to the Gospel.[39] No one should think that all of the problems of religion and of faith will be completely solved by academic studies; nevertheless, we are convinced that a school is a privileged place for finding adequate ways to deal with these problems. The declaration *Gravissimum Educationis*,[40] echoing *Gaudium et spes*,[41] indicates that one of the characteristics of a Catholic school is that it interpret and give order to human culture in the light of faith.

53 As the Council points out, giving order to human culture in the light of the message of salvation cannot mean a lack of respect for the autonomy of the different academic disciplines and the methodology proper to them; nor can it mean that these disciplines are to be seen merely as subservient to faith. On the other hand, it is necessary to point out that a proper autonomy of culture has to be distinguished from a vision of the human person or of the world as totally autonomous, implying that one can negate spiritual values or prescind from them. We must always remember that, while faith is not to be identified with any one culture and is independent of all cultures, it must inspire every culture: "Faith which does not become culture is faith which is not received fully, not assimilated entirely, not lived faithfully."[42]

54 In a number of countries, renewal in school programming has given increased attention to science and technology. Those teaching these subject areas must not ignore the religious dimension. They should help their students to understand that positive science, and the technology allied to it, is a part of the universe created by God. Understanding this can help encourage an interest in research: the whole of creation, from the distant celestial bodies and the immeasurable cosmic forces down to the infinitesimal particles and waves of matter and energy, all bear the imprint of the Creator's wisdom and power, The wonder that past ages felt when contemplating this universe, recorded by the Biblical authors,[43] is still valid for the students of today; the only difference is that we have a knowledge that is much more vast and profound. There can be

39. Cf. the address of Pope John Paul II to the teachers and students of Catholic schools in Melbourne, Australia, on the occasion of his pastoral journey to East Asia and Oceania: *Insegnamenti* November 28, 1986; IX/2, 1986, pp. 1710ff.

40. Cf. *Gravissimum Educationis*, 8.

41. Cf. *Gaudium et Spes*, 53–62.

42. Pope John Paul II, speaking at the National Congress of Catholic Cultural Organizations: *Insegnamenti*, V/1, 1982, p. 131. See also John Paul II, *Epistula qua Pontificium Consilium pro Hominum Cultura Instituitur: AAS* 74 (1982), p. 685.

43. *Wis* 13:5: "Through the grandeur and beauty of the creatures we may, by analogy, contemplate their Author." *Ps* 18(19):2ff.: "The heavens tell of the glory of God. . . ."

no conflict between faith and true scientific knowledge; both find their source in God.

The student who is able to discover the harmony between faith and science will, in future professional life, be better able to put science and technology to the service of men and women, and to the service of God. It is a way of giving back to God what he has first given to us.[44]

55 A Catholic school must be committed to the development of a program which will overcome the problems of a fragmented and insufficient curriculum. Teachers dealing with areas such as anthropology, biology, psychology, sociology and philosophy all have the opportunity to present a complete picture of the human person, including the religious dimension. Students should be helped to see the human person as a living creature having both a physical and a spiritual nature; each of us has an immortal soul, and we are in need of redemption. The older students can gradually come to a more mature understanding of all that is implied in the concept of "person": intelligence and will, freedom and feelings, the capacity to be an active and creative agent; a being endowed with both rights and duties, capable of interpersonal relationships, called to a specific mission in the world.

56 The religious dimension makes a true understanding of the human person possible. A human being has a dignity and a greatness exceeding that of all other creatures: a work of God that has been elevated to the supernatural order as a child of God, and therefore having both a divine origin and an eternal destiny which transcend this physical universe.[45] Religion teachers will find the way already prepared for an organic presentation of Christian anthropology.

57 Every society has its own heritage of accumulated wisdom. Many people find inspiration in these philosophical and religious concepts which have endured for millennia. The systematic genius of classical Greek and European thought has, over the centuries, generated countless different doctrinal systems, but it has also given us a set of truths which we can recognize as a part of our permanent philosophical heritage. A Catholic school conforms to the generally accepted school programming of today, but implements these programs within an overall religious perspective. This perspective includes criteria such as the following:

Respect for those who seek the truth, who raise fundamental questions about human existence.[46] Confidence in our ability to attain truth, at least in a limited

44. Cf. *Mt* 25:14–30.
45. Cf. *Gaudium et Spes*, 12; 14; 17; 22.

way—a confidence based not on feeling but on faith. God created us "in his own image and likeness" and will not deprive us of the truth necessary to orient our lives.[47] The ability to make judgments about what is true and what is false; and to make choices based on these judgments.[48] Making use of a systematic framework, such as that offered by our philosophical heritage, with which to find the best possible human responses to questions regarding the human person, the world, and God.[49] Lively dialogue between culture and the Gospel message.[50] The fullness of truth contained in the Gospel message itself, which embraces and integrates the wisdom of all cultures, and enriches them with the divine mysteries known only to God but which, out of love, he has chosen to reveal to us.[51] With such criteria as a basis, the student's careful and reflective study of philosophy will bring human wisdom into an encounter with divine wisdom.

58 Teachers should guide the students' work in such a way that they will be able to discover a religious dimension in the world of human history. As a preliminary, they should be encouraged to develop a taste for historical truth, and therefore to realize the need to look critically at texts and curricula which, at times, are imposed by a government or distorted by the ideology of the author. The next step is to help students see history as something real: the drama of human grandeur and human misery.[52] The protagonist of history is the human person, who projects onto the world, on a larger scale, the good and the evil that is within each individual. History is, then, a monumental struggle between these two fundamental realities,[53] and is subject to moral judgments. But such judgments must always be made with understanding.

59 To this end, the teacher should help students to see history as a whole. Looking at the grand picture, they will see the development of civilizations, and learn about progress in such things as economic development, human freedom, and international cooperation. Realizing this can help to offset the disgust that comes from learning about the darker side of human history. But even

46. Cf. *Gaudium et Spes*, 10.
47. Cf. Denz.-Schön. 3004 for the ability to know God through human reason, and 3005 for the ability to know other truths.
48. *1 Thess* 5:21: "Examine all things, hold on to what is good." *Phil* 4:8: "Everything that is true, noble, or just . . . let all this be the object of your thoughts."
49. Cf. *Gaudium et Spes*, 61, on the need to hold on to certain fundamental concepts.
50. *Ibid.*, 44: "At the same time there should be a vital exchange between the Church and the diverse cultures of peoples."
51. Cf. *Dei Verbum* 2.
52. Cf. Blaise Pascal, *Pensées*, fr. 397.
53. *Gaudium et Spes*, 37: "The whole of human history is permeated with the gigantic struggle against the powers of darkness."

this is not the whole story. When they are ready to appreciate it, students can be invited to reflect on the fact that this human struggle takes place within the divine history of universal salvation. At this moment, the religious dimension of history begins to shine forth in all its luminous grandeur.[54]

60 The increased attention given to science and technology must not lead to a neglect of the humanities: philosophy, history, literature and art. Since earliest times, each society has developed and handed on its artistic and literary heritage, and our human patrimony is nothing more than the sum total of this cultural wealth. Thus, while teachers are helping students to develop an aesthetic sense, they can bring them to a deeper awareness of all peoples as one great human family. The simplest way to uncover the religious dimension of the artistic and literary world is to start with its concrete expressions: in every human culture, art and literature have been closely linked to religious beliefs. The artistic and literary patrimony of Christianity is vast and gives visible testimony to a faith that has been handed down through centuries.

61 Literary and artistic works depict the struggles of societies, of families, and of individuals. They spring from the depths of the human heart, revealing its lights and its shadows, its hope and its despair. The Christian perspective goes beyond the merely human, and offers more penetrating criteria for understanding the human struggle and the mysteries of the human spirit.[55] Furthermore, an adequate religious formation has been the starting point for the vocation of a number of Christian artists and art critics. In the upper grades, a teacher can bring students to an even more profound appreciation of artistic works as a reflection of the divine beauty in tangible form. Both the Fathers of the Church and the masters of Christian philosophy teach this in their writings on aesthetics—St. Augustine invites us to go beyond the intention of the artists in order to find the eternal order of God in the work of art; St. Thomas sees the presence of the Divine Word in art.[56]

62 A Catholic school is often attentive to issues having to do with educational methods, and this can be of great service both to civil society and to the Church. Government requirements for teacher preparation usually require historical and systematic courses in pedagogy, psychology and teaching methods. In more recent times, educational science has been subdivided into a number of areas of

---

54. Invaluable material for presenting the divine history of salvation can be found in *Lumen Gentium* and *Dei Verbum*.

55. Cf. *Gaudium et Spes*, 62.

56. Cf. St. Augustine, *De Libero Arbitrio*, II, 16, 42. *PL* 32, 1264. St. Thomas, *Contra Gentiles*, IV, 42.

specialization and has been subjected to a variety of different philosophies and political ideologies; those preparing to become teachers may feel that the whole field is confused and fragmented. Teachers of pedagogical science can help these students in their bewilderment, and guide them in the formulation of a carefully thought-out synthesis, whose elaboration begins with the premise that every pedagogical current of thought contains things which are true and useful. But then one must begin to reflect, judge, and choose.

63 Future teachers should be helped to realize that any genuine educational philosophy has to be based on the nature of the human person, and therefore must take into account all of the physical and spiritual powers of each individual, along with the call of each one to be an active and creative agent in service to society. And this philosophy must be open to a religious dimension. Human beings are fundamentally free; they are not the property of the state or of any human organization. The entire process of education, therefore, is a service to the individual students, helping each one to achieve the most complete formation possible.

The Christian model, based on the person of Christ, is then linked to this human concept of the person—that is, the model begins with an educational framework based on the person as human, and then enriches it with supernatural gifts, virtues, and values—and a supernatural call. It is indeed possible to speak about Christian education; the Conciliar declaration provides us with a clear synthesis of it.[57] Proper pedagogical formation, finally, will guide these students to a self-formation that is both human and Christian, because this is the best possible preparation for one who is preparing to educate others.

64 Interdisciplinary work has been introduced into Catholic schools with positive results, for there are questions and topics that are not easily treated within the limitations of a single subject area. Religious themes should be included; they arise naturally when dealing with topics such as the human person, the family, society, or history. Teachers should be adequately prepared to deal with such questions and be ready to give them the attention they deserve.

65 Religion teachers are not excluded. While their primary mission must be the systematic presentation of religion, they can also be invited—within the limitations of what is concretely possible—to assist in clarifying religious questions that come up in other classes. Conversely, they may wish to invite one of their colleagues to attend a religion class, in order to have the help of an expert when dealing with some specific issue. Whenever this happens, students will

---

57. Cf. *Gravissimum Educationis*, 1–2.

be favorably impressed by the cooperative spirit among the teachers: the one purpose all of them have in mind is to help these students grow in knowledge and in commitment.

IV. RELIGIOUS INSTRUCTION IN THE CLASSROOM AND THE RELIGIOUS DIMENSION OF FORMATION

The Nature of Religious Instruction

66 The mission of the Church is to evangelize, for the interior transformation and the renewal of humanity.[58] For young people, the school is one of the ways for this evangelization to take place.[59] It may be profitable to recall what the Magisterium has said: "Together with and in collaboration with the family, schools provide possibilities for catechesis that must not be neglected. . . . This refers especially to the Catholic school, of course: it would no longer deserve the title if, no matter how good its reputation for teaching in other areas there were just grounds for a reproach of negligence or deviation in religious education properly so-called. It is not true that such education is always given implicitly or indirectly. The special character of the Catholic school and the underlying reason for its existence, the reason why Catholic parents should prefer it, is precisely the quality of the religious instruction integrated into the overall education of the students."[60]

67 Sometimes there is an uncertainty, a difference of opinion, or an uneasiness about the underlying principles governing religious formation in a Catholic school, and therefore about the concrete approach to be taken in religious instruction. On the one hand, a Catholic school is a "civic institution;" its aim, methods and characteristics are the same as those of every other school. On the other hand, it is a "Christian community," whose educational goals are rooted in Christ and his Gospel. It is not always easy to bring these two aspects into harmony; the task requires constant attention, so that the tension between a serious effort to transmit culture and a forceful witness to the Gospel does not turn into a conflict harmful to both.

68 There is a close connection, and at the same time a clear distinction,

---

58. *Evangelii Nuntiandi*, 18: "For the Church to evangelize is to bring the Good News to all aspects of humanity and, through its influence, to transform it from within, making humanity itself into something new."

59. *Ibid.*, 44: "The effort to evangelize will bring great profit, through catechetical instruction given at Church, in schools wherever this is possible, and always within the Christian family."

60. *Catechesi Tradendae*, 69.

between religious instruction and catechesis, or the handing on of the Gospel message.[61] The close connection makes it possible for a school to remain a school and still integrate culture with the message of Christianity. The distinction comes from the fact that, unlike religious instruction, catechesis presupposes that the hearer is receiving the Christian message as a salvific reality. Moreover, catechesis takes place within a community living out its faith at a level of space and time not available to a school: a whole lifetime.

69 The aim of catechesis, or handing on the Gospel message, is maturity: spiritual, liturgical, sacramental and apostolic; this happens most especially in a local Church community. The aim of the school however, is knowledge. While it uses the same elements of the Gospel message, it tries to convey a sense of the nature of Christianity, and of how Christians are trying to live their lives. It is evident, of course, that religious instruction cannot help but strengthen the faith of a believing student, just as catechesis cannot help but increase one's knowledge of the Christian message.

The distinction between religious instruction and catechesis does not change the fact that a school can and must play its specific role in the work of catechesis. Since its educational goals are rooted in Christian principles, the school as a whole is inserted into the evangelical function of the Church. It assists in and promotes faith education.

70 Recent Church teaching has added an essential note: "The basic principle which must guide us in our commitment to this sensitive area of pastoral activity is that religious instruction and catechesis are at the same time distinct and complementary. A school has as its purpose the students' integral formation. Religious instruction, therefore, should be integrated into the objectives and criteria which characterize a modern school."[62] School directors should keep this directive of the Magisterium in mind, and they should respect the distinctive characteristics of religious instruction. It should have a place in the weekly order alongside the other classes, for example; it should have its own syllabus, approved by those in authority; it should seek appropriate interdisciplinary links with other course material so that there is a coordination between human learning and religious awareness. Like other course work, it should promote culture, and it should make use of the best educational methods available to schools today. In some countries, the results of examinations in religious

61. Cf. Address of Paul VI at the Wednesday audience of May 31, 1967, *Insegnamenti*, V, 1967, p. 788.

62. Address of John Paul II to the priests of the diocese of Rome, March 5, 1981, *Insegnamenti*, IV/1, pp. 629ff.

knowledge are included within the overall measure of student progress.

Finally, religious instruction in the school needs to be coordinated with the catechesis offered in parishes, in the family, and in youth associations.

Some Basic Presuppositions About Religious Instruction

71 It should be no surprise that young people bring with them into the classroom what they see and hear in the world around them, along with the impressions gained from the "world" of mass media. Perhaps some have become indifferent or insensitive. The school curriculum as such does not take these attitudes into account, but teachers must be very aware of them. With kindness and understanding, they will accept the students as they are, helping them to see that doubt and indifference are common phenomena, and that the reasons for this are readily understandable. But they will invite students in a friendly manner to seek and discover together the message of the Gospel, the source of joy and peace.

The teachers' attitudes and behavior should be those of one preparing the soil.[63] They then add their own spiritual lives, and the prayers they offer for the students entrusted to them.[64]

72 An excellent way to establish rapport with students is simply to talk to them—and to let them talk. Once a warm and trusting atmosphere has been established, various questions will come up naturally. These obviously depend on age and living situation, but many of the questions seem to be common among all of today's youth; and they tend to raise them at a younger age.[65] These questions are serious ones for young people, and they make a calm study of the Christian faith very difficult. Teachers should respond with patience and humility, and should avoid the type of peremptory statements that can be so easily contradicted:

Experts in history and science could be invited to class. One's own experiences and study should be used to help the students. Inspiration can be found in the numerous and carefully worked out responses which Vatican II gives to these kinds of questions. In theory at least, this patient work of clarification should take place at the beginning of each year, since it is almost certain that

63. Cf. *Mt* 3:1–3 on the mission of the Precursor.
64. Cf. *Jn* 17:9, the prayer of the Lord for those entrusted to him.
65. Apart from strictly local concerns, these questions are generally the ones treated in university "apologetics" manuals, and are about the "preambles to the faith." But the questions acquire a specific nuance for today's students, because of the material they are studying and the world they are living in. Typical questions have to do with atheism, non-Christian religions, divisions among Christians, events in the life of the Church, the violence and injustice of supposedly Christian nations, etc.

new questions and new difficulties will have come up during the vacation period. And experience suggests that every other opportune occasion should be taken advantage of.

73 It is not easy to develop a course syllabus for religious instruction classes which will present the Christian faith systematically and in a way suited to the young people of today.

The Second Extraordinary General Assembly of the Synod of Bishops in 1985 suggested that a new catechism be developed for the universal Church, and the Holy Father immediately created a commission to begin the preparatory work on this project. When the catechism becomes available, adaptations will be necessary in order to develop course outlines that conform to the requirements of education authorities and respond to the concrete situations that depend on local circumstances of time and place.

While we await the new synthesis of Christian doctrine—the completion of the work mandated by the Synod—we present by way of example an outline which is the fruit of experience. It is complete in content, faithful to the Gospel message, organic in form, and is developed according to a methodology based on the words and deeds of the Lord.

An Outline for an Organic Presentation of the Christian Event and the Christian Message

74 As expressed by Vatican II, the task of the teacher is to summarize Christology and present it in everyday language. Depending on the level of the class, this should be preceded by a presentation of some basic ideas about Sacred Scripture, especially those having to do with the Gospels, Divine Revelation, and the Tradition that is alive in the Church.[66] With this as a base, the class begins to learn about the Lord Jesus. His person, his message, his deeds, and the historical fact of his resurrection lead to the mystery of his divinity: "You are the Christ, the Son of the living God."[67] For more mature students, this study can be expanded to include Jesus as Savior, Priest, Teacher, and Lord of the universe. At his side is Mary his Mother, who cooperates in his mission.[68]

The discovery process is an important pedagogical method. The person of Jesus will come alive for the students. They will see again the example of his life,

---

66. Revelation, Scripture, Tradition and Christology are themes developed in *Dei Verbum*, *Lumen Gentium*, and *Gaudium et Spes*. Study of the Gospels should be extended to include a study of these documents.

67. *Mt* 16:16.

68. Concerning the Blessed Virgin Mary in the life of the Pilgrim Church, cf. the encyclical *Redemptoris Mater* of Pope John Paul II, number 39.

listen to his words, hear his invitation as addressed to them: "Come to me, all of you...."[69] Faith is thus based on knowing Jesus and following him; its growth depends on each one's good will and cooperation with grace.

75 The teacher has a reliable way to bring young people closer to the mystery of the revealed God, to the extent that this can ever be humanly possible.[70] It is the way indicated by the Savior: "Whoever has seen me, has seen the Father."[71] Through his person and his message we learn about God: we examine what he has said about the Father, and what he has done in the name of the Father. Through the Lord Jesus, therefore, we come to the mystery of God the Father, who created the universe and who sent his Son into the world so that all men and women might be saved.[72] Through Christ we come to the mystery of the Holy Spirit, sent into the world to bring the mission of the Son to fulfillment.[73] And thus we approach the supreme mystery of the Holy Trinity, in itself and as operative in the world. It is this mystery that the Church venerates and proclaims whenever it recites the Creed, repeating the words of the first Christian communities.

The process has great educational value. Its successful completion will help to strengthen the virtues of faith and of Christian religion, both of which have God as their object: Father, Son and Holy Spirit; known, loved and served in this life as we await an eternal life in union with them.

76 Students learn many things about the human person by studying science; but science has nothing to say about mystery. Teachers should help students begin to discover the mystery within the human person, just as Paul tried to help the people of Athens discover the "Unknown God." The text of John already cited[74] demonstrates that, in and through Christ, a close relationship has been established between God and each human being. The relationship has its beginning in the love of the Father; it is expressed in the love of Jesus, which led to the ultimate sacrifice of himself: "No one has greater love than this: to lay down one's life for one's friends."[75] A crowd of people constantly surrounded Jesus; they were of all types, as if representing all of humanity. As the students see this, they will begin to ask themselves why Jesus loves everyone, why he

---

69. *Mt* 11:28.
70. Cf. Denz.-Schön. 2854: one cannot speak about God in the same way that one speaks about the objects of human knowledge.
71. *Jn* 14:9.
72. Cf. *Lk* 12:24–28; *Jn* 3:16ff.
73. Cf. *Jn* 16:13.
74. Cf. *Jn* 3:16ff.
75. *Jn* 15:13.

offers an invitation to all, why he gives his life for us all. And they will be forced to conclude that each person must be a very privileged creature of God, to be the object of so much love. This is the point at which students will begin to discover another mystery—that human history unfolds within a divine history of salvation: from creation, through the first sin, the covenant with the ancient people of God, the long period of waiting until finally Jesus our Savior came, so that now we are the new People of God, pilgrims on earth journeying toward our eternal home.[76]

The educational value of Christian anthropology is obvious. Here is where students discover the true value of the human person: loved by God, with a mission on earth and a destiny that is immortal. As a result, they learn the virtues of self-respect and self-love, and of love for others—a love that is universal. In addition, each student will develop a willingness to embrace life, and also his or her own unique vocation, as a fulfillment of God's will.

77 The history of salvation continues in the Church, an historical reality that is visible to the students. They should be encouraged to discover its origins in the Gospels, in Acts, and in the Apostolic Letters; as they study these works they will see the Church at its birth, and then as it begins to grow and take its place in the world. From the way it comes into being, from its miraculous growth, and from its fidelity to the Gospel message the transition is made to the Church as a mystery. The teacher will help students to discover the Church as the People of God, composed of women and men just like ourselves, bringing salvation to all of humanity. The Church is guided by Jesus the Eternal Shepherd; guided by his Spirit, which sustains it and is forever renewing it; guided visibly by the pastors he has ordained: the Holy Father and the bishops, assisted by priests and the deacons who are their collaborators in priesthood and in ministry. The Church, called by God to be holy in all its members, continues to be at work in the world. This is the mystery of the One, Holy, Catholic, and Apostolic Church that we celebrate in the Creed.[77]

Ecclesiology has an extremely important educational value: the ideal of a universal human family is realized in the Church. As young people come to a better knowledge of the Church they belong to, they will learn to love it with a filial affection; this has obvious consequences for life, for apostolate, and for a Christian vision of the world.

---

76. From the point of view of Christian anthropology, it is essential that the history of salvation presented in *Lumen Gentium* and *Gaudium et Spes* be a part of what is studied in class.

77. Important and valuable material for teaching about the Church can be found in *Lumen Gentium*.

78 As they get older, many young people stop receiving the Sacraments; this may be a sign that their meaning has not been grasped. Perhaps they are seen as devotional, practices for children, or a popular devotion joined to a secular feast. Teachers are familiar with this phenomenon and its dangers. They will, therefore, help students to discover the real value of the Sacraments: they accompany the believer on his or her journey through life. This journey takes place within the Church, and therefore becomes more comprehensible as students grow in an understanding of what it means to be a member of the Church. The essential point for students to understand is that Jesus Christ is always truly present in the Sacraments which he has instituted,[78] and his presence makes them efficacious means of grace. The moment of closest encounter with the Lord Jesus occurs in the Eucharist, which is both Sacrifice and Sacrament. In the Eucharist, two supreme acts of love are united: Our Lord renews his sacrifice of salvation for us, and he truly gives himself to us.

79 An understanding of the sacramental journey has profound educational implications. Students become aware that being a member of the Church is something dynamic, responding to every person's need to continue growing all through life. When we meet the Lord in the Sacraments, we are never left unchanged. Through the Spirit, he causes us to grow in the Church, offering us "grace upon grace;"[79] the only thing he asks is our cooperation. The educational consequences of this touch on our relationship with God, our witness as a Christian, and our choice of a personal vocation.[80]

80 Young people today are assaulted by distractions; the circumstances are not ideal for reflecting on the last things. An effective way to approach this mystery of faith is, however, available to the teacher: the Lord proposes it in his own unique way. In the story of Lazarus, he calls himself "the resurrection and the life."[81] In the parable of the rich man he helps us to understand that a personal judgment awaits each one of us.[82] In the impressive drama of the last judgment he points to an eternal destiny which each of us merits through our own works.[83] The good or evil done to each human being is as if done to him.[84]

---

78. *Sacrosanctum Concilium*, 7: "Christ is present in the Sacraments with his own authority, so that when one baptizes it is Christ himself who baptizes. . . ."

79. *Jn* 1:16.

80. The content and the methods for teaching about the Sacraments can be enriched through studying parts of *Lumen Gentium* and *Sacrosanctum Concilium*.

81. *Jn* 11:25–27.

82. Cf. *Lk* 16:19–31.

83. Cf. *Mt* 25:31–46.

84. Cf. *Ibid.* 25:40.

81 Then, using the Creed as a pattern, the teacher can help students to learn about the Kingdom of Heaven: that it consists of those who have believed in him and spent their lives in his service. The Church calls them "saints" even if not all are formally venerated under that title. First among them is Mary, the Mother of Jesus, living a glorified life at the side of her Son. Those who have died are not separated from us. They, with us, form the one Church, the People of God, united in the "communion of saints." Those dear to us who have left us are alive and are in communion with us.[85]

These truths of faith contribute to human and Christian maturity in several important areas. They provide a sense of the dignity of the person, as destined to immortality. Christian hope offers comfort in life's difficulties. We are personally responsible in everything we do, because we must render an account to God.

An Outline for a Systematic Presentation of the Christian Life

82 As we have seen, each truth of faith has educational and ethical implications, and students should be helped to learn about these from the time when they first begin the study of religion. But a systematic presentation of Christian ethics is also needed; to assist in this task, we present here a sample outline.

As an introduction to a study of the relationship between faith and life through religious ethics it can be helpful to reflect on the first Christian communities, where the Gospel message was accompanied by prayer and the celebration of the Sacraments.[86] This has permanent value. Students will begin to understand the meaning of the virtue of faith: helped by grace, to give complete, free, personal and affective loyalty to the God who reveals himself through his Son.

This commitment is not automatic; it is itself a gift of God. We must ask for it and wait for it patiently. And students must be given time to grow and to mature.

83 The life of faith is expressed in acts of religion. The teacher will assist students to open their hearts in confidence to Father, Son, and Holy Spirit through personal and liturgical prayer. The latter is not just another way of praying; it is the official prayer of the Church, which makes the mystery of Christ present in our lives—especially through the Eucharist, Sacrifice and Sacrament, and

85. Cf. *Lumen Gentium*, Chapter VII on the eschatological nature of the pilgrim Church and its union with the heavenly Church.

86. Cf. *Eph* 1:1–14 and *Col* 1:13–20 for doxologies which witness to the faith of the early communities. *Acts* 10 speaks of evangelization, conversion, faith, and the gift of the Spirit in the house of the Roman official Cornelius. *Acts* 20:7–12 describes evangelization and the Eucharist in a house at Troas.

through the Sacrament of Reconciliation. Religious experiences are then seen, not as something externally imposed, but as a free and loving response to the God who first loved us.[87] The virtues of faith and religion, thus rooted and cultivated, are enabled to develop during childhood, youth, and in all the years that follow.

84 The human person is present in all the truths of faith: created in "the image and likeness" of God; elevated by God to the dignity of a child of God; unfaithful to God in original sin, but redeemed by Christ; a temple of the Holy Spirit; a member of the Church; destined to eternal life.

Students may well object that we are a long way from this ideal. The teacher must listen to these pessimistic responses, but point out that they are also found in the Gospel.[88] Students may need to be convinced that it is better to know the positive picture of personal Christian ethics rather than to get lost in an analysis of human misery. In practice, this means respect for oneself and for others. We must cultivate intelligence and the other spiritual gifts, especially through scholastic work. We must learn to care for our body and its health, and this includes physical activity and sports. And we must be careful of our sexual integrity through the virtue of chastity, because sexual energies are also a gift of God, contributing to the perfection of the person and having a providential function for the life of society and of the Church.[89] Thus, gradually, the teacher will guide students to the idea, and then to the realization, of a process of total formation.

85 Christian love is neither sentimentalism nor humanitarianism; it is a new reality, born of faith. Teachers must remember that the love of God governs the divine plan of universal salvation. The Lord Jesus came to live among us in order to show us the Father's love. His ultimate sacrifice testifies to his love for his friends. And the Lord's new commandment is at the center of our faith: "This is my commandment: that you love one another as I have loved you."[90] The "as" is the model and the measure of Christian love.

86 Students will raise the standard objections: violence in the world, racial hatred, daily crime, both young and old concerned only with themselves and what they can get for themselves. Teachers cannot avoid discussing these issues, but they should insist that the commandment of Christ is new and revolution-

---

87. *1 Jn* 4:10: "It is not we who have loved God, but God who first loved us. . . ."

88. Cf. *Mt* 15:19ff.

89. Cf. the document of the Congregation for Catholic Education already referred to— *Educational Guidance in Human Love: Outlines for Sex Education.*

90. *Jn* 15:12.

ary, and that it stands in opposition to all that is evil and to every form of egoism. The new Christian ethic needs to be understood and put into practice.

87 It begins at the level of family and school: affection, respect, obedience, gratitude, gentleness, goodness, helpfulness, service and good example. All manifestations of egoism, rebellion, antipathy, jealousy, hatred or revenge must be rooted out. At the broader level of Church: a love for all that excludes no one because of religion, nationality or race; prayer for all, so that all may know the Lord; laboring together in apostolic works and in efforts to relieve human suffering; a preferential option for the less fortunate, the sick, the poor, the handicapped, the lonely. As love grows in the Church, more young people may choose a life of service in it, responding to a call to the priesthood or to Religious life.

As they begin to prepare for marriage: rejecting anything that would hint at a desecration of love; discovering the newness and the depth of Christian love between man and woman, including the mutuality and reserve with which it is expressed and the sincere tenderness by which it is preserved. Young people should experience love in this way from their first friendships, gradually leading to the possibility of a commitment, until finally love is consecrated for the whole of life in the Sacrament of Matrimony.

88 Christian, social ethics must always be founded on faith. From this starting point it can shed light on related disciplines such as law, economics and political science, all of which study the human situation,[91] and this is an obvious area for fruitful interdisciplinary study. But it is important to remind ourselves that God has put the world at the service of the human family.[92] As our Lord pointed out,[93] violence and injustice in society come from men and women, and they are contrary to the will of God. But in saving us, God also saves our works: a renewed world flows from a renewed heart. The works of the new Christian order of humanity are love, justice, freedom and grace.[94]

89 These, then, are the basic elements of a Christian social ethic: the human person, the central focus of the social order; justice, the recognition of the rights of each individual; honesty, the basic condition for all human relationships; freedom, the basic right of each individual and of society. World peace must then be founded on good order and the justice to which all men and women

91. Cf. *Gaudium et Spes*, 63–66 and related applications.
92. Cf. *Gen* 1:27ff.
93. Again cf. *Mt* 15:19ff.
94. Cf. *Gaudium et Spes*, 93.

have a right as children of God; national and international well-being depend on the fact that the goods of the earth are gifts of God, and are not the privilege of some individuals or groups while others are deprived of them. Misery and hunger weigh on the conscience of humanity and cry out to God for justice.

90 This is an area which can open up broad possibilities. Students will be enriched by the principles and values they learn, and their service of society will be more effective. The Church supports and enlightens them with a social doctrine which is waiting to be put into practice by courageous and generous men and women of faith.[95]

91 The guidelines developed up to this point seem excessively optimistic. While the presentation of the Christian message as "good news" is pedagogically sound,[96] the realism of revelation, history and daily experience all require that students have a clear awareness of the evil that is at work in the world and in the human person. The Lord spoke about the "power of darkness."[97] Men and women wander far away from God, and rebel against the Gospel message; they continue to poison the world with war, violence, injustice and crime.

92 A teacher can invite the students to examine their own consciences. Which one of us can honestly claim to be without sin?[98] Thus they will acquire a sense of sin: the great sin of humanity as a whole and the personal sin which all of us discover within ourselves. Sin drives us away from God, rejects the message of Christ, and transgresses the law of love; sin betrays conscience, abuses the gift of freedom, offends the other children of God, and harms the Church of which we are all members.

93 But we are not in a hopeless situation. The teacher should help students to see, in the light of faith, that this reality has another side to it. On the world scale, the Gospel message continues to "die" as the "seed" in the soil of the earth only to blossom and bear fruit in due season.[99] At the personal level, the Lord waits for us in the Sacrament of Reconciliation. It is not just a devotional practice, but

---

95. Students should become aware of at least some of the Church's major social documents.

96. *Lk* 2:10: "I bring you news of great joy. . . ."

97. *Lk* 22: 53: "But this is your hour; this is the reign of darkness." Evidence of this is easily found in various abuses, acts of injustice, attacks on freedom, the overwhelming weight of misery that leads to sickness, decline and death, the scandalous inequality between rich and poor, the lack of any equity or sense of solidarity in international relations. (Cf. *Some Aspects of the "Theology of Liberation,"* published by the Congregation for the Doctrine of the Faith, Introduction and Part I).

98. *Jn* 8:7: "Let the one who is without sin cast the first stone. . . ."

99. Cf. *Lk* 8:4–15.

rather a personal encounter with him, through the mediation of his minister. After this celebration we can resume our journey with renewed strength and joy.

94 These truths can lead to a new and more mature understanding of Christianity. The Lord calls us to an endless struggle: to resist the forces of evil and, with his help, to have the courage to overpower it. This is a Christianity which is alive and healthy, at work in history and within the life of each individual.[100]

The call to be a Christian involves a call to help liberate the human family from its radical slavery to sin and, therefore, from the effects of sin in the cultural, economic, social and political orders. Ultimately, these effects all result from sin; they are obstacles which prevent men and women from living according to the dignity which is theirs.[101]

95 Perfection is a theme which must be part of this systematic presentation of the Christian message. To pass over it would be disloyal: to the Lord, who calls us to limitless perfection;[102] to the Church, which invites us all to perfection;[103] and to the young people themselves, who have the right to know what the Lord and the Church expect of them. The teacher will begin by reminding believing students that, through their baptism, they have become members of the Church. The Christian perfection to which we are all called is a gift of Jesus through the mediation of the Spirit; but the gift requires our cooperation. Our apostolic witness must make this perfection visible in the world, today and in the future.

Once they get beyond feeling that too much is being asked of them, students will realize that perfection is actually within their grasp. The only thing they have to do is live their lives as students as well as they can:[104] do their best in study and work; put into practice the virtues they already know in theory—especially love, which must be lived in the classroom, at home, and among friends; accept difficulties with courage; help those in need; give good example. In addition, they must find the inspiration for their daily lives in the words and the example of Jesus. They must converse with him in prayer and receive him in the Eucharist. No student can say that these are impossible demands.

The ideal would be for each student to have an opportunity for spiritual

100. Cf. *Eph* 6:10–17, a characteristically vigorous Pauline description.

101. Cf. the Introduction to *Some Aspects of the "Theology of Liberation"* published by the Congregation for the Doctrine of the Faith, August 6, 1984.

102. *Mt* 5:48: "You must be perfect as your heavenly Father is perfect."

103. *Lumen Gentium*, 42: "All the faithful are invited and called to holiness and to perfection within their own state of live."

104. *Ibid.*, 39: "This holiness of the Church . . . is expressed in various forms according to each individual, who in their lives and their activities join perfection to love."

guidance, to help in interior formation. It is the best way of giving orientation and completion to the religious instruction given in the classroom and, at the same time, of integrating this instruction into the personal experiences of each individual.

The Religion Teacher

96 The fruits of an organic presentation of the faith and of Christian ethics depend in great part on the religion teachers: who they are and what they do.

The religion teacher is the key, the vital component, if the educational goals of the school are to be achieved. But the effectiveness of religious instruction is closely tied to the personal witness given by the teacher; this witness is what brings the content of the lessons to life. Teachers of religion, therefore, must be men and women endowed with many gifts, both natural and supernatural, who are also capable of giving witness to these gifts; they must have a thorough cultural, professional, and pedagogical training, and they must be capable of genuine dialogue.

Most of all, students should be able to recognize authentic human qualities in their teachers. They are teachers of the faith; however, like Christ, they must also be teachers of what it means to be human. This includes culture, but it also includes such things as affection, tact, understanding, serenity of spirit, a balanced judgment, patience in listening to others and prudence in the way they respond, and, finally, availability for personal meetings and conversations with the students. A teacher who has a clear vision of the Christian milieu and lives in accord with it will be able to help young people develop a similar vision, and will give them the inspiration they need to put it into practice.

97 In this area, especially, an unprepared teacher can do a great deal of harm. Everything possible must be done to ensure that Catholic schools have adequately trained religion teachers; it is a vital necessity and a legitimate expectation. In Catholic schools today, these teachers tend more and more to be lay people, and they should have the opportunity of receiving the specific experiential knowledge of the mystery of Christ and of the Church that priests and Religious automatically acquire in the course of their formation. We need to look to the future and promote the establishment of formation centers for these teachers; ecclesiastical universities and faculties should do what they can to develop appropriate programs so that the teachers of tomorrow will be able to carry out their task with the competence and efficacy that is expected of them.[105]

105. Some aspects of this are treated in the documents already referred to: *The Catholic School*, 78–80; *Lay Catholics in Schools: Witnesses to the Faith*, especially 56–59. What is said there does not apply only to the lay teachers.

V. A GENERAL SUMMARY: THE RELIGIOUS
DIMENSION OF THE FORMATION PROCESS AS A WHOLE

What is a Christian Formation Process?

98 The declaration of the Council insists on the dynamic nature of integral human formation,[106] but it adds immediately that, from a Christian point of view, human development by itself is not sufficient. Education "does not merely strive to foster in the human person the maturity already described. Rather, its principal aims are these: that as the baptized person is gradually introduced into a knowledge of the mystery of salvation, he or she may daily grow more conscious of the gift of faith which has been received. . . ."[107] What characterizes a Catholic school, therefore, is that it guide students in such a way "that the development of each one's own personality will be matched by the growth of that new creation which he or she became by baptism."[108] We need to think of Christian education as a movement or a growth process, directed toward an ideal goal which goes beyond the limitations of anything human.[109] At the same time the process must be harmonious, so that Christian formation takes place within and in the course of human formation. The two are not separate and parallel paths; they are complementary forms of education which become one in the goals of the teacher and the willing reception of the students. The Gospel notes this harmonious growth in the child Jesus.[110]

99 A Christian formation process might therefore be described as an organic set of elements with a single purpose: the gradual development of every capability of every student, enabling each one to attain an integral formation within a context that includes the Christian religious dimension and recognizes the help of grace. But what really matters is not the terminology but the reality, and this reality will be assured only if all the teachers unite their educational efforts in the pursuit of a common goal. Sporadic, partial, or uncoordinated efforts, or a situation in which there is a conflict of opinion among the teachers, will interfere with rather than assist in the students' personal development.

---

106. *Gravissimum Educationis*, 1: "Children and young people should be assisted in the harmonious development of their physical, moral and intellectual gifts. . . . They should be helped to acquire gradually a more mature sense of responsibility. . . ."

107. *Ibid.*, 2.

108. *Ibid.*, 8.

109. Cf. *Mt* 5:48.

110. *Lk* 2:40: "The child grew and became strong, filled with wisdom; and the favor of God was upon him." *Lk* 2:52: "And Jesus grew in wisdom and in stature, and in favor with God and with men."

Educational Goals

100 The responsibility of a Catholic school is enormous and complex. It must respect and obey the laws that define methods, programs, structure, etc., and at the same time it must fulfill its own educational goals by blending human culture with the message of salvation into a coordinated program; it must help each of the students to actually become the "new creature" that each one is potentially, and at the same time prepare them for the responsibilities of an adult member of society. This means that a Catholic school needs to have a set of educational goals which are "distinctive" in the sense that the school has a specific objective in mind, and all of the goals are related to this objective. Concretely, the educational goals provide a frame of reference which:

- defines the school's identity: in particular, the Gospel values which are its inspiration must be explicitly mentioned;
- gives a precise description of the pedagogical, educational and cultural aims of the school;
- presents the course content, along with the values that are to be transmitted through these courses;
- describes the organization and the management of the school;
- determines which policy decisions are to be reserved to professional staff (governors and teachers), which policies are to be developed with the help of parents and students, and which activities are to be left to the free initiative of teachers, parents, or students;
- indicates ways in which student progress is to be tested and evaluated.

101 In addition, careful attention must be given to the development of general criteria which will enable each aspect of school activity to assist in the attainment of the educational objective, so that the cultural, pedagogical, social, civil and political aspects of school life are all integrated:

a. Fidelity to the Gospel as proclaimed by the Church. The activity of a Catholic school is, above all else, an activity that shares in the evangelizing mission of the Church; it is a part of the particular local Church of the country in which it is situated, and shares in the life and work of the local Christian community.

b. Careful rigor in the study of culture and the development of a critical sense, maintaining a respect for the autonomy of human knowledge and for the rules and methods proper to each of the disciplines, and at the same time orienting the whole process toward the integral formation of the person.

c. Adapting the educational process in a way that respects the particular circumstances of individual students and their families.

d. Sharing responsibility with the Church. While school authorities are the ones primarily responsible for the educational and cultural activities of the school, the local Church should also be involved in appropriate ways; the educational goals should be the result of dialogue with this ecclesial community.

It is clear, then, that the set of educational goals is something quite distinct from internal school regulations or teaching methods; and it is not just a description of vague intentions.

102 The educational goals should be revised each year on the basis of experience and need. They will be achieved through a formation process which takes place in stages; it has a starting point, various intermediate points, and a conclusion. At each stage, teachers, students and families should determine the degree of success in achieving these goals; where there is insufficient progress they should look for the reasons and find suitable remedies. It is essential that this evaluation be seen as a common responsibility, and that it be carried out faithfully.

The end of each school year is one appropriate time for such an evaluation. From a Christian perspective, it is not enough to say that this is the time for examinations. The academic program is only one part of the process, and the end of the school year is also the time for a serious and intelligent examination of which educational goals have been achieved and which have not. A much more decisive time comes at the completion of a student's years in the school, because this is the moment when students should have reached the maximum level of an education that integrates the human and the Christian.[111]

103 The religious dimension of the school climate strengthens the quality of the formation process, so long as certain conditions are verified—conditions that depend both on teachers and students. It is worth noting, once again, that the students are not spectators; they help to determine the quality of this climate.

Some of the conditions for creating a positive and supportive climate are the following: that everyone agree with the educational goals and cooperate in achieving them; that interpersonal relationships be based on love and Christian freedom; that each individual, in daily life, be a witness to Gospel values; that every student be challenged to strive for the highest possible level of formation, both human and Christian. In addition, the climate must be one in which families are welcomed, the local Church is an active participant, and civil society—

---

111. Cf. once again *Gravissimum Educationis*, 1–2.

local, national, and international—is included. If all share a common faith, this can be an added advantage.

104 Strong determination is needed to do everything possible to eliminate conditions which threaten the health of the school climate. Some examples of potential problems are these: the educational goals are either not defined or are defined badly; those responsible for the school are not sufficiently trained; concern for academic achievement is excessive; relations between teachers and students are cold and impersonal; teachers are antagonistic toward one another; discipline is imposed from on high without any participation or cooperation from the students; relationships with families are formal or even strained, and families are not involved in helping to determine the educational goals; some within the school community are giving a negative witness; individuals are unwilling to work together for the common good; the school is isolated from the local Church; there is no interest in or concern for the problems of society; religious instruction is "routine." Whenever some combination of these symptoms is present, the religious dimension of the school is seriously threatened. Religious instruction can become empty words falling on deaf ears, because the authentically Christian witness that reinforces it is absent from the school climate. All symptoms of ill health have to be faced honestly and directly, remembering that the Gospel calls us to a continuous process of conversion.

105 A school exerts a great deal of effort in trying to obtain the students' active cooperation. Since they are active agents in their own formation process, this cooperation is essential. To be human is to be endowed with intelligence and freedom; it is impossible for education to be genuine without the active involvement of the one being educated. Students must act and react; with their intelligence, freedom, will, and the whole complex range of human emotions. The formation process comes to a halt when students are uninvolved and unmoved. Experienced teachers are familiar with the causes of such "blocks" in young people; the roots are both psychological and theological, and original sin is not excluded.

106 There are many ways to encourage students to become active participants in their own formation. Those with sufficient knowledge and maturity can be asked to help in the development of educational goals. While they are clearly not yet able to determine the final objective, they can help in determining the concrete means which will help to attain this objective. When students are trusted and given responsibility, when they are invited to contribute their own ideas and efforts for the common good, their gratitude rules out indifference and inertia. The more that students can be helped to realize that a school and all its activities have only one purpose—to help them in their growth toward maturity—the more those students will be willing to become actively involved.

Even students who are very young can sense whether the atmosphere in the school is pleasant or not. They are more willing to cooperate when they feel respected, trusted and loved. And their willingness to cooperate will be reinforced by a school climate which is warm and friendly, when teachers are ready to help, and when they find it easy to get along with the other students.

107 One important result of religious instruction is the development of religious values and religious motivation; these can be a great help in obtaining the willing participation of the students. But we must remember that religious values and motivation are cultivated in all subject areas and, indeed, in all of the various activities going on in the school. One way that teachers can encourage an understanding of and commitment to religious values is by frequent references to God. Teachers learn through experience how to help the students understand and appreciate the religious truths they are being taught, and this appreciation can easily develop into love, a truth which is loved by the teacher, and communicated in such a way that it is seen to be something valuable in itself, then becomes valuable to the student. One advantage of the Christological approach to religious instruction is that it can develop this love more easily in young people. The approach we have suggested concentrates on the person of Jesus. It is possible to love a person; it is rather difficult to love a formula. This love for Christ is then transferred to his message which, because it is loved, has value.

But every true educator knows that a further step is necessary: values must lead to action; they are the motivation for action. Finally, truth becomes fully alive through the supernatural dynamism of grace, which enlightens and leads to faith, to love, to action that is in accord with the will of God, through the Lord Jesus, in the Holy Spirit. The Christian process of formation is, therefore, the result of a constant interaction involving the expert labor of the teachers, the free cooperation of the students, and the help of grace.

108 We have already referred to the fact that, in many parts of the world, the student body in a Catholic school includes increasing numbers of young people from different faiths and different ideological backgrounds. In these situations it is essential to clarify the relationship between religious development and cultural growth. It is a question which must not be ignored, and dealing with it is the responsibility of each Christian member of the educational community.

In these situations, however, evangelization is not easy—it may not even be possible. We should look to pre-evangelization: to the development of a religious sense of life. In order to do this, the process of formation must constantly raise questions about the "how" and the "why" and the "what" and then point out and deepen the positive results of this investigation.

The transmission of a culture ought to be especially attentive to the practical effects of that culture, and strengthen those aspects of it which will make a person more human. In particular, it ought to pay attention to the religious dimension of the culture and the emerging ethical requirements to be found in it.

There can be unity in the midst of pluralism, and we need to exercise a wise discernment in order to distinguish between what is essential and what is accidental. Prudent use of the "why" and the "what" and the "how" will lead to integral human development in the formation process, and this is what we mean by a genuine pre-evangelization. It is fertile ground which may, at some future time, be able to bear fruit.

109 In order to describe the formation process, we have had to proceed by an analysis of its various elements; this, of course, is not the way things happen in the real world. The Catholic school is a center of life, and life is synthetic, in this vital center, the formation process is a constant interplay of action and reaction. The interplay has both a horizontal and a vertical dimension, and it is this qualification that makes the Catholic school distinctive from those other schools whose educational objectives are not inspired by Christianity.

110 The teachers love their students, and they show this love in the way they interact with them. They take advantage of every opportunity to encourage and strengthen them in those areas which will help to achieve the goals of the educational process. Their words, their witness, their encouragement and help, their advice and friendly correction are all important in achieving these goals, which must always be understood to include academic achievement, moral behavior, and a religious dimension.

When students feel loved, they will love in return. Their questioning, their trust, their critical observations and suggestions for improvement in the classroom and the school milieu will enrich the teachers and also help to facilitate a shared commitment to the formation process.

111 In a Catholic school, even this is not enough. There is also a continuous vertical interaction, through prayer; this is the fullest and most complete expression of the religious dimension.

Each of the students has his or her own life, family and social background, and these are not always happy situations. They feel the unrest of the child or adolescent, which grows more intense as they face the problems and worries of a young person approaching maturity. Teachers will pray for each of them, that the grace present in the Catholic school's milieu may permeate their whole person, enlightening them and helping them to respond adequately to all that is demanded of them in order to live Christian lives.

And the students will learn that they must pray for their teachers. As they get older, they will come to appreciate the pain and the difficulties that teaching involves. They will pray that the educational gifts of their teachers may be more effective, that they may be comforted by success in their work, that grace may sustain their dedication and bring them peace in their work.

112 Thus a relationship is built up which is both human and divine; there is a flow of love, and also of grace. And this will make the Catholic school truly authentic. As the years go by, students will have the joy of seeing themselves nearing maturity; not only physically, but also intellectually and spiritually. When they look back, they will realize that, with their cooperation, the educational objectives of the school have become a reality. And as they look forward, they will feel free and secure, because they will be able to face the new, and now proximate, life commitments.

Conclusion

113 The Congregation for Catholic Education asks local ordinaries and superiors of Religious Congregations dedicated to the education of youth to bring these reflections to the attention of all teachers and directors of Catholic schools, At the same time, the Congregation wishes to affirm once again that it is fully conscious of the important service they offer—to youth and to the Church.

114 Therefore the Congregation extends warm thanks to all those engaged in this work: for all they have done, and for all that they continue to do in spite of political, economic, and practical difficulties. For many, to continue in this mission involves great sacrifice. The Church is deeply grateful to everyone dedicated to the educational mission in a Catholic school; it is confident that, with the help of God, many others will be called to join in this mission and will respond generously.

115 The Congregation would like to suggest that further study, research, and experimentation be done in all areas that affect the religious dimension of education in Catholic schools. Much has been done, but many people are asking for even more. This is surely possible in every school whose freedom is sufficiently protected by civil law. It may be difficult in those countries which allow the Catholic school as an academic institution, but where the religious dimension leads to constant conflict. Local experience must be the determining factor

in such situations; however, to the extent that it is possible, a religious dimension should always be present—either in the school or outside its walls. There has never been a shortage of families and students, of different faiths and religions, who choose a Catholic school because they appreciate the value of an education where instruction is enhanced by a religious dimension.

Educators will know the best way to respond to their expectations, knowing that, in a world of cultural pluralism, dialogue always gives grounds for hope.

Rome, April 7, 1988, Feast of Saint John Baptist de La Salle, Principal Patron of teachers.

WILLIAM Cardinal BAUM, *Prefect*
† ANTONIO M. JAVIERRE ORTAS
Titular Archbishop of Meta
Secretary

ON CATHOLIC UNIVERSITIES
EX CORDE ECCLESIAE

APOSTOLIC CONSTITUTION OF THE SUPREME PONTIFF
JOHN PAUL II

Introduction

1 Born from the heart of the Church, a Catholic University is located in that course of tradition which may be traced back to the very origin of the University as an institution. It has always been recognized as an incomparable center of creativity and dissemination of knowledge for the good of humanity. By vocation, the *Universitas magistrorum et scholarium* is dedicated to research, to teaching and to the education of students who freely associate with their teachers in a common love of knowledge.[1] With every other University it shares that *gaudium de veritate,* so precious to Saint Augustine, which is that joy of searching for, discovering and communicating truth[2] in every field of knowledge. A Catholic University's privileged task is "to unite existentially by intellectual effort two orders of reality that too frequently tend to be placed in opposition as though they were antithetical: the search for truth, and the certainty of already knowing the fount of truth."[3]

2 For many years I myself was deeply enriched by the beneficial experience of university life: the ardent search for truth and its unselfish transmission to youth and to all those learning to think rigorously, so as to act rightly and to serve humanity better.

Therefore, I desire to share with everyone my profound respect for Catholic Universities, and to express my great appreciation for the work that is being done in them in the various spheres of knowledge. In a particular way, I wish to manifest my joy at the numerous meetings which the Lord has permitted me to have in the course of my apostolic journeys with the Catholic University communities of various continents. They are for me a lively and promising sign of the fecundity of the Christian mind in the heart of every culture. They give me

---

1. Cf. The letter of Pope Alexander IV to the University of Paris, 14 April 1255, Introduction: *Bullarium Diplomatum. . .* , vol. III, Turin, 1858, p. 602.

2. Saint Augustine, *Confes.* X, xxiii, 33: "In fact, the blessed life consists in *the joy that comes from the truth,* since this joy comes from You who are Truth, God my light, salvation of my face, my God." PL 32, 793–794. Cf. Saint Thomas Aquinas, *De Malo,* IX, 1: "It is actually natural to man to strive for knowledge of the truth."

3. John Paul II, Discourse to the "Institut Catholique de Paris," 1 June 1980: *Insegnamenti di Giovanni Paolo II,* Vol. III/1 (1980), p. 1581.

a well-founded hope for a new flowering of Christian culture in the rich and varied context of our changing times, which certainly face serious challenges but which also bear so much promise under the action of the Spirit of truth and of love.

It is also my desire to express my pleasure and gratitude to the very many Catholic scholars engaged in teaching and research in non-Catholic Universities. Their task as academics and scientists, lived out in the light of the Christian faith, is to be considered precious for the good of the Universities in which they teach. Their presence, in fact, is a continuous stimulus to the selfless search for truth and for the wisdom that comes from above.

3 Since the beginning of this Pontificate, I have shared these ideas and sentiments with my closest collaborators, the Cardinals, with the Congregation for Catholic Education, and with men and women of culture throughout the world. In fact, the dialogue of the Church with the cultures of our times is that vital area where "the future of the Church and of the world is being played out as we conclude the twentieth century."[4] There is only one culture: that of man, by man and for man.[5] And thanks to her Catholic Universities and their humanistic and scientific inheritance, the Church, expert in humanity, as my predecessor, Paul VI, expressed it at the United Nations,[6] explores the mysteries of humanity and of the world, clarifying them in the light of Revelation.

4 It is the honor and responsibility of a Catholic University to consecrate itself without reserve to *the cause of truth*. This is its way of serving at one and the same time both the dignity of man and the good of the Church, which has "an intimate conviction that truth is (its) real ally . . . and that knowledge and reason are sure ministers to faith."[7] Without in any way neglecting the acquisition of useful knowledge, a Catholic University is distinguished by its free search for the whole truth about nature, man and God. The present age is in urgent need of this kind of disinterested service, namely of *proclaiming the meaning of truth*, that fundamental value without which freedom, justice and human dignity are extinguished. By means of a kind of universal humanism a Catholic University is completely dedicated to the research of all aspects of truth in their essential

---

4. John Paul II, Discourse to the Cardinals, 10 November 1979: *Insegnamenti di Giovanni Paolo II*, Vol. II/2 (1979), p. 1096; cf. Discourse to UNESCO, Paris, 2 June 1980: AAS 72 (1980), pp. 735–752.

5. Cf. John Paul II, Discourse to the University of Coimbra, 15 May 1982: *Insegnamenti di Giovanni Paolo II*, Vol. V/2 (1982), p. 1692.

6. Paul VI, Allocution to Representatives of States, 4 October 1965: *Insegnamenti di Paolo VI*, Vol. III (1965), p. 508.

7. John Henry Cardinal Newman, *The Idea of a University*, London, Longmans, Green and Company, 1931, p. xi.

connection with the supreme Truth, who is God. It does this without fear but rather with enthusiasm, dedicating itself to every path of knowledge, aware of being preceded by him who is "the Way, the Truth, and the Life,"[8] the *Logos*, whose Spirit of intelligence and love enables the human person with his or her own intelligence to find the ultimate reality of which he is the source and end and who alone is capable of giving fully that Wisdom without which the future of the world would be in danger.

5 It is in the context of the impartial search for truth that the relationship between faith and reason is brought to light and meaning. The invitation of Saint Augustine, "*Intellege ut credas; crede ut intellegas,*"[9] is relevant to Catholic Universities that are called to explore courageously the riches of Revelation and of nature so that the united endeavor of intelligence and faith will enable people to come to the full measure of their humanity, created in the image and likeness of God, renewed even more marvelously, after sin, in Christ, and called to shine forth in the light of the Spirit.

6 Through the encounter which it establishes between the unfathomable richness of the salvific message of the Gospel and the variety and immensity of the fields of knowledge in which that richness is incarnated by it, a Catholic University enables the Church to institute an incomparably fertile dialogue with people of every culture. Man's life is given dignity by culture, and, while he finds his fullness in Christ, there can be no doubt that the Gospel which reaches and renews him in every dimension is also fruitful for the culture in which he lives.

7 In the world today, characterized by such rapid developments in science and technology, the tasks of a Catholic University assume an ever greater importance and urgency. Scientific and technological discoveries create an enormous economic and industrial growth, but they also inescapably require the correspondingly necessary *search for meaning* in order to guarantee that the new discoveries be used for the authentic good of individuals and of human society as a whole. If it is the responsibility of every University to search for such meaning, a Catholic University is called in a particular way to respond to this need: its Christian inspiration enables it to include the moral, spiritual and religious dimension in its research, and to evaluate the attainments of science and technology in the perspective of the totality of the human person.

---

8. *Jn* 14:6.

9. Cf. Saint Augustine, Serm. 43, 9: PL 38, 258. Cf. also Saint Anselm, *Proslogion*, chap. I: PL 158, 227.

In this context, Catholic Universities are called to a continuous renewal, both as "Universities" and as "Catholic." For, "What is at stake is the *very meaning of scientific and technological research, of social life and of culture,* but, on an even more profound level, what is at stake is *the very meaning of the human person.*"[10] Such renewal requires a clear awareness that, by its Catholic character, a University is made more capable of conducting an *impartial* search for truth, a search that is neither subordinated to nor conditioned by particular interests of any kind.

8 Having already dedicated the Apostolic Constitution *Sapientia Christiana* to Ecclesiastical Faculties and Universities,[11] I then felt obliged to propose an analogous Document for Catholic Universities as a sort of "magna carta," enriched by the long and fruitful experience of the Church in the realm of Universities and open to the promise of future achievements that will require courageous creativity and rigorous fidelity.

9 The present Document is addressed especially to those who conduct Catholic Universities, to the respective academic communities, to all those who have an interest in them, particularly the Bishops, Religious Congregations and ecclesial *Institutions,* and to the numerous laity who are committed to the great mission of higher education. Its purpose is that "the Christian mind may achieve, as it were, a public, persistent and universal presence in the whole enterprise of advancing higher culture and that the students of these institutions become people outstanding in learning, ready to shoulder society's heavier burdens and to witness the faith to the world."[12]

10 In addition to Catholic Universities, I also turn to the many Catholic Institutions of higher education. According to their nature and proper objectives, they share some or all of the characteristics of a University and they offer their own contribution to the Church and to society, whether through research, education or professional training. While this Document specifically concerns Catholic Universities, it is also meant to include all Catholic Institutions of higher education engaged in instilling the Gospel message of Christ in souls and cultures.

---

10. Cf. John Paul II, Allocution to the International Congress on Catholic Universities, 25 April 1989, n. 3: *AAS* 18 (1989), p. 1218.

11. John Paul II, Apostolic Constitution *Sapientia Christiana* concerning the Ecclesiastical Universities and Faculties, 15 April 1979: *AAS* 71 (1979), pp. 469–521.

12. Vatican Council II, Declaration on Catholic Education *Gravissimum Educationis*, n. 10: *AAS* 58 (1966), p. 737.

Therefore, it is with great trust and hope that I invite all Catholic Universities to pursue their irreplaceable task. Their mission appears increasingly necessary for the encounter of the Church with the development of the sciences and with the cultures of our age.

Together with all my brother Bishops who share pastoral responsibility with me, I would like to manifest my deep conviction that a Catholic University is without any doubt one of the best instruments that the Church offers to our age which is searching for certainty and wisdom. Having the mission of bringing the Good News to everyone, the Church should never fail to interest herself in this Institution. By research and teaching, Catholic Universities assist the Church in the manner most appropriate to modern times to find cultural treasures both old and new, "*nova et vetera,*" according to the words of Jesus.[13]

11 Finally, I turn to the whole Church, convinced that Catholic Universities are essential to her growth and to the development of Christian culture and human progress. For this reason, the entire ecclesial Community is invited to give its support to Catholic Institutions of higher education and to assist them in their process of development and renewal. It is invited in a special way to guard the rights and freedom of these Institutions in civil society, and to offer them economic aid, especially in those countries where they have more urgent need of it, and to furnish assistance in founding new Catholic Universities wherever this might be necessary.

My hope is that these prescriptions, based on the teaching of Vatican Council II and the directives of the Code of Canon Law, will enable Catholic Universities and other Institutes of higher studies to fulfill their indispensable mission in the new advent of grace that is opening up to the new Millennium.

PART I: IDENTITY AND MISSION

A. The Identity of the Catholic University

1. *Nature and Objectives*

12 Every Catholic University, *as a university,* is an academic community which, in a rigorous and critical fashion, assists in the protection and advancement of human dignity and of a cultural heritage through research, teaching and various services offered to the local, national and international communities.[14] It possesses that institutional autonomy necessary to perform its functions effectively

---

13. *Mt* 13:52.

14. Cf. *The Magna Carta of the European Universities,* Bologna, Italy, 18 September 1988, "Fundamental Principles."

and guarantees its members academic freedom, so long as the rights of the individual person and of the community are preserved within the confines of the truth and the common good.[15]

13 Since the objective of a Catholic University is to assure in an institutional manner a Christian presence in the university world confronting the great problems of society and culture,[16] every Catholic University, as *Catholic*, must have the following *essential characteristics:*

1. a Christian inspiration not only of individuals but of the university community as such;
2. a continuing reflection in the light of the Catholic faith upon the growing treasury of human knowledge, to which it seeks to contribute by its own research;
3. fidelity to the Christian message as it comes to us through the Church;
4. an institutional commitment to the service of the people of God and of the human family in their pilgrimage to the transcendent goal which gives meaning to life.[17]

14 "In the light of these four characteristics, it is evident that besides the teaching, research and services common to all Universities, a Catholic University, by *institutional commitment*, brings to its task the inspiration and light of the *Christian message*. In a Catholic University, therefore, Catholic ideals, attitudes

15. Cf. Vatican Council II, Pastoral Constitution on the Church in the Modern World *Gaudium et Spes*, n. 59: *AAS* 58 (1966), p. 1080; Declaration on Catholic Education *Gravissimum Educationis*, n. 10: *AAS* 58 (1966), p. 737. "Institutional autonomy" means that the governance of an academic institution is and remains internal to the institution; "academic freedom" is the guarantee given to those involved in teaching and research that, within their specific specialized branch of knowledge, and according to the methods proper to that specific area, they may search for the truth wherever analysis and evidence leads them, and may teach and publish the results of this search, keeping in mind the cited criteria, that is, safeguarding the rights of the individual and of society within the confines of the truth and the common good.

16. There is a two-fold notion of *culture* used in this document: the *humanistic* and the *socio-historical*. "The word 'culture' in its general sense indicates all those factors by which man refines and unfolds his manifold spiritual and bodily qualities. It means his effort to bring the world itself under his control by his knowledge and his labor. It includes the fact that by improving customs and institutions he renders social life more human both within the family and in the civic community. Finally, it is a feature of culture that throughout the course of time man expresses, communicates, and conserves in his works great spiritual experiences and desires, so that these may be of advantage to the progress of many, even of the whole human family. Hence it follows that human culture necessarily has a historical and social aspect and that the word 'culture' often takes on a sociological and ethnological sense." Vatican Council II, Pastoral Constitution on the Church in the Modern World *Gaudium et Spes*, n. 53: *AAS* 58 (1966), p. 1075.

17. *L'Université Catholique dans le monde moderne. Document final du 2ème Congrès des Délégués des Universités Catholiques*, Rome, 20–29 November 1972, § 1.

and principles penetrate and inform university activities in accordance with the proper nature and autonomy of these activities. In a word, being both a University and Catholic, it must be both a community of scholars representing various branches of human knowledge, and an academic institution in which Catholicism is vitally present and operative."[18]

15 A Catholic University, therefore, is a place of research, where scholars *scrutinize reality* with the methods proper to each academic discipline, and so contribute to the treasury of human knowledge. Each individual discipline is studied in a systematic manner; moreover, the various disciplines are brought into dialogue for their mutual enhancement.

In addition to assisting men and women in their continuing quest for the truth, this research provides an effective witness, especially necessary today, to the Church's belief in the intrinsic value of knowledge and research.

In a Catholic University, research necessarily includes (*a*) the search for an *integration of knowledge*, (*b*) a *dialogue between faith and reason*, (*c*) an *ethical concern*, and (*d*) a *theological perspective*.

16 *Integration of knowledge* is a process, one which will always remain incomplete; moreover, the explosion of knowledge in recent decades, together with the rigid compartmentalization of knowledge within individual academic disciplines, makes the task increasingly difficult. But a University, and especially a Catholic University, "*has to be a 'living union' of individual organisms* dedicated to the search for truth.... It is necessary *to work towards a higher synthesis* of knowledge, in which alone lies the possibility of satisfying that thirst for truth which is profoundly inscribed on the heart of the human person."[19] Aided by the specific contributions of philosophy and theology, university scholars will be engaged in a constant effort to determine the relative place and meaning of each of the various disciplines within the context of a vision of the human person and the world that is enlightened by the Gospel, and therefore by a faith in Christ, the *Logos*, as the center of creation and of human history.

17 In promoting this integration of knowledge, a specific part of a Catholic University's task is to promote *dialogue between faith and reason*, so that it can

---

18. *Ibid.*

19. John Paul II, Allocution to the International Congress on Catholic Universities, 25 April 1989, n. 4: *AAS* 81 (1989), p. 1219. Cf. also Vatican Council II, Pastoral Constitution on the Church in the Modern World *Gaudium et Spes*, n. 61: *AAS* 58 (1966), pp. 1081–1082. Cardinal Newman observes that a University "professes to assign to each study which it receives, its proper place and its just boundaries; to define the rights, to establish the mutual relations and to affect the intercommunion of one and all." (Op. cit., p. 457).

be seen more profoundly how faith and reason bear harmonious witness to the unity of all truth. While each academic discipline retains its own integrity and has its own methods, this dialogue demonstrates that "methodical research within every branch of learning, when carried out in a truly scientific manner and in accord with moral norms, can never truly conflict with faith. For the things of the earth and the concerns of faith derive from the same God."[20] A vital interaction of two distinct levels of coming to know the one truth leads to a greater love for truth itself, and contributes to a more comprehensive understanding of the meaning of human life and of the purpose of God's creation.

18 Because knowledge is meant to serve the human person, research in a Catholic University is always carried out with a concern for the *ethical* and *moral implications* both of its methods and of its discoveries. This concern, while it must be present in all research, is particularly important in the areas of science and technology. "It is essential that we be convinced of the priority of the ethical over the technical, of the primacy of the person over things, of the superiority of the spirit over matter. The cause of the human person will only be served if knowledge is joined to conscience. Men and women of science will truly aid humanity only if they preserve the sense of the transcendence of the human person over the world and of God over the human person."[21]

19 *Theology* plays a particularly important role in the search for a synthesis of knowledge as well as in the dialogue between faith and reason. It serves all other disciplines in their search for meaning, not only by helping them to investigate how their discoveries will affect individuals and society but also by bringing a perspective and an orientation not contained within their own methodologies. In turn, interaction with these other disciplines and their discoveries enriches theology, offering it a better understanding of the world today, and making theological research more relevant to current needs. Because of its specific importance among the academic disciplines, every Catholic University should have a faculty, or at least a chair, of theology.[22]

---

20. Vatican Council II, Pastoral Constitution on the Church in the Modern World *Gaudium et Spes*, n. 36: *AAS* 58 (1966), p. 1054. To a group of scientists I pointed out that "while reason and faith surely represent two distinct orders of knowledge, each autonomous with regard to its own methods, the two must finally converge in the discovery of a single whole reality which has its origin in God." (John Paul II, *Address at the Meeting on Galileo*, 9 May 1983, n. 3: *AAS* 75 [1983], p. 690).

21. John Paul II, Address at UNESCO, 2 June 1980, n. 22: *AAS* 72 (1980), p. 750. The last part of the quotation uses words directed to the Pontifical Academy of Sciences, 10 November 1979: *Insegnamenti di Giovanni Paolo II*, Vol. II/2 (1979), p. 1109.

22. Cf. Vatican Council II, Declaration on Catholic Education *Gravissimum Educationis*, n. 10: *AAS* 58 (1966), p. 737.

20 Given the close connection between research and teaching, the research qualities indicated above will have their influence on all teaching. While each discipline is taught systematically and according to its own methods, *interdisciplinary studies,* assisted by a careful and thorough study of philosophy and theology, enable students to acquire an organic vision of reality and to develop a continuing desire for intellectual progress. In the communication of knowledge, emphasis is then placed on how *human reason in its reflection* opens to increasingly broader questions, and how the complete answer to them can only come from above through faith. Furthermore, the *moral implications* that are present in each discipline are examined as an integral part of the teaching of that discipline so that the entire educative process be directed towards the whole development of the person. Finally, Catholic theology, taught in a manner faithful to Scripture, Tradition, and the Church's Magisterium, provides an awareness of the Gospel principles which will enrich the meaning of human life and give it a new dignity.

Through research and teaching the students are educated in the various disciplines so as to become truly competent in the specific sectors in which they will devote themselves to the service of society and of the Church, but at the same time prepared to give the witness of their faith to the world.

2. *The University Community*

21 A Catholic University pursues its objectives through its formation of an authentic human community animated by the spirit of Christ. The source of its unity springs from a common dedication to the truth, a common vision of the dignity of the human person and, ultimately, the person and message of Christ which gives the Institution its distinctive character. As a result of this inspiration, the community is animated by a spirit of freedom and charity; it is characterized by mutual respect, sincere dialogue, and protection of the rights of individuals. It assists each of its members to achieve wholeness as human persons; in turn, everyone in the community helps in promoting unity, and each one, according to his or her role and capacity, contributes towards decisions which affect the community, and also towards maintaining and strengthening the distinctive Catholic character of the Institution.

22 *University teachers* should seek to improve their competence and endeavor to set the content, objectives, methods, and results of research in an individual discipline within the framework of a coherent world vision. Christians among the teachers are called to be witnesses and educators of authentic Christian life, which evidences attained integration between faith and life, and between professional competence and Christian wisdom. All teachers are to be inspired by academic ideals and by the principles of an authentically human life.

23 *Students* are challenged to pursue an education that combines excellence in humanistic and cultural development with specialized professional training. Most especially, they are challenged to continue the search for truth and for meaning throughout their lives, since "the human spirit must be cultivated in such a way that there results a growth in its ability to wonder, to understand, to contemplate, to make personal judgments, and to develop a religious, moral, and social sense."[23] This enables them to acquire or, if they have already done so, to deepen a Christian way of life that is authentic. They should realize the responsibility of their professional life, the enthusiasm of being the trained 'leaders' of tomorrow, of being witnesses to Christ in whatever place they may exercise their profession.

24 *Directors* and *administrators* in a Catholic University promote the constant growth of the University and its community through a leadership of service; the dedication and witness of the *non-academic staff* are vital for the identity and life of the University.

25 Many Catholic Universities were founded by Religious Congregations, and continue to depend on their support; those Religious Congregations dedicated to the apostolate of higher education are urged to assist these Institutions in the renewal of their commitment, and to continue to prepare religious men and women who can positively contribute to the mission of a Catholic University.

Lay people have found in university activities a means by which they too could exercise an important apostolic role in the Church and, in most Catholic Universities today, the academic community is largely composed of laity; in increasing numbers, lay men and women are assuming important functions and responsibilities for the direction of these Institutions. These lay Catholics are responding to the Church's call "to be present, as signs of courage and intellectual creativity, in the privileged places of culture, that is, the world of education-school and university."[24] The future of Catholic Universities depends to a great extent on the competent and dedicated service of lay Catholics. The Church sees their developing presence in these institutions both as a sign of hope and as a confirmation of the irreplaceable lay vocation in the Church and

---

23. Vatican Council II, Pastoral Constitution on the Church in the Modern World *Gaudium et Spes*, n. 59: *AAS* 58 (1966), p. 1080. Cardinal Newman describes the ideal to be sought in this way: "A habit of mind is formed which lasts through life, of which the attributes are freedom, equitableness, calmness, moderation and wisdom." *(Op. cit.,* pp. 101–102).

24. John Paul II, Post-Synodal Apostolic Exhortation *Christifideles Laici*, 30 December 1988, n. 44: *AAS* 81 (1989), p. 479.

in the world, confident that lay people will, in the exercise of their own distinctive role, "illumine and organize these (temporal) affairs in such a way that they always start out, develop, and continue according to Christ's mind, to the praise of the Creator and the Redeemer."[25]

26 The university community of many Catholic institutions includes members of other Churches, ecclesial communities and religions, and also those who profess no religious belief. These men and women offer their training and experience in furthering the various academic disciplines or other university tasks.

3. The Catholic University in the Church

27 Every Catholic University, without ceasing to be a University, has a relationship to the Church that is essential to its institutional identity. As such, it participates most directly in the life of the local Church in which it is situated; at the same time, because it is an academic institution and therefore a part of the international community of scholarship and inquiry, each institution participates in and contributes to the life and the mission of the universal Church, assuming consequently a special bond with the Holy See by reason of the service to unity which it is called to render to the whole Church. One consequence of its essential relationship to the Church is that the *institutional* fidelity of the University to the Christian message includes a recognition of and adherence to the teaching authority of the Church in matters of faith and morals. Catholic members of the university community are also called to a personal fidelity to the Church with all that this implies. Non-Catholic members are required to respect the Catholic character of the University, while the University in turn respects their religious liberty.[26]

28 Bishops have a particular responsibility to promote Catholic Universities, and especially to promote and assist in the preservation and strengthening of their Catholic identity, including the protection of their Catholic identity in relation to civil authorities. This will be achieved more effectively if close personal and pastoral relationships exist between University and Church authorities, characterized by mutual trust, close and consistent cooperation and continuing dialogue. Even when they do not enter directly into the internal

---

25. Vatican Council II, Dogmatic Constitution on the Church *Lumen Gentium*, n. 31: *AAS* 57 (1965), pp. 37–38. Cf. Decree on the Apostolate of the Laity *Apostolicam Actuositatem*, passim: *AAS* 58 (1966), pp. 837ff. Cf. also *Gaudium et Spes*, n. 43: *AAS* 58 (1966), pp. 1061–1064.

26. Cf. Vatican Council II, Declaration on Religious Liberty *Dignitatis Humanae*, n. 2: *AAS* 58 (1966), pp. 930–931.

governance of the University, Bishops "should be seen not as external agents but as participants in the life of the Catholic University."[27]

29 The Church, accepting "the legitimate autonomy of human culture and especially of the sciences," recognizes the academic freedom of scholars in each discipline in accordance with its own principles and proper methods,[28] and within the confines of the truth and the common good.

Theology has its legitimate place in the University alongside other disciplines. It has proper principles and methods which define it as a branch of knowledge. Theologians enjoy this same freedom so long as they are faithful to these principles and methods.

Bishops should encourage the creative work of theologians. They serve the Church through research done in a way that respects theological method. They seek to understand better, further develop and more effectively communicate the meaning of Christian Revelation as transmitted in Scripture and Tradition and in the Church's Magisterium. They also investigate the ways in which theology can shed light on specific questions raised by contemporary culture. At the same time, since theology seeks an understanding of revealed truth whose authentic interpretation is entrusted to the Bishops of the Church,[29] it is intrinsic to the principles and methods of their research and teaching in their academic discipline that theologians respect the authority of the Bishops, and assent to Catholic doctrine according to the degree of authority with which it is taught.[30] Because of their interrelated roles, dialogue between Bishops and theologians is essential; this is especially true today, when the results of research are so quickly and so widely communicated through the media.[31]

B. THE MISSION OF SERVICE OF A CATHOLIC UNIVERSITY

30 The basic mission of a University is a continuous quest for truth through its research, and the preservation and communication of knowledge for the good of society. A Catholic University participates in this mission with its own specific characteristics and purposes.

---

27. John Paul II, Address to Leaders of Catholic Higher Education, Xavier University of Louisiana, U.S.A., 12 September 1987, n. 4: *AAS* 80 (1988), p. 764.

28. Vatican Council II, Pastoral Constitution on the Church in the Modern World *Gaudium et Spes*, n. 59: *AAS* 58 (1966), p. 1080.

29. Cf. Vatican Council II, Dogmatic Constitution on Divine Revelation *Dei Verbum*, nn. 8–10: *AAS* 58 (1966), pp. 820-822.

30. Cf. Vatican Council II, Dogmatic Constitution on the Church *Lumen Gentium*, n. 25: *AAS* 57 (1965), pp. 29–31.

31. Cf. "Instruction on the Ecclesial Vocation of the Theologian" of the Congregation for the Doctrine of the Faith of 24 May 1990.

1. *Service to Church and Society*

31 Through teaching and research, a Catholic University offers an indispensable contribution to the Church. In fact, it prepares men and women who, inspired by Christian principles and helped to live their Christian vocation in a mature and responsible manner, will be able to assume positions of responsibility in the Church. Moreover, by offering the results of its scientific research, a Catholic University will be able to help the Church respond to the problems and needs of this age.

32 A Catholic University, as any University, is immersed in human society; as an extension of its service to the Church, and always within its proper competence, it is called on to become an ever more effective instrument of cultural progress for individuals as well as for society. Included among its research activities, therefore, will be a study of *serious contemporary problems* in areas such as the dignity of human life, the promotion of justice for all, the quality of personal and family life, the protection of nature, the search for peace and political stability, a more just sharing in the world's resources, and a new economic and political order that will better serve the human community at a national and international level. University research will seek to discover the roots and causes of the serious problems of our time, paying special attention to their ethical and religious dimensions.

If need be, a Catholic University must have the courage to speak uncomfortable truths which do not please public opinion, but which are necessary to safeguard the authentic good of society.

33 A specific priority is the need to examine and evaluate the predominant values and norms of modern society and culture in a Christian perspective, and the responsibility to try to communicate to society those *ethical and religious principles which give full meaning to human life*. In this way a University can contribute further to the development of a true Christian anthropology, founded on the person of Christ, which will bring the dynamism of the creation and redemption to bear on reality and on the correct solution to the problems of life.

34 The Christian spirit of service to others for the *promotion of social justice* is of particular importance for each Catholic University, to be shared by its teachers and developed in its students. The Church is firmly committed to the integral growth of all men and women.[32] The Gospel, interpreted in the social teachings of the Church, is an urgent call to promote "the development of those

---

32. Cf. John Paul II, Encyclical Letter *Sollicitudo Rei Socialis*, nn. 27–34: *AAS* 80 (1988), pp. 547–560.

peoples who are striving to escape from hunger, misery, endemic diseases and ignorance; of those who are looking for a wider share in the benefits of civilization and a more active improvement of their human qualities; of those who are aiming purposefully at their complete fulfillment."[33] Every Catholic University feels responsible to contribute concretely to the progress of the society within which it works: for example it will be capable of searching for ways to make university education accessible to all those who are able to benefit from it, especially the poor or members of minority groups who customarily have been deprived of it. A Catholic University also has the responsibility, to the degree that it is able, to help to promote the development of the emerging nations.

35 In its attempts to resolve these complex issues that touch on so many different dimensions of human life and of society, a Catholic University will insist on cooperation among the different academic disciplines, each offering its distinct contribution in the search for solutions; moreover, since the economic and personal resources of a single Institution are limited, cooperation in *common research projects* among Catholic Universities, as well as with other private and governmental institutions, is imperative. In this regard, and also in what pertains to the other fields of the specific activity of a Catholic University, the role played by various national and international associations of Catholic Universities is to be emphasized. Among these associations the mission of *The International Federation of Catholic Universities*, founded by the Holy See,[34] is particularly to be remembered. The Holy See anticipates further fruitful collaboration with this Federation.

36 Through programs of *continuing education* offered to the wider community, by making its scholars available for consulting services, by taking advantage of modern means of communication, and in a variety of other ways, a Catholic University can assist in making the growing body of human knowledge and a developing understanding of the faith available to a wider public, thus expanding university services beyond its own academic community.

37 In its service to society, a Catholic University *will relate especially to the academic, cultural and scientific world* of the region in which it is located. Original

33. Paul VI, Encyclical Letter *Populorum Progressio*, n. 1: *AAS* 59(1967), p. 257.

34. "Therefore, in that there has been a pleasing multiplication of centers of higher learning, it has become apparent that it would be opportune for the faculty and the alumni to unite in common association which, working in reciprocal understanding and close collaboration, and based upon the authority of the Supreme Pontiff, as father and universal doctor, they might more efficaciously spread and extend the light of Christ." (Pius XII, Apostolic Letter *Catholicas Studiorum Universitates*, with which The International Federation of Catholic Universities was established: *AAS* 42 [1950], p. 386).

forms of dialogue and collaboration are to be encouraged between the Catholic Universities and the other Universities of a nation on behalf of development, of understanding between cultures, and of the defense of nature in accordance with an awareness of the international ecological situation.

Catholic Universities join other private and public Institutions in serving the public interest through higher education and research; they are one among the variety of different types of institution that are necessary for the free expression of cultural diversity, and they are committed to the promotion of solidarity and its meaning in society and in the world. Therefore they have the full right to expect that civil society and public authorities will recognize and defend their institutional autonomy and academic freedom; moreover, they have the right to the financial support that is necessary for their continued existence and development.

2. *Pastoral Ministry*

38 Pastoral ministry is that activity of the University which offers the members of the university community an opportunity to integrate religious and moral principles with their academic study and non-academic activities, *thus integrating faith with life.* It is part of the mission of the Church within the University, and is also a constitutive element of a Catholic University itself, both in its structure and in its life. A university community concerned with promoting the Institution's Catholic character will be conscious of this pastoral dimension and sensitive to the ways in which it can have an influence on all university activities.

39 As a natural expression of the Catholic identity of the University, the university community *should give a practical demonstration of its faith in its daily activity,* with important moments of reflection and of prayer. Catholic members of this community will be offered opportunities to assimilate Catholic teaching and practice into their lives and will be encouraged to participate in the celebration of the sacraments, especially the Eucharist as the most perfect act of community worship. When the academic community includes members of other Churches, ecclesial communities or religions, their initiatives for reflection and prayer in accordance with their own beliefs are to be respected.

40 Those involved in pastoral ministry will encourage teachers and students to become more aware of their responsibility towards those who are suffering physically or spiritually. Following the example of Christ, they will be particularly attentive to the poorest and to those who suffer economic, social, cultural or religious injustice. This responsibility begins within the academic community, but it also finds application beyond it.

41 Pastoral ministry is an indispensable means by which Catholic students can, in fulfillment of their baptism, *be prepared for active participation in the life of the Church;* it can assist in developing and nurturing the value of marriage and family life, fostering vocations to the priesthood and religious life, stimulating the Christian commitment of the laity and imbuing every activity with the spirit of the Gospel. Close cooperation between pastoral ministry in a Catholic University and the other activities within the local Church, under the guidance or with the approval of the diocesan Bishop, will contribute to their mutual growth.[35]

42 Various associations or movements of spiritual and apostolic life, especially those developed specifically for students, can be of great assistance in developing the pastoral aspects of university life.

3. *Cultural Dialogue*

43 By its very nature, a University develops culture through its research, helps to transmit the local culture to each succeeding generation through its teaching, and assists cultural activities through its educational services. It is open to all human experience and is ready to dialogue with and learn from any culture. A Catholic University shares in this, offering the rich experience of the Church's own culture. In addition, a Catholic University, aware that human culture is open to Revelation and transcendence, is also a primary and privileged place for a *fruitful dialogue between the Gospel and culture.*

44 Through this dialogue a Catholic University assists the Church, enabling it to come to a better knowledge of diverse cultures, discern their positive and negative aspects, to receive their authentically human contributions, and to develop means by which it can make the faith better understood by the men and women of a particular culture.[36] While it is true that the Gospel cannot be identified with any particular culture and transcends all cultures, it is also true that "the Kingdom which the Gospel proclaims is lived by men and women who are pro-

---

35. The Code of Canon Law indicates the general responsibility of the Bishop toward university students: "The diocesan bishop is to have serious pastoral concern for students by erecting a parish for them or by assigning priests for this purpose on a stable basis; he is also to provide for Catholic university centers at universities, even non-Catholic ones, to give assistance, especially spiritual to young people." (*CIC*, can. 813).

36. "Living in various circumstances during the course of time, the Church, too, has used in her preaching the discoveries of different cultures to spread and explain the message of Christ to all nations, to probe it and more deeply understand it, and to give it better expression in liturgical celebrations and in the life of the diversified community of the faithful." (Vatican Council II, Pastoral Constitution on the Church in the Modern World *Gaudium et Spes,* n. 58: *AAS* 58 [1966], p. 1079).

foundly linked to a culture, and the building up of the Kingdom cannot avoid borrowing the elements of human culture or cultures."[37] A faith that places itself on the margin of what is human, of what is therefore culture, would be a faith unfaithful to the fullness of what the Word of God manifests and reveals, a decapitated faith, worse still, a faith in the process of self-annihilation.[38]

45 A Catholic University must become *more attentive to the cultures of the world of today,* and to the *various cultural traditions existing within the Church* in a way that will promote a continuous and profitable dialogue between the Gospel and modern society. Among the criteria that characterize the values of a culture are above all, the *meaning of the human person,* his or her liberty, dignity, *sense of responsibility,* and openness to the transcendent. To a respect for persons is joined *the preeminent value of the family,* the primary unit of every human culture.

Catholic Universities will seek to discern and evaluate both the aspirations and the contradictions of modern culture, in order to make it more suited to the total development of individuals and peoples. In particular, it is recommended that by means of appropriate studies, the impact of modern technology and especially of the mass media on persons, the family, and the institutions and whole of modern culture be studied deeply. Traditional cultures are to be defended in their identity, helping them to receive modern values without sacrificing their own heritage, which is a wealth for the whole of the human family. Universities, situated within the ambience of these cultures, will seek to harmonize local cultures with the positive contributions of modern cultures.

46 An area that particularly interests a Catholic University is the *dialogue between Christian thought and the modern sciences.* This task requires persons particularly well versed in the individual disciplines and who are at the same time adequately prepared theologically, and who are capable of confronting epistemological questions at the level of the relationship between faith and reason. Such dialogue concerns the natural sciences as much as the human sciences which posit new and complex philosophical and ethical problems. The Christian researcher should demonstrate the way in which human intelligence is enriched by the higher truth that comes from the Gospel: "The intelligence is never diminished, rather, it is stimulated and reinforced by that interior fount of

37. Paul VI, Apostolic Exhortation *Evangelii Nuntiandi,* n. 20: *AAS* 68 (1976), p. 18. Cf. Vatican Council II, Pastoral Constitution on the Church in the Modern World *Gaudium et Spes,* n. 58: *AAS* 58 (1966), p. 1079.

38. John Paul II, Address to Intellectuals, to Students and to University Personnel at Medellín, Colombia, 5 July 1986, n. 3: *AAS* 79 (1987), p. 99. Cf. also Vatican Council II, Pastoral Constitution on the Church in the Modern World *Gaudium et Spes,* n. 58: *AAS* 58 (1966), p. 1079.

deep understanding that is the Word of God, and by the hierarchy of values that results from it. . . . In its unique manner, the Catholic University helps to manifest the superiority of the spirit, that can never, without the risk of losing its very self, be placed at the service of something other than the search for truth."[39]

47 Besides cultural dialogue, a Catholic University, in accordance with its specific ends, and keeping in mind the various religious-cultural contexts, following the directives promulgated by competent ecclesiastical authority, can offer a contribution to ecumenical dialogue. It does so to further the search for unity among all Christians. In inter-religious dialogue it will assist in discerning the spiritual values that are present in the different religions.

4. *Evangelization*

48 The primary mission of the Church is to preach the Gospel in such a way that a relationship between faith and life is established in each individual and in the socio-cultural context in which individuals live and act and communicate with one another. Evangelization means "bringing the Good News into all the strata of humanity, and through its influence transforming humanity from within and making it new. . . . It is a question not only of preaching the Gospel in ever wider geographic areas or to ever greater numbers of people, but also of affecting and, as it were, upsetting, through the power of the Gospel, humanity's criteria of judgment, determining values, points of interest, lines of thought, sources of inspiration and models of life, which are in contrast with the Word of God and the plan of salvation."[40]

49 By its very nature, each Catholic University makes an important contribution to the Church's work of evangelization. It is a living *institutional* witness to Christ and his message, so vitally important in cultures marked by secularism, or where Christ and his message are still virtually unknown. Moreover, all the basic academic activities of a Catholic University are connected with and in harmony with the evangelizing mission of the Church: research carried out in the light of the Christian message which puts new human discoveries at the service of individuals and society; education offered in a faith-context that forms men and women capable of rational and critical judgment and conscious of the transcendent dignity of the human person; professional training that incorporates ethical values and a sense of service to individuals and to society; the dialogue with culture that makes the faith better understood, and the theological

---

39. Paul VI, to the Delegates of The International Federation of Catholic Universities, 27 November 1972: *AAS* 64 (1972), p. 770.

40. Paul VI, Apostolic Exhortation *Evangelii Nuntiandi*, nn. 18ff.: *AAS* 68 (1976), pp. 17–18.

research that translates the faith into contemporary language. "Precisely because it is more and more conscious of its salvific mission in this world, the Church wants to have these centers closely connected with it; it wants to have them present and operative in spreading the authentic message of Christ."[41]

PART II: GENERAL NORMS

Article 1. *The Nature of These General Norms*

§ 1. These General Norms are based on, and are a further development of, the Code of Canon Law[42] and the complementary Church legislation, without prejudice to the right of the Holy See to intervene should this become necessary. They are valid for all Catholic Universities and other Catholic Institutes of Higher Studies throughout the world.

§ 2. The General Norms are to be applied concretely at the local and regional levels by Episcopal Conferences and other Assemblies of Catholic Hierarchy[43] in conformity with the Code of Canon Law and complementary Church legislation, taking into account the Statutes of each University or Institute and, as far as possible and appropriate, civil law. After review by the Holy See,[44] these local or regional "Ordinances" will be valid for all Catholic Universities and other Catholic Institutes of Higher Studies in the region, except for Ecclesiastical Universities and Faculties. These latter Institutions, including Ecclesiastical Faculties which are part of a Catholic University, are governed by the norms of the Apostolic Constitution Sapientia Christiana.[45]

§ 3. A University established or approved by the Holy See, by an Episcopal Conference or another Assembly of Catholic Hierarchy, or by a diocesan Bishop is

---

41. Paul VI, Address to Presidents and Rectors of the Universities of the Society of Jesus, 6 August 1975, n. 2: *AAS* 67 (1975), p. 533. Speaking to the participants of the International Congress on Catholic Universities, 25 April 1989, I added (n. 5): "Within a Catholic University the evangelical mission of the Church and the mission of research and teaching become *interrelated* and *coordinated:*" Cf. *AAS* 81 (1989), p. 1220.

42. Cf. in particular the Chapter of the Code: "Catholic Universities and other Institutes of Higher Studies" *(CIC*, can. 807–814).

43. Episcopal Conferences were established in the Latin Rite. Other Rites have other Assemblies of Catholic Hierarchy.

44. Cf. *CIC*, can. 455, § 2.

45. Cf. *Sapientia Christiana: AAS* 71 (1979), pp. 469–521. Ecclesiastical Universities and Faculties are those that have the right to confer academic degrees by the authority of the Holy See.

to incorporate these General Norms and their local and regional applications into its governing documents, and conform its existing Statutes both to the General Norms and to their applications, and submit them for approval to the competent ecclesiastical Authority. It is contemplated that other Catholic Universities, that is, those not established or approved in any of the above ways, with the agreement of the local ecclesiastical Authority, will make their own the General Norms and their local and regional applications, internalizing them into their governing documents, and, as far as possible, will conform their existing Statutes both to these General Norms and to their applications.

Article 2. *The Nature of a Catholic University*

§ 1. A Catholic University, like every university, is a community of scholars representing various branches of human knowledge. It is dedicated to research, to teaching, and to various kinds of service in accordance with its cultural mission.

§ 2. A Catholic University, as Catholic, informs and carries out its research, teaching, and all other activities with Catholic ideals, principles and attitudes. It is linked with the Church either by a formal, constitutive and statutory bond or by reason of an institutional commitment made by those responsible for it.

§ 3. Every Catholic University is to make known its Catholic identity, either in a mission statement or in some other appropriate public document, unless authorized otherwise by the competent ecclesiastical Authority. The University, particularly through its structure and its regulations, is to provide means which will guarantee the expression and the preservation of this identity in a manner consistent with §2.

§ 4. Catholic teaching and discipline are to influence all university activities, while the freedom of conscience of each person is to be fully respected.[46] Any official action or commitment of the University is to be in accord with its Catholic identity.

§ 5. A Catholic University possesses the autonomy necessary to develop its distinctive identity and pursue its proper mission. Freedom in research and teaching is recognized and respected according to the principles and methods of each individual discipline, so long as the rights of the individual and of the

---

46. Cf. Vatican Council II, Declaration on Religious Liberty *Dignitatis Humanae*, n. 2: *AAS* 58 (1966), pp. 930–931.

community are preserved within the confines of the truth and the common good.[47]

Article 3. *The Establishment of a Catholic University*

§ 1. A Catholic University may be established or approved by the Holy See, by an Episcopal Conference or another Assembly of Catholic Hierarchy, or by a diocesan Bishop.

§ 2. With the consent of the diocesan Bishop, a Catholic University may also be established by a Religious Institute or other public juridical person.

§ 3. A Catholic University may also be established by other ecclesiastical or lay persons; such a University may refer to itself as a Catholic University only with the consent of the competent ecclesiastical Authority, in accordance with the conditions upon which both parties shall agree.[48]

§ 4. In the cases of §§ 1 and 2, the Statutes must be approved by the competent ecclesiastical Authority.

Article 4. *The University Community*

§1. The responsibility for maintaining and strengthening the Catholic identity of the University rests primarily with the University itself. While this responsibility is entrusted principally to university authorities (including, when the positions exist, the Chancellor and/or a Board of Trustees or equivalent body), it is shared in varying degrees by all members of the university community, and therefore calls for the recruitment of adequate university personnel, especially teachers and administrators, who are both willing and able to promote that identity. The identity of a Catholic University is essentially linked to the quality of its teachers and to respect for Catholic doctrine. It is the responsibility of the competent Authority to watch over these two fundamental needs in accordance with what is indicated in Canon Law.[49]

---

47. Cf. Vatican Council II, Pastoral Constitution on the Church in the Modern World *Gaudium et Spes,* nn. 57 and 59: *AAS* 58 (1966), pp. 1077–1080; *Gravissimum Educationis,* n. 10: *AAS* 58 (1966), p. 737.

48. Both the establishment of such a university and the conditions by which it may refer to itself as a Catholic University are to be in accordance with the prescriptions issued by the Holy See, Episcopal Conference or other Assembly of Catholic Hierarchy.

49. Canon 810 of CIC, specifies the responsibility of the competent Authorities in this area: § 1 "It is the responsibility of the authority who is competent in accord with the statutes to provide for the appointment of teachers to Catholic universities who, besides their scientific and pedagogical

§ 2. All teachers and all administrators, at the time of their appointment, are to be informed about the Catholic identity of the Institution and its implications, and about their responsibility to promote, or at least to respect, that identity.

§ 3. In ways appropriate to the different academic disciplines, all Catholic teachers are to be faithful to, and all other teachers are to respect, Catholic doctrine and morals in their research and teaching. In particular, Catholic theologians, aware that they fulfill a mandate received from the Church, are to be faithful to the Magisterium of the Church as the authentic interpreter of Sacred Scripture and Sacred Tradition.[50]

§ 4. Those university teachers and administrators who belong to other Churches, ecclesial communities, or religions, as well as those who profess no religious belief, and also all students, are to recognize and respect the distinctive Catholic identity of the University. In order not to endanger the Catholic identity of the University or Institute of Higher Studies, the number of non-Catholic teachers should not be allowed to constitute a majority within the Institution, which is and must remain Catholic.

§ 5. The education of students is to combine academic and professional development with formation in moral and religious principles and the social teachings of the Church; the program of studies for each of the various professions is to include an appropriate ethical formation in that profession. Courses in Catholic doctrine are to be made available to all students.[51]

Article 5. *The Catholic University Within the Church*

§ 1. Every Catholic University is to maintain communion with the universal Church and the Holy See; it is to be in close communion with the local Church and in particular with the diocesan Bishops of the region or nation in which it is located. In ways consistent with its nature as a University, a Catholic University will contribute to the Church's work of evangelization.

suitability, are also outstanding in their integrity of doctrine and probity of life; when those requisite qualities are lacking they are to be removed from their positions in accord with the procedure set forth in the statutes. § 2 The conference of bishops and the diocesan bishops concerned have the duty and right of being vigilant that in these universities the principles of Catholic doctrine are faithfully observed." Cf. also Article 5, 2 ahead in these "Norms."

50. Vatican Council II, Dogmatic Constitution on the Church *Lumen Gentium,* n. 25: *AAS* 57 (1965), p. 29; *Dei Verbum,* nn. 8–10: *AAS* 58 (1966), pp. 820–822; Cf. *CIC,* can. 812: "It is necessary that those who teach theological disciplines in any institute of higher studies have a mandate from the competent ecclesiastical authority."

51. Cf. *CIC,* can. 811 § 2.

§2. Each Bishop has a responsibility to promote the welfare of the Catholic Universities in his diocese and has the right and duty to watch over the preservation and strengthening of their Catholic character. If problems should arise concerning this Catholic character, the local Bishop is to take the initiatives necessary to resolve the matter, working with the competent university authorities in accordance with established procedures[52] and, if necessary, with the help of the Holy See.

§3. Periodically, each Catholic University, to which Article 3, 1 and 2 refers, is to communicate relevant information about the University and its activities to the competent ecclesiastical Authority. Other Catholic Universities are to communicate this information to the Bishop of the diocese in which the principal seat of the Institution is located.

Article 6. *Pastoral Ministry*

§1. A Catholic University is to promote the pastoral care of all members of the university community, and to be especially attentive to the spiritual development of those who are Catholics. Priority is to be given to those means which will facilitate the integration of human and professional education with religious values in the light of Catholic doctrine, in order to unite intellectual learning with the religious dimension of life.

§2. A sufficient number of qualified people-priests, religious, and lay persons-are to be appointed to provide pastoral ministry for the university community, carried on in harmony and cooperation with the pastoral activities of the local Church under the guidance or with the approval of the diocesan Bishop. All members of the university community are to be invited to assist the work of pastoral ministry, and to collaborate in its activities.

Article 7. *Cooperation*

§1. In order better to confront the complex problems facing modern society, and in order to strengthen the Catholic identity of the Institutions, regional, national and international cooperation is to be promoted in research, teaching, and other university activities among all Catholic Universities, including Ecclesiastical Universities and Faculties.[53] Such cooperation is also to be promoted

---

52. For Universities to which Article 3 §§ 1 and 2 refer, these procedures are to be established in the university statutes approved by the competent ecclesiastical Authority; for other Catholic Universities, they are to be determined by Episcopal Conferences or other Assemblies of Catholic Hierarchy.

53. Cf. *CIC*, can. 820. Cf. also *Sapientia Christiana*, Norms of Application, Article 49: *AAS* 71 (1979), p. 512.

between Catholic Universities and other Universities, and with other research and educational Institutions, both private and governmental.

§2. Catholic Universities will, when possible and in accord with Catholic principles and doctrine, cooperate with government programs and the programs of other national and international Organizations on behalf of justice, development and progress.

TRANSITIONAL NORMS

Art. 8. The present Constitution will come into effect on the first day of the academic year 1991.

Art. 9. The application of the Constitution is committed to the Congregation for Catholic Education, which has the duty to promulgate the necessary directives that will serve towards that end.

Art. 10. It will be the competence of the Congregation for Catholic Education, when with the passage of time circumstances require it, to propose changes to be made in the present Constitution in order that it may be adapted continuously to the needs of Catholic Universities.

Art. 11. Any particular laws or customs presently in effect that are contrary to this Constitution are abolished. Also, any privileges granted up to this day by the Holy See whether to physical or moral persons that are contrary to this present Constitution are abolished.

Conclusion

The mission that the Church, with great hope, entrusts to Catholic Universities holds a cultural and religious meaning of vital importance because it concerns the very future of humanity. The renewal requested of Catholic Universities will make them better able to respond to the task of bringing the message of Christ to man, to society, to the various cultures: "Every human reality, both individual and social has been liberated by Christ: persons, as well as the activities of men and women, of which culture is the highest and incarnate expression. The salvific action of the Church on cultures is achieved, first of all, by means of persons, families and educators. . . . Jesus Christ, our Savior, offers his light and his hope to all those who promote the sciences, the arts, letters and the numerous fields developed by modern culture. Therefore, all the sons and daughters of the Church should become aware of their mission and discover how the strength of the Gospel can penetrate and regenerate the mentalities and dominant values that inspire individual cultures, as well as the opinions and mental attitudes that are derived from it."[54]

It is with fervent hope that I address this Document to all the men and women engaged in various ways in the significant mission of Catholic higher education.

Beloved Brothers and Sisters, my encouragement and my trust go with you in your weighty daily task that becomes ever more important, more urgent and necessary on behalf of Evangelization for the future of culture and of all cultures. The Church and the world have great need of your witness and of your capable, free, and responsible contribution.

Given in Rome, at Saint Peter's, on 15 August, the Solemnity of the Assumption of the Blessed Virgin Mary into Heaven, in the year 1990, the twelfth of the Pontificate.

---

54. John Paul II, to the Pontifical Council for Culture, 13 January 1989, n. 2: *AAS* 81 (1989), pp. 857–858.

THE CATHOLIC SCHOOL ON THE THRESHOLD OF THE THIRD MILLENNIUM

CONGREGATION FOR CATHOLIC EDUCATION
(for Seminaries and Educational Institutions)

Introduction

1 On the threshold of the third millennium education faces new challenges which are the result of a new socio-political and cultural context. First and foremost, we have a crisis of values which, in highly developed societies in particular, assumes the form, often exalted by the media, of subjectivism, moral relativism and nihilism. The extreme pluralism pervading contemporary society leads to behavior patterns which are at times so opposed to one another as to undermine any idea of community identity. Rapid structural changes, profound technical innovations and the globalization of the economy affect human life more and more throughout the world. Rather than prospects of development for all, we witness the widening of the gap between rich and poor, as well as massive migration from underdeveloped to highly-developed countries. The phenomena of multiculturalism and an increasingly multi-ethnic and multi-religious society is at the same time an enrichment and a source of further problems. To this we must add, in countries of long-standing evangelization, a growing marginalization of the Christian faith as a reference point and a source of light for an effective and convincing interpretation of existence.

2 In the specifically educational field, the scope of educational functions has broadened, becoming more complex, more specialized. The sciences of education, which concentrated in the past on the study of the child and teacher-training, have been widened to include the various stages of life, and the different spheres and situations beyond the school. New requirements have given force to the demand for new contents, new capabilities and new educational models besides those followed traditionally. Thus education and schooling become particularly difficult today.

3 Such an outlook calls for courageous renewal on the part of the Catholic school. The precious heritage of the experience gained over the centuries reveals its vitality precisely in the capacity for prudent innovation. And so, now as in the past, the Catholic school must be able to speak for itself effectively and convincingly. It is not merely a question of adaptation, but of missionary thrust, the fundamental duty to evangelize, to go towards men and women wherever they are, so that they may receive the gift of salvation.

4 Accordingly, the Congregation for Catholic Education, during this time of immediate preparation for the great jubilee of the year 2000, and as it celebrates the thirtieth anniversary of the creation of the Schools Office[1] and the twentieth anniversary of *The Catholic School*, published on 19th March 1977, proposes to "focus attention on the nature and distinctive characteristics of a school which would present itself as *Catholic*."[2] It therefore addresses this circular letter to all those who are engaged in Catholic schooling, in order to convey to them a word of encouragement and hope. In particular, by means of the present letter, the Congregation shares their joy for the positive fruits yielded by the Catholic school and their anxiety about the difficulties which it encounters. Furthermore, the teachings of the Second Vatican Council, innumerable interventions of the Holy Father, ordinary and extraordinary Assemblies of the Synod of Bishops, Episcopal Conferences and the pastoral solicitude of diocesan Ordinaries, as well as international Catholic organizations involved in education and schooling, all support our conviction that it is opportune to devote careful attention to certain fundamental characteristics of the Catholic school, which are of great importance if its educational activity is to be effectual in the Church and in society. Such are: *the Catholic school as a place of integral education of the human person through a clear educational project of which Christ is the foundation;*[3] *its ecclesial and cultural identity; its mission of education as a work of love; its service to society; the traits which should characterize the educating community.*

Joys and Difficulties

5 We retrace with satisfaction the positive course of the Catholic school over the past decades. First and foremost, we must recognize the contribution it makes to the evangelizing mission of the Church throughout the world, including those areas in which no other form of pastoral work is possible. Moreover, in spite of numerous obstacles, the Catholic school has continued to share responsibility for the social and cultural development of the different communities and peoples to which it belongs, participating in their joys and hopes, their sufferings and difficulties, their efforts to achieve genuine human and communitarian progress. In this respect, mention must be made of the invaluable services of the Catholic school to the spiritual and material development of

---

1. The Sacred Congregation for Catholic Education was the new name given to the Sacred Congregation for Seminaries and Universities by the Apostolic Constitution *Regimini Ecclesiae Universae*, which was published on 15 August 1967 and in force as from 1 March 1968 (*AAS*, LIX [1967] pp. 885–928). The Congregation now comprised a third section, the Schools Office, intended "to develop further" the fundamental principles of education, especially in schools (cf. II Vatican Council, Declaration on Christian Education *Gravissimum Educationis*, Preface).
2. S. Congregation for Catholic Education, *The Catholic School*, n. 2.
3. Cf. S. Congregation for Catholic Education, *The Catholic School*, n. 34.

less fortunate peoples. It is our duty to express appreciation for the Catholic school's contribution to innovation in the fields of pedagogy and didactics, and the strenuous commitment of so many men and women, especially of all those religious and laity who see their teaching as a mission and true apostolate.[4] Finally, we cannot forget the part played by Catholic schools in organic pastoral work and in pastoral care for the family in particular, emphasizing in this respect their discreet insertion in the educational dynamics between parents and their children and, very especially the unpretentious yet caring and sensitive help offered in those cases, more and more numerous above all in wealthy nations, of families which are "fragile" or have broken up.

6 The school is undoubtedly a sensitive meeting-point for the problems which besiege this restless end of the millennium. The Catholic school is thus confronted with children and young people who experience the difficulties of the present time. Pupils who shun effort, are incapable of self-sacrifice and perseverance and who lack authentic models to guide them, often even in their own families. In an increasing number of instances they are not only indifferent and non-practicing, but also totally lacking in religious or moral formation. To this we must add —on the part of numerous pupils and families —a profound apathy where ethical and religious formation is concerned, to the extent that what is in fact required of the Catholic school is a certificate of studies or, at the most, quality instruction and training for employment. The atmosphere we have described produces a certain degree of pedagogical tiredness, which intensifies the ever increasing difficulty of conciliating the role of the teacher with that of the educator in today's context.

7 Among existing difficulties, there are also situations in the political, social and cultural sphere which make it harder or even impossible to attend a Catholic school. The drama of large-scale poverty and hunger in many parts of the world, internal conflicts and civil wars, urban deterioration, the spread of crime in large cities, impede the implementation of projects for formation and education. In other parts of the world, governments themselves put obstacles in the way, when they do not actually prevent the Catholic school from operating, in spite of the progress which has been made as far as attitude, democratic practice and sensitivity to human rights are concerned. Finance is a source of further difficulties, which are felt more acutely in those states in which no government aid is provided for non-state schools. This places an almost unbearable financial burden on families choosing not to send their children to state schools and constitutes a serious threat to the survival of the schools them-

---

4. Cf. II Vatican Council, Declaration on Christian Education *Gravissimum Educationis*, n. 8.

selves. Moreover, such financial strain not only affects the recruiting and stability of teachers, but can also result in the exclusion from Catholic schools of those who cannot afford to pay, leading to a selection according to means which deprives the Catholic school of one of its distinguishing features, which is to be a school for all.

Looking Ahead

8 This overview of the joys and difficulties of the Catholic school, although not pretending to exhaust its entire breadth and depth, does prompt us to reflect on the contribution it can make to the formation of the younger generation on the threshold of the third millennium, recognizing, as John Paul II has written, that "the future of the world and of the Church belongs to the *younger generation*, to those who, born in this century, will reach maturity in the next, the first century of the new millennium."[5] Thus the Catholic school should be able to offer young people the means to acquire the knowledge they need in order to find a place in a society which is strongly characterized by technical and scientific skill. But at the same time, it should be able, above all, to impart a solid Christian formation. And for the Catholic school to be a means of education in the modern world, we are convinced that certain fundamental characteristics need to be strengthened.

The Human Person and His or Her Education

9 The Catholic school sets out to be a school for the human person and of human persons. "The person of each individual human being, in his or her material and spiritual needs, is at the heart of Christ's teaching: this is why the promotion of the human person is the goal of the Catholic school."[6] This affirmation, stressing man's vital relationship with Christ, reminds us that it is in His person that the fullness of the truth concerning man is to be found. For this reason the Catholic school, in committing itself to the development of the whole man, does so in obedience to the solicitude of the Church, in the awareness that all human values find their fulfillment and unity in Christ.[7] This awareness expresses the centrality of the human person in the educational project of the Catholic school, strengthens its educational endeavor and renders it fit to form strong personalities.

5. John Paul II, Apostolic Letter *Tertio Millennio Adveniente*, n. 58.
6. Cf. John Paul II, *Address to the National Meeting of the Catholic School in Italy*, in *L'Osservatore Romano*, 24 November 1991, p. 4.
7. Cf. S. Congregation for Catholic Education, *The Catholic School*, n. 35.

10 The social and cultural context of our time is in danger of obscuring "the educational value of the Catholic school, in which its fundamental reason for existing and the basis of its genuine apostolate is to be found."[8] Indeed, although it is true to say that in recent years there has been an increased interest and a greater sensitivity on the part of public opinion, international organizations and governments with regard to schooling and education, there has also been a noticeable tendency to reduce education to its purely technical and practical aspects. Pedagogy and the sciences of education themselves have appeared to devote greater attention to the study of phenomenology and didactics than to the essence of education as such, centered on deeply meaningful values and vision. The fragmentation of education, the generic character of the values frequently invoked and which obtain ample and easy consensus at the price of a dangerous obscuring of their content, tend to make the school step back into a supposed neutrality, which enervates its educating potential and reflects negatively on the formation of the pupils. There is a tendency to forget that education always presupposes and involves a definite concept of man and life. To claim neutrality for schools signifies in practice, more times than not, banning all reference to religion from the cultural and educational field, whereas a correct pedagogical approach ought to be open to the more decisive sphere of ultimate objectives, attending not only to "how," but also to "why," overcoming any misunderstanding as regards the claim to neutrality in education, restoring to the educational process the unity which saves it from dispersion amid the meandering of knowledge and acquired facts, and focuses on the human person in his or her integral, transcendent, historical identity. With its educational project inspired by the Gospel, the Catholic school is called to take up this challenge and respond to it in the conviction that "it is only in the mystery of the Word made flesh that the mystery of man truly becomes clear."[9]

The Catholic School at the Heart of the Church

11 The complexity of the modern world makes it all the more necessary to increase awareness of the ecclesial identity of the Catholic school. It is from its Catholic identity that the school derives its original characteristics and its "structure" as a genuine instrument of the Church, a place of real and specific pastoral ministry. The Catholic school participates in the evangelizing mission of the Church and is the privileged environment in which Christian education is carried out. In this way "Catholic schools are at once places of evangelization, of complete formation, of inculturation, of apprenticeship in a lively dialogue

8. S. Congregation for Catholic Education, *The Catholic School*, n. 3.

9. II Vatican Council, Pastoral Constitution on the Church in the Modern World *Gaudium et Spes*, n. 22.

between young people of different religions and social backgrounds."[10] The ecclesial nature of the Catholic school, therefore, is written in the very heart of its identity as a teaching institution. It is a true and proper ecclesial entity by reason of its educational activity, "in which faith, culture and life are brought into harmony."[11] Thus it must be strongly emphasized that this ecclesial dimension is not a mere adjunct, but is a proper and specific attribute, a distinctive characteristic which penetrates and informs every moment of its educational activity, a fundamental part of its very identity and the focus of its mission.[12] The fostering of this dimension should be the aim of all those who make up the educating community.

12 By reason of its identity, therefore, the Catholic school is a place of ecclesial experience, which is molded in the Christian community. However, it should not be forgotten that the school fulfills its vocation to be a genuine experience of Church only if it takes its stand within the organic pastoral work of the Christian community. In a very special way the Catholic school affords the opportunity to meet young people in an environment which favors their Christian formation. Unfortunately, there are instances in which the Catholic school is not perceived as an integral part of organic pastoral work, at times it is considered alien, or very nearly so, to the community. It is urgent, therefore, to sensitize parochial and diocesan communities to the necessity of their devoting special care to education and schools.

13 In the life of the Church, the Catholic school is recognized above all as an expression of those Religious Institutes which, according to their proper charism or specific apostolate, have dedicated themselves generously to education. The present time is not without its difficulties, not only on account of the alarming decrease in numbers, but also of a serious misunderstanding which induces some Religious to abandon the teaching apostolate. In other words, on the one hand the commitment to schooling is separated from pastoral activity, while on the other it is not easy to reconcile concrete activities with the specific demands of religious life. The fertile intuitions of saintly founders and foundresses demonstrate, more radically than any other argumentation, the groundless and precarious nature of such attitudes. We should also remember that the presence of consecrated religious within the educating community is indispensable, since "consecrated persons are able to be especially effective in educational activi-

---

10. John Paul II, Apostolic Exhortation *Ecclesia in Africa*, n. 102.

11. Congregation for Catholic Education, *Religious Dimension of Education in a Catholic School*, n. 34.

12. Cf. Congregation for Catholic Education, *Religious Dimension of Education in a Catholic School*, n. 33.

ties;"[13] they are an example of the unreserved and gratuitous "gift" of self to the service of others in the spirit of their religious consecration. The presence of men and women religious, side by side with priests and lay teachers, affords pupils "a vivid image of the Church and makes recognition of its riches easier."[14]

Cultural Identity of the Catholic School

14 From the nature of the Catholic school also stems one of the most significant elements of its educational project: the synthesis between culture and faith. Indeed, knowledge set in the context of faith becomes wisdom and life vision. The endeavor to interweave reason and faith, which has become the heart of individual subjects, makes for unity, articulation and coordination, bringing forth within what is learnt in school a Christian vision of the world, of life, of culture and of history. In the Catholic school's educational project there is no separation between time for learning and time for formation, between acquiring notions and growing in wisdom. The various school subjects do not present only knowledge to be attained, but also values to be acquired and truths to be discovered.[15] All of which demands an atmosphere characterized by the search for truth, in which competent, convinced and coherent educators, teachers of learning and of life, may be a reflection, albeit imperfect but still vivid, of the one Teacher. In this perspective, in the Christian educational project all subjects collaborate, each with its own specific content, to the formation of mature personalities.

"Care for Learning Means Loving" (Sap 6, 17)

15 In its ecclesial dimension another characteristic of the Catholic school has its root: it is a school for all, with special attention to those who are weakest. In the past, the establishment of the majority of Catholic educational institutions has responded to the needs of the socially and economically disadvantaged. It is no novelty to affirm that Catholic schools have their origin in a deep concern for the education of children and young people left to their own devices and deprived of any form of schooling. In many parts of the world even today material poverty prevents many youths and children from having access to formal education and adequate human and Christian formation. In other areas new forms of poverty challenge the Catholic school. As in the past, it can come up against situations of incomprehension, mistrust and lack of material resources. The girls from poor families that were taught by the Ursuline nuns in the 15th

---

13. John Paul II, Apostolic Exhortation *Vita Consecrata*, n. 96.
14. John Paul II, Apostolic Exhortation *Christifideles Laici*, n. 62.
15. Cf. S. Congregation for Catholic Education, *The Catholic School*, n. 39.

Century, the boys that Saint Joseph of Calasanz saw running and shouting through the streets of Rome, those that De la Salle came across in the villages of France, or those that were offered shelter by Don Bosco, can be found again among those who have lost all sense of meaning in life and lack any type of inspiring ideal, those to whom no values are proposed and who do not know the beauty of faith, who come from families which are broken and incapable of love, often living in situations of material and spiritual poverty, slaves to the new idols of a society, which, not infrequently, promises them only a future of unemployment and marginalization. To these new poor the Catholic school turns in a spirit of love. Spurred on by the aim of offering to all, and especially to the poor and marginalized, the opportunity of an education, of training for a job, of human and Christian formation, it can and must find in the context of the old and new forms of poverty that original synthesis of ardor and fervent dedication which is a manifestation of Christ's love for the poor, the humble, the masses seeking for truth.

The Catholic School at the Service of Society

16 The school cannot be considered separately from other educational institutions and administered as an entity apart, but must be related to the world of politics, economy, culture and society as a whole. For her part the Catholic school must be firmly resolved to take the new cultural situation in her stride and, by her refusal to accept unquestioningly educational projects which are merely partial, be an example and stimulus for other educational institutions, in the forefront of ecclesial community's concern for education. In this way the Catholic school's public role is clearly perceived. It has not come into being as a private initiative, but as an expression of the reality of the Church, having by its very nature a public character. It fulfills a service of public usefulness and, although clearly and decidedly configured in the perspective of the Catholic faith, is not reserved to Catholics only, but is open to all those who appreciate and share its qualified educational project. This dimension of openness becomes particularly evident in countries in which Christians are not in the majority or developing countries, where Catholic schools have always promoted civil progress and human development without discrimination of any kind.[16] Catholic schools, moreover, like state schools, fulfill a public role, for their presence guarantees cultural and educational pluralism and, above all, the freedom and right of families to see that their children receive the sort of education they wish for them.[17]

---

16. Cf. Vatican Council II, Declaration on Christian Education *Gravissimum Educationis*, n. 9.
17. Cf. Holy See, *Charter of Rights of the Family*, art. 5.

17 The Catholic school, therefore, undertakes a cordial and constructive dialogue with states and civil authorities. Such dialogue and collaboration must be based on mutual respect, on the reciprocal recognition of each other's role and on a common service to mankind. To achieve this end, the Catholic school willingly occupies its place within the school system of the different countries and in the legislation of the individual states, when the latter respect the fundamental rights of the human person, starting with respect for life and religious freedom. A correct relationship between state and school, not only a Catholic school, is based not so much on institutional relations as on the right of each person to receive a suitable education of their free choice. This right is acknowledged according to the principle of subsidiarity.[18] For "The public authority, therefore, whose duty it is to protect and defend the liberty of the citizens, is bound according to the principle of distributive justice to ensure that public subsidies are so allocated that parents are truly free to select schools for their children in accordance with their conscience."[19] In the framework not only of the formal proclamation, but also in the effective exercise of this fundamental human right, in some countries there exists the crucial problem of the juridical and financial recognition of non-state schools. We share John Paul II's earnest hope, expressed yet again recently, that in all democratic countries "concrete steps finally be taken to implement true equality for non-state schools and that it be at the same time respectful of their educational project."[20]

Climate of the Educating Community

18 Before concluding, we should like to dwell briefly on the climate and role of the educating community, which is constituted by the interaction and collaboration of its various components: students, parents, teachers, directors and non-teaching staff.[21] Attention is rightly given to the importance of the relations existing between all those who make up the educating community. During childhood and adolescence a student needs to experience personal relations with outstanding educators, and what is taught has greater influence on the student's formation when placed in a context of personal involvement, genuine reciprocity, coherence of attitudes, life-styles and day to day behavior. While respecting individual roles, the community dimension should be fostered, since

18. Cf. John Paul II, Apostolic Exhortation *Familiaris Consortio*, n. 40; cf. Congregation for the Doctrine of the Faith, Instruction *Libertatis Conscientia*, n. 94.

19. II Vatican Council, Declaration on Christian Education *Gravissimum Educationis*, n. 6.

20. John Paul II, *Letter to the Superior General of the Piarists*, in *L'Osservatore Romano*, 28 June 1997, p. 5.

21. Cf. S. Congregation for Catholic Education, *Lay Catholics in Schools: Witnesses to Faith*, n. 22.

it is one of the most enriching developments for the contemporary school.[22] It is also helpful to bear in mind, in harmony with the Second Vatican Council,[23] that this community dimension in the Catholic school is not a merely sociological category; it has a theological foundation as well. The educating community, taken as a whole, is thus called to further the objective of a school as a place of complete formation through interpersonal relations.

19 In the Catholic school, "prime responsibility for creating this unique Christian school climate rests with the teachers, as individuals and as a community."[24] Teaching has an extraordinary moral depth and is one of man's most excellent and creative activities, for the teacher does not write on inanimate material, but on the very spirits of human beings. The personal relations between the teacher and the students, therefore, assume an enormous importance and are not limited simply to giving and taking. Moreover, we must remember that teachers and educators fulfill a specific Christian vocation and share an equally specific participation in the mission of the Church, to the extent that "it depends chiefly on them whether the Catholic school achieves its purpose."[25]

20 Parents have a particularly important part to play in the educating community, since it is to them that primary and natural responsibility for their children's education belongs. Unfortunately in our day there is a widespread tendency to delegate this unique role. Therefore it is necessary to foster initiatives which encourage commitment, but which provide at the same time the right sort of concrete support which the family needs and which involve it in the Catholic school's educational project.[26] The constant aim of the school therefore, should be contact and dialogue with the pupils' families, which should also be encouraged through the promotion of parents' associations, in order to clarify with their indispensable collaboration that personalized approach which is needed for an educational project to be efficacious.

Conclusion

21 The Holy Father has pointed out in a meaningful expression how "man is the primary and fundamental way for the Church, the way traced out by Christ

22. Cf. *Ibid.*
23. Cf. Vatican Council II, Declaration on Christian Education *Gravissimum Educationis*, n. 8.
24. Congregation for Catholic Education, *Religious Dimension of Education in a Catholic school*, n. 26.
25. Cf. Vatican Council II, Declaration on Christian Education *Gravissimum Educationis*, n. 8.
26. Cf. John Paul II, Apostolic Exhortation *Familiaris Consortio*, n. 40.

himself."[27] This way cannot, then, be foreign to those who evangelize. Travelling along it, they will experience the challenge of education in all its urgency. Thus it follows that the work of the school is irreplaceable and the investment of human and material resources in the school becomes a prophetic choice. On the threshold of the third millennium we perceive the full strength of the mandate which the Church handed down to the Catholic school in that "Pentecost" which was the Second Vatican Council: "Since the Catholic school can be of such service in developing the mission of the People of God and in promoting dialogue between the Church and the community at large to the advantage of both, it is still of vital importance even in our times."[28]

Prot. N. 29096
Rome, 28th December 1997,
Solemnity of the Holy Family
Pio Card. Laghi, *Prefect*
José Saraiva Martins
Tit. Archbishop of Tuburnica
Secretary

27. Cf. John Paul II, Encyclical Letter *Redemptor Hominis*, n. 14.
28. Vatican Council II, Declaration on Christian Education *Gravissimum Educationis*, n. 8.

CONSECRATED PERSONS AND THEIR MISSION IN SCHOOLS REFLECTIONS AND GUIDELINES

CONGREGATION FOR CATHOLIC EDUCATION

Introduction

At the Beginning of the Third Millennium

1 The celebration of the two thousandth anniversary of the incarnation of the Word was for many believers a time of conversion and of opening to God's plan for the human person created in his image. The grace of the Jubilee incited in the People of God an urgency to proclaim the mystery of Jesus Christ "yesterday, today and forever" with the testimony of their lives and, in Him, the truth about the human person. Young people, moreover, expressed a surprising interest with regard to the explicit announcement of Jesus. Consecrated persons, for their part, grasped the strong call to live in a state of conversion for accomplishing their specific mission in the Church: to be witnesses of Christ, *epiphany of the love of God in the world,* recognizable signs of reconciled humanity.[1]

A Prophetic Task

2 The complex cultural situations of the beginning of the 21st century are a further appeal to a responsibility to live the present as *kairós,* a favorable time, so that the Gospel may effectively reach the men and women of today. Consecrated persons feel the importance of the prophetic task entrusted to them by the Church in these momentous but fascinating times,[2] *"recalling and serving the divine plan for humanity,* as it is announced in Scripture and as also emerges from the attentive reading of the signs of God's providential action in history."[3] This task requires the courage of testimony and the patience of dialogue; it is a duty before the cultural tendencies that threaten the dignity of human life, especially in the crucial moments of its beginning and its ending, the harmony of creation, and the existence of peoples and peace.

---

1. Cf. John Paul II, Apostolic exhortation *Vita Consecrata,* 25th March 1996, nn. 72–73, *AAS* 88 (1996), 447–449.
2. Cf. John Paul II, Encyclical letter *Redemptoris Missio,* 7th December 1990, n. 38, *AAS* 83 (1991), 286.
3. John Paul II, Apostolic exhortation *Vita Consecrata,* n. 73, *AAS* 88 (1996), 448.

The Reason for These Reflections

3 Within the context of the profound changes that assail the world of education and schools, the Congregation for Catholic Education wishes to share some reflections, offer some guidelines and incite some further investigations of the educational mission and the presence of consecrated persons in schools in general, not only Catholic schools. This document is mainly addressed to members of institutes of consecrated life and of societies of apostolic life, as well as to those who, involved in the educational mission of the Church, have assumed the evangelical counsels in other forms.

As a Continuation of Previous Ecclesial Guidelines

4 These considerations are within the lines of the Second Vatican Council, the Magisterium of the universal Church and the documents of the continental Synods regarding evangelization, the consecrated life and education, especially scholastic education. In recent years, this Congregation has offered guidelines on Catholic schools[4] and on lay people who bear witness to faith in schools.[5] As a continuation of the document on lay people, it now intends reflecting on the specific contribution of consecrated persons to the educational mission in schools in the light of the Apostolic Exhortation *Vita Consecrata* and of the more recent developments of pastoral care for culture.[6] This is a result of its conviction that: "a faith that does not become culture is a faith that has not been fully received, not entirely thought through, not loyally lived."[7]

The Cultural Mediation of the Faith Today

5 The necessity for a cultural mediation of the faith is an invitation for consecrated persons to consider the meaning of their presence in schools. The altered circumstances in which they operate, in environments that are often laicized and in reduced numbers in educational communities, make it necessary to clearly express their specific contribution in cooperation with the other vocations present in schools. A time emerges in which to process answers to the fundamental questions of the young generations and to present a clear cultural proposal that clarifies the type of person and society to which it is desired to

---

4. Cf. Sacred Congregation for Catholic Education, *The Catholic School*, 19th March 1977; cf. Congregation for Catholic Education, *The Catholic School on the Threshold of the Third Millennium*, 28th December 1997.

5. Cf. Sacred Congregation for Catholic Education, *Lay Catholics in Schools: Witnesses to Faith*, 15th October 1982.

6. Cf. Pontifical Council for Culture, *Toward a Pastoral Approach to Culture*, 23rd May 1999, *L'Osservatore Romano* (English), N. 23, 9 June 1999.

7. John Paul II, *Letter Instituting the Pontifical Council for Culture*, 20th May 1982, *AAS* 74 (1982), 685.

educate, and the reference to the anthropological vision inspired by the values of the gospel, in a respectful and constructive dialogue with the other concepts of life.

A Renewed Commitment in the Educational Sphere

6 The challenges of modern life give new motivations to the mission of consecrated persons, called to live the evangelic councils and bring the humanism of the beatitudes to the field of education and schools. This is not at all foreign to the mandate of the Church to announce salvation to all.[8] "At the same time, however, we are painfully aware of certain difficulties which induce your Communities to abandon the school sector. The dearth of religious vocations, estrangement from the teaching apostolate, the attraction of alternative forms of apostolate seemingly more gratifying."[9] Far from discouraging, these difficulties can be a source of purification and characterize a time *of grace and salvation* (cf. *2 Cor* 6:2). They invite discernment and an attitude of constant *renewal*. The Holy Spirit, moreover, guides us to rediscover the charism, the roots and the modalities for our presence in schools, concentrating on the essential: the importance of the testimony of Christ, the poor, humble and chaste one; the priority of the person and of relationships based on love; the search for truth; the synthesis between faith, life and culture and the valid proposal of a view of man that respects God's plan.

Evangelize by Educating

It thus becomes clear that consecrated persons in schools, in communion with the Bishops, carry out an ecclesial mission that is vitally important inasmuch as while they educate they are also evangelizing. This mission requires a commitment of holiness, generosity and skilled educational professionalism so that the truth about the person as revealed by Jesus may enlighten the growth of the young generations and of the entire community. This Dicastery feels therefore that it is opportune to call attention to the profile of consecrated persons and to reflect on some well-known aspects of their educational mission in schools today.

---

8. Cf. John Paul II, Apostolic exhortation *Vita Consecrata*, n. 96, *AAS* 88 (1996), 471.

9. Congregation for Catholic Education, *Circular Letter to the Reverend General Superiors and Presidents of Societies of Apostolic Life Responsible for Catholic Schools,* 15th October 1996, in *Enchiridion Vaticanum,* vol. 15, 837.

I. PROFILE OF CONSECRATED PERSONS

At the School of Christ the Teacher

Ecclesial Gift for Revealing the Word

7 "The consecrated life, deeply rooted in the example and teaching of Christ the Lord, is a gift of God the Father to his Church through the Holy Spirit. By the profession of the evangelical counsels *the characteristic features of Jesus*—the chaste, poor and obedient one—*are made constantly 'visible' in the midst of the world* and the eyes of the faithful are directed towards the mystery of the Kingdom of God already at work in history, even as it awaits its full realization in heaven."[10] The aim of the consecrated life is "conformity to the Lord Jesus in *his total self-giving*,"[11] so that every consecrated person is called to assume "his mind and his way of life,"[12] his way of thinking and of acting, of being and of loving.

Identity of Consecrated Life

8 *The direct reference to Christ* and the *intimate nature of a gift* for the Church and the world, [13] are elements that define the identity and scope of the consecrated life. In them the consecrated life finds itself, its point of departure, God and his love, and its point of arrival, the human community and its requirements. It is through these elements that every religious family traces its own physiognomy, from its spirituality to its apostolate, from its style of community life to its ascetic plan, to the sharing and participation in the richness of its own charisms.

At Christ's School to Have His Mind

9 The consecrated life can be compared in some ways to a *school*, that every consecrated person is called to attend for his whole life. In fact, having the mind of the Son means to attend his school daily, to learn from him to have a heart that is meek and humble, courageous and passionate. It means allowing oneself to be *educated* by Christ, the eternal Word of the Father and, to be drawn to him, the heart and center of the world, choosing his same *form* of life.

---

10. John Paul II, Apostolic exhortation *Vita Consecrata*, n. 1, *AAS* 88 (1996), 377.

11. *Ibid.*, n. 65, 441.

12. *Ibid.*, n. 18, 391.

13. Cf. Second Vatican Ecumenical Council, Dogmatic Constitution on the Church *Lumen Gentium*, nn. 43–44.

*Allowing Oneself to be Educated and Formed by Christ,
to be Similar to Him*

10 The life of a consecrated person is therefore an *educational-formative* rise
and fall that educates to the truth of life and forms it to the freedom of the gift
of oneself, according to the model of the Easter of the Lord. Every moment of
consecrated life forms part of this rise and fall, in its double educational and formative aspect. A consecrated person does in fact gradually learn to have the
mind of the Son in him and to reveal it in *a life that is increasingly similar to his,*
both at individual and community level, in initial and permanent formation.
Thus the vows are an expression of the lifestyle chosen by Jesus on this earth that
was essential, chaste and completely dedicated to the Father. Prayer becomes a
continuation on earth of the praise of the Son to the Father for the salvation of
all mankind. Community life is the demonstration that, in the name of the
Lord, stronger bonds than those that come from flesh and blood can be tied.
These are bonds that are able to overcome what can divide. The apostolate is the
impassioned announcement of he by whom we have been conquered.

Gift for Everyone

11 The school of the mind of the Son gradually opens the consecrated life to
the urgency for testimony, so that *the gift may reach everyone.* In fact, Christ
"did not count equality with God a thing to be grasped" (*Phil* 2:6), he kept
nothing for himself, but shared his wealth of being Son with all men. That is
why, even when the testimony contests some elements of the local culture, consecrated persons try to enter into a dialogue in order to share the wealth which
they bring. This means that the testimony must be distinct and unequivocal,
clear and comprehensible for everyone, in order to demonstrate that religious
consecration has much to say to every culture inasmuch as it helps to reveal the
truth about human beings.

Radical Response

Anthropological Value of the Consecrated Life

12 Among the challenges that the consecrated life faces today is that of trying
to demonstrate the *anthropological value* of consecration. It is a question of
demonstrating that a poor, chaste and obedient life enhances intimate human
dignity; that *everyone* is called, in a different way, according to his or her vocation, to be poor, obedient and chaste. The evangelical counsels do, in fact,
transfigure authentically human values and desires, but they also relativize the
human "by pointing to God as the absolute good."[14] The consecrated life,

---

14. John Paul II, Apostolic exhortation *Vita Consecrata*, n. 87, *AAS* 88 (1996), 463.

moreover, must be able to show that the evangelical message possesses considerable importance for living in today's world and is also comprehensible for those who live in a competitive society such as ours. Lastly, the consecrated life must try to testify that holiness is the highest humanizing proposal of man and of history; it is a project that everyone on earth can make his or her own.[15]

Charismatic Circularity

13 Consecrated persons communicate the richness of their specific vocation to the extent that they live their consecration commitments to the full. On the other hand, such a communication also arouses in the receiver a capacity for an enriching response through the participation of his personal gift and his specific vocation. This "confrontation-sharing" with the Church and with the world is of great importance for the vitality of the various religious charisms and for their interpretation in line with the modern context and their respective spiritual roots. It is the principle of *charismatic circularity*, as a result of which the charism *returns* in a sort of way to where it was born, but without simply repeating itself. In this way, the consecrated life itself is renewed, in the listening and interpretation of the signs of the times and in the creative and active fidelity of its origins.

Constructive Dialogue in the Past and in the Present

14 The validity of this principle is confirmed by history; the consecrated life has always woven a constructive dialogue with local culture, sometimes questioning and provoking it, at others defending and preserving it, but in any case allowing it to stimulate and interrogate, in a confrontation that was in some cases dialectic, but always fruitful. It is important that such a confrontation continues even in these times of renewal for the consecrated life and of cultural disorientation that risks frustrating the human heart's insuppressible need for truth.

In the Church Communion

The Church Mystery of Communion

15 The study of the ecclesial situation as a mystery of communion has led the Church, under the action of the Spirit, to increasingly understand itself as the pilgrim people of God and, at the same time as the body of Christ the members of which are in a mutual relationship with each other and with the head.

At a pastoral level, "to make the Church *the home and the school of commun-*

---

15. Cf. John Paul II, Apostolic letter *Novo Millennio Ineunte*, 6th January 2001, n. 30, *AAS* 93 (2001), 287.

ion"[16] is the great challenge that we must know how to face, at the beginning of the new millennium, in order to be faithful to God's plan and to the world's deep expectations. It is first and foremost necessary to promote a *spirituality of communion* capable of becoming the educational principle in the various environments in which the human person is formed. This *spirituality* is learned by making our hearts ponder on the mystery of the Trinity, whose light is reflected in the face of every person, and welcomed and appreciated as a gift.

Consecrated Persons in the Church-Communion

16 Demands for communion have offered consecrated persons the chance to rediscover the mutual relationship with the other vocations in the people of God. In the Church they are called, in a special way, to reveal that participation in the Trinitarian communion can change human relations creating a new kind of solidarity. By professing to live *for God and of God*, consecrated persons do, in fact, undertake to preach the power of the peacemaking action of grace that overcomes the disruptive dynamisms present in the human heart.

With the Dynamism of the Specific Charism

17 Whatever the specific charism that characterizes them, consecrated persons are called, through their vocations, to be *experts of communion*, to promote human and spiritual bonds that promote the mutual exchange of gifts between all the members of the people of God. The acknowledgement of the *many forms* of vocations in the Church gives a new meaning to the presence of consecrated persons in the field of scholastic education. For them a school is a place of mission, where the prophetic role conferred by baptism and lived according to the requirements of the radicalism typical of the evangelical counsels is fulfilled. The gift of special consecration that they have received will lead them to recognizing in schools and in the educational commitment the fruitful furrow in which the Kingdom of God can grow and bear fruit.

A Consecrated Person Educates...

18 This commitment responds perfectly to the nature and to the scope of the consecrated life itself and is carried out according to that double *educational and formative* model that accompanies the growth of the individual consecrated person. Through schools, men and women religious educate, help young people to grasp their own identity and to reveal those authentic needs and desires that inhabit everyone's heart, but which often remain unknown and underestimated: thirst for authenticity and honesty, for love and fidelity, for

---

16. *Ibid.*, n. 43, 296.

truth and consistency, for happiness and fullness of life. Desires which in the final analysis converge in the supreme human desire: *to see the face of God.*

...Forms

19 The second modality is that regarding formation. A school *forms* when it offers a precise proposal for fulfilling those desires, preventing them from being deformed, or only partially or weakly achieved. With the testimony of their lives consecrated persons, who are at the school of the Lord, propose that form of existence which is inspired by Christ, so that even a young person may live the freedom of being a child of God and may experiment the true joy and authentic fulfillment that spring from the project of the Father. Consecrated persons have a providential mission in schools, in the modern context, where the educational proposals seem to be increasingly poorer and man's aspirations seem to be increasingly unanswered!

In Schools, Educational Communities

20 There is no need for consecrated persons to reserve exclusive tasks for themselves in educational communities. The specificity of the consecrated life lies in its being a sign, a memory and prophecy of the values of the Gospel. Its characteristic is "to bring to bear on the world of education their radical witness to the values of the Kingdom,"[17] in cooperation with the laity called to express, in the sign of secularity, the realism of the Incarnation of God in our midst, "the intimate dependency of earthly situations on God in Christ."[18]

By Developing the Specificity of All the Vocations Present in the Educational Community

21 The different vocations operate for the growth of the body of Christ and of his mission in the world. The commitment to evangelical testimony according to the typical form of every vocation gives rise to a dynamism of mutual help to fully live membership of the mystery of Christ and of the Church in its many dimensions; a stimulus for each one to discover the evangelical richness of his or her own vocation in a gratitude-filled comparison with others.

By avoiding both confrontation and homologation, the reciprocity of vocations seems to be a particularly fertile prospect for enriching the ecclesial value of educational communities. In them the various vocations carry out a service for achieving a culture of communion. They are correlative, different and mutual paths that converge to bring to fulfillment the charism of charisms: love.

17. John Paul II, Apostolic exhortation *Vita Consecrata*, n. 96, *AAS* 88 (1996), 472.

18. Sacred Congregation for Catholic Education, *Lay Catholics in Schools: Witnesses to Faith*, n. 43.

Before the World

Accounting for Hope

22 The awareness that they are living in a time that is full of challenges and new possibilities urges consecrated persons, involved in the educational mission in schools, to make good use of the gift received by accounting for the hope that animates them. Fruit of the faith in the God of history, hope is based on the word and on the life of Jesus, who lived *in the world*, without being *of the world*. He asks the same attitude from those who follow him: to live and work in history, without however allowing oneself to be imprisoned by it. Hope demands insertion in the world, but also separation; it requires prophecy and sometimes involves following or withdrawing in order to educate the children of God to freedom in a context of influences that lead to new forms of slavery.

Discernment and Contemplative Gaze

23 This way of being in history requires a deep capacity for discernment. Born from daily listening to the Word of God, this facilitates the interpreting events and prepares for becoming, as if to say, a *critical conscience*. The deeper and more authentic this commitment, the more likely it will be to grasp the action of the Spirit in the life of people and in the events of history. Such a capacity finds its foundation in contemplation and in prayer, which teach us to see persons and things from God's viewpoint. This is the contrary of a superficial glance and of an activism that is incapable of reflecting on the important and the essential. When there is no contemplation and prayer—and consecrated persons are not exempt from this risk—passion for the announcement of the Gospel is also lacking as is the capacity to fight for the life and salvation of mankind.

In Schools for Educating to Silence and to Meeting God

24 By living their vocations with generosity and eagerness, consecrated persons bring to schools their experience of a relationship with God, based on prayer, the Eucharist, the sacrament of Reconciliation and the spirituality of communion that characterizes the life of religious communities. The evangelical position that results facilitates discernment and the formation of a critical sense, a fundamental and necessary aspect of the educational process. Whatever their specific task, the presence of consecrated persons in schools *infects* the contemplative glance by educating to a silence that leads to listening to God, to paying attention to others, to the situation that surrounds us, to creation. Furthermore, by aiming at the essential, consecrated persons provoke the need for authentic encounters, they renew the capacity to be amazed and to take care of the other, rediscovered like a brother.

For Living the Gospel to the Full

25 Because of their role, consecrated persons are "*a living memorial of Jesus' way of living and acting* as the Incarnate Word in relation to the Father and in relation to the brethren."[19] The first and fundamental contribution to the educational mission in schools by consecrated persons is the evangelical completeness of their lives. This way of shaping their lives, based on their generous response to God's call, becomes an invitation to all the members of the educational community to make their lives a response to God, according to their various states of life.

And Testifying a Chaste, Poor and Obedient Life

26 In this perspective, consecrated persons testify that the *chastity* of their hearts, bodies, lives is the full and strong expression of a total love for God that renders a person free, full of deep joy and ready for their mission. Thus consecrated persons contribute to guiding young men and women towards the full development of their capacity to love and a complete maturation of their personalities. This is a very important testimony in a culture that increasingly tends to trivialize human love and close itself to life. In a society where everything tends to be free, consecrated persons, through their freely chosen *poverty*, take on a simple and essential lifestyle, promoting a correct relationship with things and trusting in Divine Providence. Freedom from things makes them unreservedly ready for an educational service to the young that becomes a sign of the availability of God's love in a world where materialism and having seem to prevail over being. Finally, by living *obedience*, they remind everyone of the lordship of the only God and, against the temptation of dominion, they indicate a choice of faith that counters forms of individualism and self-sufficiency.

And Expressing Their Donation

27 Just as Jesus did for his disciples, so consecrated persons live their donation for the benefit of the receivers of their mission: students, in the first place, but also their parents and other educators. This encourages them to live prayer and their daily response to their following Christ to become an increasingly more suitable instrument for the work that God achieves through them.

The call to give themselves fully to schools, in deep and true freedom, means that consecrated men and women become a living testimony to the Lord who offers himself for everyone. This excess of gratuitousness and love makes their donation assessable over and above any type of usefulness.[20]

---

19. John Paul II, Apostolic exhortation *Vita Consecrata*, n. 22, *AAS* 88 (1996), 396.
20. Cf. *Ibid.*, n. 105, 481.

Looking at Mary

28 Consecrated persons find in Mary the model to inspire them in their relations with God and in living human history. Mary is the icon of prophetic hope because of her capacity to welcome and meditate at length on the Word in her heart, of interpreting history according to God's plan, of contemplating God present and working in time. In her eyes we see the wisdom that unites in harmony the ecstasy of her meeting with God and the greatest critical realism with regard to the world. The *Magnificat* is the prophecy *par excellence* of the Virgin. It always sounds new in the spirit of a consecrated person, as a constant praise to the Lord who bends down to the least and to the poor to give them life and mercy.

II. THE EDUCATIONAL MISSION OF
CONSECRATED PERSONS TODAY

29 A profile of consecrated persons clearly shows how their educational commitment in schools is suited to the nature of the consecrated life. In fact "thanks to their experience of the particular gifts of the Spirit, their careful listening to the Word, their constant practice of discernment and their rich heritage of pedagogical traditions amassed since the establishment of their Institutes ... consecrated persons give life to educational undertakings"[21] in the educational field. This requires the promotion within the consecrated life, on the one hand, of a "renewed cultural commitment which seeks to raise the level of personal preparation,"[22] and on the other of a constant conversion to follow Jesus, *the way, the truth and the life* (cf. Jn 14:6). It is an uncomfortable and tiring road that does however make it possible to take up the challenges of the present time and undertake the educational mission entrusted to the Church. While aware that it cannot be exhaustive, the Congregation for Catholic Education, intends pausing to consider just some elements of this mission. In particular it wishes to reflect on three specific contributions of the presence of consecrated persons to scholastic education: first of all the link of education to evangelization; then formation to "vertical" relationism, that is to the opening to God and lastly formation to "horizontal" relationism, that is to say to welcoming the other and to living together.

---

21. Congregation for Institutes of Consecrated Life and Societies of Apostolic Life, *Starting Afresh from Christ*, 19th May 2002, n. 39.

22. *Ibid.*, n. 39.

Educators Called to Evangelize
Go... preach the Gospel to the whole creation (Mk 16:15)

The Educational Experience of Consecrated Persons

30 "To fulfill the mandate she has received from her divine founder of proclaiming the mystery of salvation to all men and of restoring all things in Christ, Holy Mother the Church must be concerned with the whole of men's life, even the secular part of it insofar as it has a bearing on his heavenly calling."[23] Both in Catholic and in other types of schools, the educational commitment for consecrated persons is a vocation and choice of life, a path to holiness, a demand for justice and solidarity especially towards the poorest young people, threatened by various forms of deviancy and risk. By devoting themselves to the educational mission in schools, consecrated persons contribute to making the bread of culture reach those in most need of it. They see in culture a fundamental condition for people to completely fulfill themselves, achieve a level of life that conforms to their dignity and open themselves to encounter with Christ and the Gospel. Such a commitment is founded on a patrimony of pedagogical wisdom that makes it possible to confirm the value of education as a force that is able to help the maturing of a person, to draw him to the faith and to respond to the challenges of such a complex society as that which we have today.

Faced with Modern Challenges

The Globalization Process

31 The process of globalization characterizes the horizon of the new century. This is a complex phenomenon in its dynamics. It has positive effects, such as the possibility for peoples and cultures to meet, but also negative aspects, which risk producing further disparities, injustices and marginalization. The rapidity and complexity of the changes produced by globalization are also reflected in schools, which risk being exploited by the demands of the productive-economic structures, or by ideological prejudices and political calculations that obscure their educational function. This situation incites schools to strongly reassert their specific role of stimulus to reflection and critical aspiration. Because of their vocation consecrated persons undertake to promote the dignity of the human person, cooperating with schools so that they may become places of overall education, evangelization and learning of a vital dialogue between persons of different cultures, religions and social backgrounds.[24]

---

23. Second Vatican Ecumenical Council, Declaration on Christian Education *Gravissimum Educationis*, Intro.

24. Cf. Congregation for Catholic Education, *The Catholic School on the Threshold of the Third Millennium*, n. 11.

New Technologies

32 The growing development and diffusion of new technologies provide means and instruments that were unconceivable up to just a few years ago. However, they also give rise to questions concerning the future of human development. The vastness and depth of technological innovations influence the processes of access to knowledge, socialization, relations with nature and they foreshadow radical, not always positive, changes in huge sectors of the life of mankind. Consecrated persons cannot shirk wondering about the impact that these technologies will have on people, on means of communication, on the future of society.

Schools' Task

33 Within the context of these changes, schools have a meaningful role to play in the formation of the personalities of the new generations. The responsible use of the new technologies, especially of internet, demands an appropriate ethical formation.[25] Together with those working in schools, consecrated persons feel the need to understand the processes, languages, opportunities and challenges of the new technologies, but above all to become *communication educators,* so that these technologies may be used with discernment and wisdom.[26]

…For the Future of Man

34 Among the challenges of modern society that schools have to face are threats to life and to families, genetic manipulations, growing pollution, plundering of natural resources, the unsolved drama of the underdevelopment and poverty that crush entire populations of the south of the world. These are vital questions for everyone, which need to be faced with extensive and responsible vision, promoting a concept of life that respects the dignity of man and of creation. This means forming persons who are able to dominate and transform processes and instruments in a sense that is humanizing and filled with solidarity. This concern is shared by the whole international community, that is active in assuring that national educational programs contribute to developing training initiatives in this regard.[27]

---

25. Cf. Pontifical Council for Social Communications, *Ethics in Internet,* 22nd February 2002, n. 15.

26. Cf. Pontifical Council for Social Communications *The Church and Internet,* 22nd February 2002, n. 7.

27. Cf. UNESCO, Conférence générale, *Résolution adoptée sur le rapport de la Commission V. Séance plénière,* 12 novembre 1997.

An Explicit Anthropological View

Necessity for an Anthropological Foundation

35 The clarification of the anthropological foundation of the formative proposal of schools is an increasingly more unavoidable urgency in our complex
societies.

The human person is defined by his *rationality*, that is by his intelligent and free
nature, and by his *relational nature,* that is by his relationship with other persons. Living with others involves both the level of the being of the human
person—man/woman—and the ethical level of his acting. The foundation of
human *ethos* is in being the image and likeness of God, the Trinity of persons in
communion. The existence of a person appears therefore as a call to the duty to
exist for one another.

36 The commitment of a spirituality of communion for the 21st century is the
expression of a concept of the human person, created in the image of God. This
view enlightens the mystery of man and woman. The human person experiences his humanity to the extent that he is able to participate in the humanity
of the other, the bearer of a unique and unrepeatable plan. This is a plan that
can only be carried out within the context of the relation and dialogue with the
you in a dimension of reciprocity and opening to God. This kind of reciprocity
is at the basis of the gift of self and of *closeness* as an opening in solidarity with
every other person. This closeness has its truest root in the mystery of Christ,
the Word Incarnate, who wished to become close to man.

Within the Dimension of a Plenary Humanism

37 Faced with ideological pluralism and the proliferation of "knowledge," consecrated men and women therefore offer the contribution of a vision of a *plenary humanism*,[28] open to God, who loves everyone and invites them to
become increasingly more "conformed to the image of his Son" (cf. *Rm* 8:29).
This divine plan is the heart of Christian humanism: "Christ . . . fully reveals
man to man himself and makes his supreme calling clear."[29] To confirm the
greatness of the human creature does not mean to ignore his fragility: the
image of God reflected in persons is in fact deformed by sin. The illusion of
freeing oneself from all dependency, even from God, always ends up in new
forms of slavery, violence and suppression. This is confirmed by the experience

---

28. Cf. Paul VI, Encyclical letter *Populorum Progressio*, 26th March 1967, n. 42, *AAS* 59 (1967),
p. 278.

29. Second Vatican Ecumenical Council, Pastoral Constitution on the Church in the Modern
World *Gaudium et Spes*, n. 22.

of each human being, by the history of bloodshed in the name of ideologies and regimes that wished to construct a *new humanity* without God.[30] On the contrary, in order to be authentic, freedom must measure itself according to the truth of the person, the fullness of which is revealed in Christ, and lead to a liberation from all that denies his dignity preventing him from achieving his own good and that of others.

Witnesses of the Truth About the Human Person

38 Consecrated persons undertake to be witnesses in schools to the truth about persons and to the transforming power of the Holy Spirit. With their lives they confirm that faith enlightens the whole field of education by raising and strengthening human values. Catholic schools especially have a priority: that of "bringing forth within what is learnt in school a Christian vision of the world, of life, of culture and of history."[31]

With Cultural Mediation

39 Hence the importance of reasserting, in a pedagogical context that tends to put it in the background, the humanistic and spiritual dimension of knowledge and of the various school subjects. Through study and research a person contributes to perfecting himself and his humanity. Study becomes the path for a personal encounter with the truth, a "place" of encounter with God himself. Taken this way, knowledge can help to motivate existence, to begin the search for God, it can be a great experience of freedom for truth, placing itself in the service of the maturation and promotion of humanity.[32] Such a commitment demands of consecrated persons an accurate analysis of the quality of their educational proposal, and also constant attention to their cultural and *professional* formation.

And Commitment in the Field of Non-Formal Education

40 Another, equally important, field of evangelization and humanization is non-formal education, that is of those who have been unable to have access to normal schooling. Consecrated persons feel that they should be present and promote innovative projects in such contexts. In these situations poorer young people should be given the chance of a suitable formation that considers their moral, spiritual and religious development and is able to promote socialization and overcome discrimination. This is no novelty, inasmuch as working classes

30. Cf. John Paul II, Encyclical letter *Redemptoris Missio*, n. 8, *AAS* 83 (1991), 256.

31. Congregation for Catholic Education, *The Catholic School on the Threshold of the Third Millennium*, n. 14.

32. Cf. John Paul II, *Speech to the Plenary Session of the Pontifical Academy of Sciences*, 13th November 2000, *AAS* 93 (2001), 202–206.

have always been within the sphere of various religious families. It is a case of confirming today with suitable means and plans an attention that has never been lacking.

Educators Called to Accompany Towards the Other
We Wish to See Jesus (Jn 12:21)

The Dynamism of Reciprocity in the Educational Community

41 The educational mission is carried out in a spirit of cooperation between various subjects—students, parents, teachers, non-teaching personnel and the school management—who form the educational community. It can create an environment for living in which the values are mediated by authentic interpersonal relations between the various members of which it is composed. Its highest aim is the complete and comprehensive education of the person. In this respect, consecrated persons can offer a decisive contribution, in the light of their experience of communion that characterizes their community lives. In fact, by committing themselves to live and communicate the spirituality of communion in the school community, through a dialogue that is constructive and able to harmonize differences, they build an environment that is rooted in the evangelical values of truth and love. Consecrated persons are thus leaven that is able to create relations of increasingly deep communion, that are in themselves educational. They promote solidarity, mutual enhancement and joint responsibility in the educational plan, and, above all, they give an explicit Christian testimony, through communication of the experience of God and of the evangelical message, even sharing the awareness of being instruments of God and bearers of a charism in the service of all men.

Within the Sphere of the Church Communion

42 The task of communicating the spirituality of communion within the school community derives from being part of the Church communion. This means that consecrated persons involved in the educational mission must be integrated, starting from their charism, in the pastoral activity of the local Church. They, in fact, carry out an ecclesial ministry in the service of a concrete community and in communion with the Diocesan Ordinary. The common educational mission entrusted to them by the Church does, however, require cooperation and greater synergy between the various religious families. Apart from offering a more skilled educational service, this synergy offers the chance for sharing charisms from which the entire Church will gain. For this reason the communion that consecrated persons are called to experiment goes well beyond their own religious family or institute. Indeed, by opening themselves to communion with other forms of consecration, consecrated persons can "rediscover their common Gospel roots and together grasp the beauty of their own identity in the variety of charisms with greater clarity."[33]

The Relational Dimension

Promoting Authentic Relations

43 The educational community expresses the variety and beauty of the various vocations and the fruitfulness at educational and pedagogical level that this contributes to the life of scholastic institutions. The commitment to promote the relational dimension of the person and the care taken in establishing authentic educational relationships with young people are undoubtedly aspects that the presence of consecrated persons can facilitate in schools, considered as microcosms in which oases are created where the bases are laid for living responsibly in the macrocosm of society. It is not, however, strange to observe, even in schools, the progressive deterioration of interpersonal relations, due to the functionalization of roles, haste, fatigue and other factors that create conflicting situations. To organize schools like gymnasiums where one exercises to establish positive relationships between the various members and to search for peaceful solutions to the conflicts is a fundamental objective not just for the life of the educational community, but also for the construction of a society of peace and harmony.

Educating to Reciprocity

44 Usually in schools there are boys and girls, as well as men and women with tasks of teaching or administration. Consideration of the single-dual dimension of the human person implies the need to educate to mutual acknowledgement, in respect and acceptance of differences. The experience of man/woman reciprocity may appear paradigmatic in the positive management of other differences, including ethnic and religious ones. It does, in fact, develop and encourage positive attitudes, such as an awareness that every person can give and receive, a willingness to welcome the other, a capacity for a serene dialogue and a chance to purify and clarify one's own experience while seeking to communicate it and compare it with the other.

Through Enhancing Relations

45 In a relationship of reciprocity, interaction can be asymmetric from the point of view of roles, as it is necessarily in the educational relationship, but not from that of the dignity and uniqueness of every human person. Learning is

---

33. Congregation for Institutes of Consecrated Life and Societies of Apostolic Life, *Starting Afresh from Christ,* n. 30.

facilitated when, without undue straining with regard to roles, educational interaction is at a level that fully recognizes the equality of the dignity of every human person. In this way it is possible to form personalities capable of having their own view of life and to agree with their choice. The involvement of families and teaching staff creates a climate of trust and respect that promotes the development of the capacity for dialogue and peaceful coexistence in the search for whatever favors the common good.

The Educational Community

Creating an Educational Environment

46 Due to their experience of community life, consecrated persons are in a most favorable position for cooperating to make the educational plan of the school promote the creation of a true community. In particular they propose an alternative model of coexistence to that of a standardized or individualistic society. In actual fact, consecrated persons undertake, together with their lay colleagues, to assure that schools are structured as places of encounter, listening, communication, where students experience values in an essential way. They help, in a directed way, to guide pedagogical choices to promote overcoming individualistic self-promotion, solidarity instead of competition, assisting the weak instead of marginalization, responsible participation instead of indifference.

Aware of the Family's Task

47 The family comes first in being responsible for the education of its children. Consecrated persons appreciate the presence of parents in the educational community and try to establish a true relation of reciprocity with them. Participating bodies, personal meetings and other initiatives are aimed at rendering increasingly more active the insertion of parents in the life of institutions and for making them aware of the educational task. Acknowledgement of this task is more necessary today than it was in the past, due to the many difficulties that families now experience. When God's original plan for families is overshadowed in peoples' minds, society receives incalculable damage and the right of children to live in an environment of fully human love is infringed. On the contrary, when a family reflects God's plan, it becomes a workshop where love and true solidarity are experienced.[34]

Consecrated persons announce this truth, which does not regard just believers, but is the patrimony of all mankind, inscribed in the heart of man. The

---

34. Cf. John Paul II, *Homily for the Jubilee of Families*, Rome, 15th October 2000, nn. 4–5, *AAS* 93 (2001), 90.

chance of contact with the families of the children and young people is a favorable occasion for examining with them meaningful questions regarding life, human love and the nature of families and for agreeing to the proposed vision instead of other often dominating visions.

And of the Importance of Brotherhood as a Prophetic Sign

48 By testifying to Christ and living their typical life of communion, consecrated men and women offer the whole educational community the prophetic sign of brotherhood. Community life, when woven with deep relationships "is itself prophetic in a society which, sometimes without realizing it, has a profound yearning for a brotherhood which knows no borders."[35] This conviction becomes visible in the commitment to make the life of the community a place of growth of persons and of mutual aid in the search and fulfillment of the common mission. In this regard it is important that the sign of brotherhood can be perceived with transparency in every moment of the life of the scholastic community.

In Network With Other Educational Agencies

49 The educational community achieves its scopes in synergy with other educational institutions present in the country.

By coordinating with other educational agencies and in the more extensive communications network a school stimulates the process of personal, professional and social growth of its students, by offering a number of proposals in integrated form. Above all, it forms a most important aid for escaping various conditionings, especially of the *media*, so helping young people to pass from simple and passive consumers to critical interlocutors, capable of positively influencing public opinion and even the quality of information.

Going Towards the Other

A Lifestyle That Questions

50 When involved in the serious search for truth through the contribution of the different subjects, the life of the educational community is constantly urged to mature in reflection, to go beyond the acquisitions achieved and to question at the existential level.

With their presence, consecrated persons offer in this context the specific contribution of their identity and vocation. Even if not always consciously, young people wish to find in them the testimony of a life lived as the answer to a call, as a journey towards God, as the search for the signs through which He

---

35. John Paul II, Apostolic exhortation *Vita Consecrata*, n. 85, *AAS* 88 (1996), 462.

makes himself present. They expect to see persons who invite them to seriously question themselves, and to discover the deepest meaning of human existence and of history.

Guide in a Search for Meaning

Develop the Gift for Searching

51 An encounter with God is always a personal event, an answer that is by its nature, a person's free act in response to the gift of faith. Schools, even Catholic schools, do not demand adherence to the faith, however, they can prepare for it. Through the educational plan it is possible to create the conditions for a person to develop a gift for searching and to be guided in discovering the mystery of his being and of the reality that surrounds him, until he reaches the threshold of the faith.

To those who then decide to cross this threshold the necessary means are offered for continuing to deepen their experience of faith through prayer, the sacraments, the encounter with Christ in the Word, in the Eucharist, in events and persons.[36]

Educating to Freedom

52 An essential dimension of the path of searching is education to freedom, typical of every school loyal to its task. Education to freedom is a humanizing action, because it aims at the full development of personality. In fact, education itself must be seen as the acquisition, growth and possession of freedom. It is a matter of educating each student to free him/herself from the conditionings that prevent him/her from fully living as a person, to form him/herself into a strong and responsible personality, capable of making free and consistent choices.[37]

Preparing the Ground for the Choice of Faith

Educating truly free people is in itself already guiding them to the faith. The search for meaning favors the development of the religious dimension of a person as ground in which the Christian choice can mature and the gift of faith can develop. It is ever more frequently observed that in schools, especially in western societies, the religious dimension of a person has become a *lost link*, not only in the typically educational sphere of schools, but also in the more extensive formative process that began in the family.

---

36. Cf. Congregation for Catholic Education, *The Religious Dimension of Education in a Catholic School*, 7th April 1988, nn. 98–112.

37. Cf. Sacred Congregation for Catholic Education, *The Catholic School*, n. 31.

Yet, without it the formative process, as a whole, is strongly affected, making any search for God difficult. The immediate, the superficial, the accessory, pre-fabricated solutions, deviations towards magic and surrogates of mystery thus tend to grasp the interest of young people and leave no room for opening to the transcendent.

Even teachers, who call themselves non-believers, today feel the urgency to recover the religious dimension of education, necessary for forming personalities able to manage the powerful conditionings under way in society and to ethically guide the new discoveries of science and technology.

With a Style of Interpellant Education

53 By living the evangelical counsels, consecrated persons form an effective invitation to question themselves about God and the mystery of life. Such a question that requires a style of education that is able to stimulate fundamental questions on the origin and meaning of life passes through the search for the *whys* more than for the *hows*. For this reason, it is necessary to check how the contents of the various subjects are proposed in order that students may develop such questions and search for suitable replies. Moreover, children and young people should be encouraged to flee from the obvious and from the trivial, especially within the sphere of choices of life, of the family, of human love. This style is translated into a methodology of study and research that trains for reflection and discernment. It takes the form of a strategy that cultivates in the person, from his earliest years, an inner life as the place to listen to the voice of God, cultivate the meaning of the sacred, decide to follow values, mature the recognition of one's limits and of sin, feel the growth of the responsibility for every human being.

Teaching Religion

Specialized Religious Education Itineraries

54 The teaching of religion assumes a specific role in this context. Consecrated persons, together with other educators, but with a greater responsibility, are often called to ensure specialized paths of religious education, depending on the different school situations: in some schools the majority of the pupils are Christians, in others different religious followings predominate, or there are agnostic or atheist choices.

Cultural Proposal Offered to Everyone

Theirs is the duty to emphasize the value of the teaching of religion within the timetable of the institution and within the cultural program. Even while acknowledging that the teaching of religion in a Catholic school has a different function from that which it has in other schools, its scope is still that of opening to the understanding of the historical experience of Christianity, of guiding to knowledge of Jesus Christ and the study of his Gospel. In this sense, it can be described as a cultural proposal that can be offered to everyone over and above their personal choices of faith. In many contexts, Christianity already forms the spiritual *horizon* of the native culture.

Teaching of Religion in Catholic Schools

In Catholic schools, teaching of religion must help students to arrive at a personal position in religious matters that is consistent and respectful of the positions of others, so contributing to their growth and to a more complete understanding of reality. It is important that the whole educational community, especially in Catholic schools, recognizes the value and role of the teaching of religion and contributes to its enhancement by the students. By using words that are suited to mediating the religious message, the religion teacher is called to stimulate the pupils to study the great questions concerning the meaning of life, the significance of reality and a responsible commitment to transform it in the light of the evangelical values and modern culture.

Other Formative Opportunities

The community of a Catholic school offers not only teaching of religion but also other opportunities, other moments and ways for educating to a harmony between faith and culture, faith and life.[38]

Life as a Vocation

Life as a Gift and as a Task

55 Together with other Christian educators, consecrated persons know how to grasp and enhance the vocational dimension that is intrinsic to the educational process. Life is, in fact, a gift that is accomplished in the free response to a special call, to be discovered in the concrete circumstances of each day. Care for the vocational dimension guides the person to interpret his existence in the light of God's plan.

The absence or scarce attention to the vocational dimension not only deprives young people of the assistance to which they have a right in the important discernment on the fundamental choices of their lives, but it also impoverishes society and the Church, both of which are in need of the presence of people able to devote themselves on a stable basis to the service of God, their brothers and the common good.

---

38. Cf. *Ibid.*, nn. 37–48.

Culture of Vocations

Reawakening a Taste for the Big Questions

56 The promotion of a new vocational culture is a fundamental component of the new evangelization. Through it, one must "find courage and zest for the big questions, those related to one's future."[39] These are questions that should be reawakened even through personalized educational processes by means of which one is gradually led to discover life as a gift of God and as a task. These processes can form a real itinerary of vocational maturation, that leads to a specific vocation.

Consecrated persons especially are called to promote the *culture of vocations* in schools. They are a sign for all Christian people not only of a specific vocation, but also of vocational dynamism as a form of life, thus eloquently representing the decision of those who wish to live with attention to God's call.

Sharing Their Educational Charism

57 In the modern situation, the educational mission in schools is increasingly shared with the laity. "Whereas at times in the recent past, collaboration came about as a means of supplementing the decline of consecrated persons necessary to carry out activities, now it is growing out of the need to share responsibility not only in the carrying out of the Institute's works but especially in the hope of sharing specific aspects and moments of the spirituality and mission of the Institute."[40] Consecrated persons must therefore transmit the educational charism that animates them and promote the formation of those who feel that they are called to the same mission. To discharge this responsibility they must be careful not to get involved exclusively in academic-administrative tasks and to not be taken over by activism. What they must do is favor attention to the richness of their charism and try to develop it in response to the new social-cultural situations.

Becoming Privileged Interlocutors in the Search for God

58 In educational communities consecrated persons can promote the achievement of a mentality that is inspired by the evangelical values in a style that is typical of their charism. This in itself is already an educational service in a vocational key. Young people, in fact, and often also the other members of the educational community, more or less consciously expect to find in consecrated

---

39. Pontifical Work for Ecclesiastical Vocations, *New Vocations for a New Europe*. Final document of the Congress of Vocations to the Priesthood and to Consecrated life, Rome, 5th–10th May 1997, n.13 b.

40. Congregation for Institutes of Consecrated Life and Societies of Apostolic Life, *Starting Afresh from Christ*, n. 31.

persons privileged interlocutors in the search for God. For this type of service, the most specific of the identity of consecrated persons, there are no age limits that would justify considering oneself retired. Even when they have to retire from professional activity, they can always continue to be available for young people and adults, as experts of life according to the Spirit, men and women educators in the sphere of faith.

The presence of consecrated men and women in schools is thus a proposal of evangelical spirituality, a reference point for the members of the educational community in their itinerary of faith and of Christian maturation.

The Vocational Dimension of the Teaching Profession

59 The quality of the teachers is fundamental in creating an educational environment that is purposeful and fertile. It is for this reason that the institutions of consecrated life and religious communities, especially when in charge of Catholic schools, propose formation itineraries for teachers. It is opportune in these to emphasize the vocational dimension of the teaching profession in order to make the teachers aware that they are participating in the educational and sanctifying mission of the Church.[41] Consecrated persons can reveal, to those who so desire, the richness of the spirituality that characterizes them and of the charism of their Institute, encouraging them to live them in the educational ministry according to the lay identity and in forms that are suitable and accessible to young people.

Educators Called to Teach Coexistence
...All men will know that you are my disciples, if you have love for one another (Jn 13:35)

On a Human Scale
Priority Attention to the Person

60 A school's community dimension is inseparable from priority attention to the person, the focus of the scholastic educational program. "*Culture must correspond to the human person*, and overcome the temptation to a knowledge which yields to pragmatism or which loses itself in the endless meanderings of erudition. Such knowledge is incapable of giving meaning to life ... knowledge enlightened by faith, far from abandoning areas of daily life, invests them with all the strength of hope and prophecy. The humanism which we desire advocates a vision of society centered on the human person and his inalienable rights, on the values of justice and peace, on a correct relationship between

---

41. Cf. Sacred Congregation for Catholic Education, *Lay Catholics in Schools: Witnesses to Faith*, n. 24.

individuals, society and the State, on the logic of solidarity and subsidiarity. It is a humanism capable of giving a soul to economic progress itself, so that it may be directed to the *promotion of each individual and of the whole person*."[42]

Characterizing Concrete Choices in That Sense[43]

61 Consecrated persons must be careful to safeguard the priority of the person in their educational program. For this they must cooperate in the concrete choices that are made regarding the general school program and its formative proposal. Each pupil must be considered as an individual, bearing in mind his family environment, his personal history, his skills and his interests. In a climate of mutual trust, consecrated men and women discover and cultivate each person's talents and help young people to become responsible for their own formation and to cooperate in that of their companions. This requires the total dedication and unselfishness of those who live the educational service as a mission. This dedication and unselfishness contribute to characterizing the school environment as a vital environment in which intellectual growth is harmonized with spiritual, religious, emotional and social growth.

Personalized Accompanying

Giving Precedence to Dialogue and Attentive Listening

62 With the typical sensitivity of their formation, consecrated persons offer personalized accompanying through attentive listening and dialogue. They are, in fact, convinced that "education is a thing of the heart" and that, consequently, an authentic formative process can only be initiated through a personal relationship.

Reawakening the Desire for Internal Liberation

63 Every human being feels that he is internally oppressed by tendencies to evil, even when he flaunts limitless freedom. Consecrated men and women strive to reawaken in young people the desire for an internal liberation. This is a condition for undertaking the Christian journey that is directed towards the new life of the evangelical beatitudes. The evangelical view will allow young people to take an critical attitude towards consumerism and hedonism that have wormed their way, like the tare in the wheat, into the culture and way of life of vast areas of humanity.

---

42. John Paul II, *Jubilee of University Professors*, Rome, 9th September 2000, nn. 3, 6, *AAS* 92 (2000), 863–865.

43. St. John Bosco, *Circolare del 24 gennaio 1883*, in CERIA E. (*a cura di*), *Epistolario di S. Giovanni Bosco*, SEI, Torino 1959, vol. IV, 209.

That is Conversion of the Heart

Fully aware that all human values find their full accomplishment and their unity in Christ, consecrated persons explicitly represent the maternal care of the Church for the complete growth of the young people of our time, communicating the conviction that there can be no true liberation if there is no conversion of the heart.[44]

The Dignity of Woman and Her Vocation

The Presence and Action of Women

64 The sensitivity of consecrated persons, so attentive to the need to develop the single-dual dimension of the human person in obedience to God's original plan (cf. *Gen* 2:18), can contribute to integrating differences in the educational endeavor to make maximum use of them and overcoming homologations and stereotypes. History testifies to the commitment of consecrated men and women in favor of women. Even today consecrated persons feel they have a duty to appreciate women in the field of education. In various parts of the world Catholic schools and numerous religious families are active in assuring that women are guaranteed access to education without any discrimination and that they can give their specific contribution to the good of the entire community. Everyone is aware of the contribution of women in favor of life and of the humanization of culture,[45] their readiness to care for people and to rebuild the social tissue that has often been broken and torn by tension and hate. Many initiatives of solidarity, even among peoples at war, are born from that *female genius* that promotes sensitivity for all human beings in all circumstances.[46] In this context consecrated women are called in a very special way to be, through their dedication lived in fullness and joy, *a sign of God's tender love towards the human race.*[47] The presence and appreciation of women is therefore essential for preparing a culture that really does place at its center people, the search for the peaceful settlement of conflicts, unity in diversity, assistance and solidarity.

---

44. Cf. Paul VI, Apostolic exhortation *Evangelii Nuntiandi*, 8th December 1975, n. 36, *AAS* 68 (1976), 29.

45. Cf. John Paul II, Apostolic exhortation *Christifideles Laici*, 30th December 1988, n. 51, *AAS* 81 (1989), 492–496.

46. Cf. John Paul II, Apostolic letter *Mulieris Dignitatem*, 15th August 1988, n. 30, *AAS* 80 (1988), 1724–1727.

47. Cf. John Paul II, Apostolic exhortation *Vita Consecrata*, n. 57, *AAS* 88 (1996), 429.

Intercultural Outlook

Contribution of Consecrated Persons to Intercultural Dialogue

65 In today's complex society, schools are called to provide young generations with the elements necessary for developing an intercultural vision. Consecrated persons involved in education, who often belong to institutes that are spread throughout the world, are an expression of "multi-cultural and International communities, called to 'witness to the sense of communion among peoples, races and cultures' . . . where mutual knowledge, respect, esteem and enrichment are being experienced."[48] For this reason they can easily consider cultural differences as a richness and propose accessible paths of encounter and dialogue. This attitude is a precious contribution for true intercultural education, something that is made increasingly urgent by the considerable phenomenon of migration. The itinerary to be followed in educational communities involves passing from tolerance of the multicultural situation to welcome and a search for reasons for mutual understanding to intercultural dialogue, which leads to acknowledging the values and limits of every culture.

Intercultural Education

Education Application Necessary

66 From a Christian viewpoint, intercultural education is essentially based on the relational model that is open to reciprocity. In the same way as happens with people, cultures also develop through the typical dynamisms of dialogue and communion. "Dialogue between cultures emerges as an intrinsic demand of human nature itself, as well as of culture. It is dialogue which protects the distinctiveness of cultures as historical and creative expressions of the underlying unity of the human family, and which sustains understanding and communion between them. The notion of communion, which has its source in Christian revelation and finds its sublime prototype in the Triune God (cf. *Jn* 17:11, 21), never implies a dull uniformity or enforced homogenization or assimilation; rather it expresses the convergence of a multiform variety, and is therefore a sign of richness and a promise of growth."[49]

Coexistence of Differences

67 The intercultural prospective involves a change of paradigm at the pedagogical level. From the integration of differences one passes to a search for their

48. Congregation for Institutes of Consecrated Life and Societies of Apostolic Life, *Starting Afresh from Christ*, n. 29.

49. John Paul II, *Dialogue between Cultures for a Civilisation of Love and Peace*, Message for the Celebration of the World Day of Peace, 1st January 2001, n. 10, *AAS* 93 (2001), 239.

coexistence. This is a model that is neither simple nor easily implemented. In the past, diversity between cultures was often a source of misunderstandings and conflicts; even today, in various parts of the world, we see the arrogant establishment of some cultures over others. No less dangerous is the tendency to homologation of cultures to models of the western world inspired by forms of radical individualism and a practically atheist concept of life.

Commitment to Seek the Ethical Foundations of the Various Cultures

68 Schools must question themselves about the fundamental ethical trends that characterize the cultural experiences of a particular community. "Cultures, like the people who give rise to them, are marked by the 'mystery of evil' at work in human history (cf. *1 Th* 2:7), and they too are in need of purification and salvation. The authenticity of each human culture, the soundness of its underlying *ethos*, and hence the validity of its moral bearings, can be measured to an extent by its commitment to the human cause and by its capacity to promote human dignity at every level and in every circumstance."[50]

In his speech to the members of the 50th General Assembly of the United Nations Organization, the Pope underlined the fundamental communion between peoples, observing that the various cultures are in actual fact just different ways of dealing with the question of the meaning of personal existence. In fact, every culture is an attempt to reflect on the mystery of the world and of man, a way of expressing the transcendent dimension of human life. Seen this way, difference, rather than being a threat, can become, through respectful dialogue, a source of deep understanding of the mystery of human existence.[51]

Sharing with the Poor in Solidarity

Preferential Option for the Poor

69 The presence of consecrated persons in an educational community concurs in perfecting the sensitivity of everyone to the poverty that still torments young people, families and entire peoples. This sensitivity can become a source of profound changes in an evangelical sense, inducing a transformation of the logics of excellence and superiority into those of service, of *caring for others* and forming a heart that is open to solidarity.

The preferential option for the poor leads to avoiding all forms of exclusion. Within the school there is often an educational plan that serves the more or less well-to-do social groups, while attention for the most needy definitively takes second place. In many cases social, economic or political circumstances leave

---

50. *Ibid.*, n. 8, 238.
51. Cf. John Paul II, *Insegnamenti*, XVIII/ 2, 1995, 730–744.

no better alternative. This, however, must not mean the exclusion of a clear idea of the evangelical criteria or of trying to apply it at a personal and community level and within the scholastic institutions themselves.

Planning Starting from the Least

Poor young people at the center of the education program

70 When the preferential option for the poorest is at the center of the educational program, the best resources and most qualified persons are initially placed at the service of the least, without in this way excluding those who have less difficulties and shortages. This is the meaning of evangelical inclusion, so distant from the logic of the world. The Church does, in fact, mean to offer its educational service *in the first place* to "those who are poor in the goods of this world or who are deprived of the assistance and affection of a family or who are strangers to the gift of Faith."[52] Unjust situations often make it difficult to implement this choice. Sometimes, however, it is Catholic educational institutions themselves that have strayed from such a preferential option, which characterized the beginnings of the majority of institutes of consecrated life devoted to teaching.

This choice, typical of the consecrated life, should therefore be cultivated from the time of initial formation, so that it is not considered as reserved only for the most generous and courageous.

Identify Situations of Poverty

71 Following in the footsteps of the Good Shepherd, consecrated persons should identify among their pupils the various poverty situations that prevent the overall maturation of the person and marginalize him or her from social life, by investigating their causes. Among these, destitution occupies an undisputable place. It often brings with it the lack of a family and of health, social maladjustment, loss of human dignity, impossibility of access to culture and consequently a deep spiritual poverty. *Becoming the voice of the poor of the world is a challenge assumed by the Church, and all Christians should do the same.*[53] Due to their choices and their publicly professed commitment of a poor personal and community lifestyle, consecrated persons are more strongly sensitive to their duty to promote justice and solidarity in the environment in which they are active.

---

52. Second Vatican Ecumenical Council, Declaration on Catholic Education *Gravissimum Educationis*, n. 9.

53. Cf. John Paul II, Apostolic letter *Tertio millennio adveniente*, 10th November 1994, n. 51, *AAS* 87 (1995), 36.

Giving Voice to the Poor

Considering the Least

72 Access to education especially for the poor[54] is a commitment assumed at different levels by Catholic educational institutions. This requires arranging educational activity to suit the least, no matter what the social status of the pupils present in the scholastic institution. This involves, among other things, proposing the contents of the social doctrine of the Church through educational projects and requires checking the profile that the school foresees for its students. If a school listens to the poorest people and arranges itself to suit them, it will be able to interpret the subjects at the service of life, and avail of their contents in relation to the global growth of people.

Commitment in Formal and Non-Formal Education

73 By listening to the poor, consecrated persons know *where* to commit themselves even within the sphere of non-formal education and how to bring the most underprivileged to have access to instruction. Acquaintance with countries where schools are reserved for the few or encounter serious difficulties in accomplishing their task could give rise in the educational communities of the more developed countries to initiatives of solidarity, among which twinning between classes or schools. The formative advantages would be great for everyone, especially for the pupils of the more developed countries. They would learn what is essential in life and they would be assisted in not following the cultural fashions induced by consumerism.

And in the Defense of Children's Rights

74 The defense of children's rights is another particularly important challenge. The exploitation of children, in different, often aberrant, forms, is among the most disturbing aspects of our time. Consecrated persons involved in the educational mission have the inescapable duty to devote themselves to the protection and promotion of children's rights. The concrete contributions that they can make both as individuals and as an educational institution will probably be insufficient with respect to the needs, but not useless, inasmuch as aimed at making known the roots from which the abuses derive. Consecrated persons willingly unite their efforts to those of other civil and ecclesial organizations and persons of good will, to uphold the respect of human rights in for the good of everyone, starting from the most weak and helpless.

---

54. See, for example, Office International Pour L'enseignement Catholique (OIEC), *Déclaration de la XIVème Assemblée Générale,* Rome, 5th March 1994.

Willing Even to Give Their Lives

75 The preferential option for the poor requires living a personal and community attitude of readiness to *give one's life* where necessary. It might therefore be necessary to leave perhaps even works of prestige which are no longer able to implement suitable formative processes and consequently leave no room for the characteristics of the consecrated life. In fact, "if a school is excellent as an academic institution, but does not bear witness to authentic values, then both good pedagogy and a concern for pastoral care make it obvious that renewal is called for."[55]

Consecrated persons are therefore called to check to see if, in their educational activity, they are mainly pursuing academic prestige rather than the human and Christian maturation of the young people; if they are favoring competition rather than solidarity; if they are involved in educating, together with the other members of the school community, persons who are free, responsible and *just* according to evangelical justice.

To the Ends of the Earth

76 Precisely because of their religious consecration, consecrated persons are pre-eminently free to leave everything to go to preach the gospel even to the ends of the earth.[56] For them, even in the educational field, the announcement *"ad gentes"* of the Good News remains a priority. They are therefore aware of the fundamental role of Catholic schools in mission countries. In many cases, in fact, schools are the only possibility for the Church's presence, in others they are a privileged place of evangelizing and humanizing action, responsible both for the human and cultural development of the poorest people. It is important in this regard to consider the necessity of the participation of the educational charism between the religious families of the countries of ancient evangelization and those born in mission territories, which inspire them. In fact, "the older Institutes, many of which have been tested by the severest of hardships, which they have accepted courageously down the centuries can be enriched through dialogue and an exchange of gifts with the foundations appearing in our own days."[57] Such sharing is also transferred into the field of formation of consecrated persons, in sustaining new religious families and in cooperation between various institutes.

---

55. Congregation for Catholic Education, *The Religious Dimension of Education in a Catholic School*, n. 19.

56. Cf. Paul VI, Apostolic exhortation *Evangelii Nuntiandi*, n. 69, *AAS* 68 (1976), 58.

57. John Paul II, Apostolic exhortation *Vita Consecrata*, n. 62, *AAS* 88 (1996), 437.

Culture of Peace
Peace Through Justice

77 The path to peace passes through justice. "Only in this way can we ensure a peaceful future for our world and remove the root causes of conflicts and wars: peace is the fruit of justice . . . a justice which is not content to apportion to each his own, but one which aims at creating conditions of *equal opportunity* among citizens, and therefore favoring those who, for reasons of social status or education or health, risk being left behind or being relegated to the lowest places in society, without possibility of deliverance."[58]

Educating for Peace Starting from the Heart

Peacemakers in Their Own Environment

78 Awareness that education is the main road to peace is a fact shared by the international community. The various projects launched by international organizations for sensitizing public opinion and governments are a clear sign of this.[59] Consecrated persons, witnesses of Christ, the Prince of Peace, grasp the urgency of placing education for peace among the primary objectives of their formative action offering their specific contribution to encourage in the hearts of the pupils the desire to become peacemakers. Wars in fact are born in the hearts of men and the defenses of peace must be built in the hearts of men. By enhancing the educational process, consecrated persons undertake to excite attitudes of peace in the souls of the men of the third millennium. This "is not only the absence of conflict but requires a positive, dynamic, participatory process where dialogue is encouraged and conflicts are solved in a spirit of mutual understanding and co-operation."[60]

Consecrated persons cooperate in this undertaking with all men and women of goodwill sharing with them the effort and urgency to always seek new ways that are suited for an effective education that "has widened possibilities for strengthening a culture of peace."[61]

Through the Education to Values

79 An effective education for peace involves preparing various levels of programs and strategies. Among other things, it is a matter of proposing to the

---

58. John Paul II, *Jubilee of Government Leaders, Members of Parliament and Politicians*, Rome, 4th November 2000, n. 2, *AAS* 93 (2001), 167.

59. For example, the United Nations has promoted the *International Decade for a Culture of Peace and Non-violence*, (2000–2010).

60. The United Nations, *Résolution 53/243: Déclaration et Programme d'action sur une culture de la paix*, 6 octobre 1999.

61. *Ibid.*, A, art. 1a; art. 4.

pupils an education to suitable values and attitudes for peacefully settling disputes in the respect of human dignity; of organizing activities, even extracurricular ones such as sports and theatre that favor assimilating the values of loyalty and respect of rules; of assuring equality of access to education for women; of encouraging, when necessary, a review of curricula, including textbooks.[62]

Education is also called to transmit to students an awareness of their cultural roots and respect for other cultures. When this is achieved with solid ethical reference points, education leads to a realization of the inherent limits in one's own culture and in that of others. At the same time, however, it emphasizes a common inheritance of values to the entire human race. In this way *"education has a particular role to play in building a more united and peaceful world.* It can help to affirm that integral humanism, open to life's ethical and religious dimension, which appreciates the importance of understanding and showing esteem for other cultures and the spiritual values present in them."[63]

Educating for Coexistence

Educating for Active and Responsible Citizens

80 As a result of the negative effects of uncontrolled economic and cultural globalization, responsible participation in the life of the community at local, national and world levels acquires increasing importance at the beginning of the third millennium. This participation presupposes the realization of the causes of the phenomena that threaten the coexistence of people and of human life itself. As with every realization, this too finds in education, and in particular in schools, fertile ground for its development. Thus a new and difficult task takes shape: educate to have active and responsible citizens. The words of the Pope are enlightening in this regard: "promoting the right to peace ensures respect for all other rights, since it encourages the building of a society in which structures of power give way to structures of cooperation, with a view to the common good."[64] In this respect, consecrated persons can offer the sign of a responsible brotherhood, living in communities in which "each member has a sense of co-responsibility for the faithfulness of the others; each one contributes to a serene climate of sharing life, of understanding, and of mutual help."[65]

---

62. Cf. *Ibid.,* B, art. 9.

63. John Paul II, *Dialogue between Cultures for a Civilisation of Love and Peace,* Message for the Celebration of the World Day of Peace, 1st January 2001, n. 20, *AAS* 93 (2001), 245.

64. John Paul II, *Respect for Human Rights: the Secret of True Peace,* Message for the Celebration of the World Day of Peace, 1st January 1999, n. 11, *AAS* 91 (1999), 385.

65. Congregation for Institutes of Consecrated Life and Societies of Apostolic Life, *Fraternal Life in Community,* 2nd February 1994, n.57, in *Enchiridion Vaticanum,* vol. 14, 265.

Conclusion

81 The reflections proposed clearly indicate that the presence of consecrated persons in the world of education is a prophetic choice.[66]

The Synod on the consecrated life exhorts to assume with renewed dedication the educational mission in all levels of schools, universities and institutions of higher learning.[67] The invitation to continue the itinerary begun by those who have already offered a significant contribution to the educational mission of the Church lies within the bounds of the fidelity to their original charism: "because of their special consecration, their particular experience of the gifts of the Spirit, their constant listening to the Word of God, their practice of discernment, their rich heritage of pedagogical traditions built up since the establishment of their Institute, and their profound grasp of spiritual truth (cf. *Ef* 1:17), consecrated persons are able to be especially effective in educational activities and to offer a specific contribution to the work of other educators."[68]

82 In the dimension of ecclesial communion, there is a growing awareness in every consecrated person of the great cultural and pedagogical wealth that derives from sharing a common educational mission, even in the specificity of the various ministries and charisms. It is a matter of discovering and renewing an awareness of one's own identity, finding again the inspiring nucleuses of a skilled educational professionalism to be rediscovered as a way of being that represents an authentic vocation.

Starting Afresh from Christ

The root of this renewed awareness is Christ. Consecrated persons working in schools must start from him to find again the motivating source of their mission. Starting afresh from Christ means contemplating his face, pausing at length with him in prayer to then be able to show him to others. It is what the Church is called to accomplish at the beginning of the new millennium, conscious that only faith can enter the mystery of that face.[69] Starting again from Christ is, therefore, also for consecrated men and women, starting afresh from faith nourished by the sacraments and supported by a hope that does not fail: "I am with you always" (*Mt* 28:20).

---

66. Cf. Congregation for Catholic Education, *The Catholic School on the Threshold of the Third Millennium*, n. 21.

67. Cf. John Paul II, Apostolic exhortation *Vita Consecrata*, n. 97, *AAS* 88 (1996), 473.

68. *Ibid.*, n. 96, 472.

69. Cf. John Paul II, Apostolic letter *Novo Millennio Ineunte*, n. 19, *AAS* 93 (2001), 278–279.

In a Renewed Commitment

Encouraged by this hope, consecrated persons are called to revive their educational passion living it in school communities as a testimony of encounter between different vocations and between generations.

The task of teaching to live, discovering the deepest meaning of life and of transcendence, to mutually interact with others, to love creation, to think freely and critically, to find fulfillment in work, to plan the future, in one word to *be*, demands a new love of consecrated persons for educational and cultural commitment in schools.

And Living in a State of Permanent Formation

83 By allowing themselves to be transformed by the Spirit and living in a state of permanent formation, consecrated men and women become able to extend their horizons and understand the profound causes of events.[70] Permanent formation also becomes the key to understanding the educational mission in schools and for carrying it out in a way that is close to a reality that is so changeable and at the same time in need of responsible, timely and prophetic intervention. The cultural study that consecrated persons are called to cultivate for improving their professionalism in the subjects for which they are responsible, or in the administrative or management service, is a duty of justice, which cannot be shirked.

Participation in the life of the universal and particular Church involves demonstrating the bonds of communion and appreciating the directions of the Magisterium, especially with regard to such matters as life, the family, the issue of women, social justice, peace, ecumenism, inter-religious dialogue. In the climate of modern pluralism, the Magisterium of the Church is the voice of authority that interprets phenomena in the light of the Gospel.

Thanksgiving for the Important and Noble Task

84 The Congregation for Catholic Education wishes to conclude these reflections with sincere gratitude to all the consecrated persons who work in the field of school education. While aware of the complexity and often of the difficulties of their task, it wishes to underline the value of the *noble* educational service aimed at giving reasons for life and hope to the new generations, through critically processed knowledge and culture, on the basis of a concept of the person and of life inspired by the evangelical values.

Every school and every place of non-formal education can become a center of a greater network which, from the smallest village to the most complex

---

70. Cf. John Paul II, Apostolic exhortation *Vita Consecrata*, n. 98, *AAS* 88 (1996), 474.

metropolis, wraps the world in hope. It is in education, in fact, that the promise of a more human future and a more harmonious society lies.

No difficulty should remove consecrated men and women from schools and from education in general, when the conviction of being called to bring the Good News of the Kingdom of God to the poor and small is so deep and vital. Modern difficulties and confusion, together with the new prospects that are appearing at the dawn of the third millennium, are a strong reminder to pass one's life in educating the new generations to become bearers of a culture of communion that may reach every people and every person. The main motive and, at the same time, the goal of the commitment of every consecrated person, is to light and trim the lamp of faith of the new generations, the "morning watchmen (cf. *Is* 21:11–12) at the dawn of the new millennium."[71]

The Holy Father, during the Audience granted to the undersigned Prefect, approved this document and authorized its publication.

Rome, 28th October 2002, thirty-seventh anniversary of the promulgation of the statement *Gravissimum Educationis* of the Second Vatican Council.

† **Zenon Card. GROCHOLEWSKI,** *Prefect*
† **Joseph PITTAU, S.J.,** *Secretary*

---

71. John Paul II, Apostolic letter *Novo Millennio Ineunte*, n. 9, *AAS* 93 (2001), 272.

EDUCATING TOGETHER IN CATHOLIC SCHOOLS
A Shared Mission between Consecrated Persons and the Lay Faithful

CONGREGATION FOR CATHOLIC EDUCATION
(of Seminaries and Educational Institutions)

Introduction

1 The unexpected and often contradictory evolution of our age gives rise to educational challenges that pose questions for the school world. They force us to seek appropriate answers not only as regards contents and didactic methods, but also as regards the *community experience* that is a mark of educational activity. The relevance of these challenges transpires from the context of the social, cultural and religious complexity in which young people are actually growing up, and significantly influences their way of living. They are widespread phenomena such as lack of interest for the fundamental truths of human life, individualism, moral relativism and utilitarianism, that permeate above all rich and developed societies. Add to that rapid structural changes, globalization and the application of new technologies in the field of information that increasingly affect daily life and the process of formation. Moreover, with the process of development, the gap between rich and poor countries grows and the phenomenon of migration increases, so emphasizing the diversity of cultural identities in the same territory with the relative consequences concerning integration. In a society that is at once global and diversified, local and planetary, that hosts various and contrasting ways of interpreting the world and life, young people find themselves faced with different proposals of values, or lack thereof, that are increasingly stimulating but also increasingly less shared. There are also the difficulties that arise from problems of family stability, situations of hardship and poverty, that create a widespread feeling of disorientation at the existential and emotional level in a delicate period of their growth and maturation, exposing them to the danger of being "tossed to and fro and carried about with every wind of doctrine" (*Eph* 4:14).

2 In this context it becomes especially urgent to offer young people a course of scholastic formation which is not reduced to a simple individualistic and instrumental fruition of service with a view to obtaining a qualification. As well as gaining knowledge, students must also have a strong experience of sharing with their educators. For this experience to be happily accomplished, educators must be welcoming and well-prepared interlocutors, able to awaken and direct the best energies of students towards the search for truth and the meaning of existence, a positive construction of themselves and of life in view of an overall formation. In the end, "real education is not possible without the light of truth."[1]

3 This perspective regards all scholastic institutions, but even more directly the Catholic school, which is constantly concerned with the formational requirements of society, because "the problem of instruction has always been closely linked to the Church's mission."[2] The Catholic school participates in this mission like a true ecclesial subject, with its educational service that is enlivened by the truth of the Gospel. In fact, faithful to its vocation, it appears "as a place of integral education of the human person through a clear educational project of which Christ is the foundation,"[3] directed at creating a synthesis between faith, culture and life.

4 The project of the Catholic school is convincing only if carried out by people who are deeply motivated, because they witness to a living encounter with Christ, in whom alone "the mystery of man truly becomes clear."[4] These persons, therefore, acknowledge a *personal and communal adherence* with the Lord, assumed as the basis and constant reference of the inter-personal relationship and mutual cooperation between educator and student.

5 The implementation of a real *educational community*, built on the foundation of shared projected values, represents a serious task that must be carried out by the Catholic school. In this setting, the presence both of students and of teachers from different cultural and religious backgrounds requires an increased commitment of discernment and accompaniment. The preparation of a shared project acts as a stimulus that should force the Catholic school to be a place of ecclesial experience. Its binding force and potential for relationships derive from a set of values and a *communion of life* that is rooted in our common belonging to Christ. Derived from the recognition of evangelical values are educational norms, motivational drives and also the final goals of the school. Certainly the degree of participation can differ in relation to one's personal history, but this requires that educators be willing to offer a permanent

---

1. Benedict XVI, *Address to Rome's Ecclesial Diocesan Convention on the Family and Christian Community* (6th June 2005): *AAS* 97 (2005), 816.

2. John Paul II, Speech to UNESCO (2nd June 1980), n. 18: *AAS* 72 (1980), 747.

3. Congregation for Catholic Education, *The Catholic School on the Threshold of the Third Millennium* (28th December 1997), n. 4.

4. Vatican Council II, Pastoral Constitution on the Church in the Modern World *Gaudium et Spes* (7th December 1965), no. 22: *AAS* 58 (1966), 1042.

commitment to formation and self-formation regarding a choice of cultural and life values to be made present in the educational community.[5]

6 Having already dealt in two previous separate documents with the themes of the identity and mission of Catholic lay persons and of consecrated persons in schools respectively, this document of the Congregation for Catholic Education considers the pastoral aspects regarding cooperation between lay and consecrated persons[6] within the same educational mission. In it, the choice of the lay faithful to live their educational commitment as "a personal vocation in the Church, and not simply *as* [...] the exercise of a profession"[7] meets with the choice of consecrated persons, inasmuch as they are called "to live the evangelical councils and bring the humanism of the beatitudes to the field of education and schools."[8]

7 This document constantly refers to previous texts of the Congregation for Catholic Education regarding education and schools[9] and clearly considers the different situations encountered by Catholic Institutions in various parts of the world. It wishes to call attention to three fundamental aspects of cooperation between lay faithful and consecrated persons in the Catholic school: communion in the educational mission, the necessary course of formation for communion for a shared educational mission and, lastly, openness towards others as the fruit of that communion.

I. COMMUNION IN THE MISSION OF EDUCATION

8 Every human being is called to communion because of his nature which is created in the image and likeness of God (cf. *Gen* 1:26–27). Therefore, within the sphere of biblical anthropology, man is not an isolated individual, but a *person*: a being who is essentially relational. The communion to which man is

5. Cf. Sacred Congregation for Catholic Education, *The Catholic School* (19th March 1977), no. 32.

6. In this document reference is made to the priests, men and women religious and persons who, with different forms of consecration, choose the path of following Christ to wholeheartedly devote themselves to him (Cf. John Paul II, Post-synodal Apostolic Exhortation *Vita Consecrata* (25th March 1996), nos. 1–12: *AAS* 88 (1996), 377–385.

7. Sacred Congregation for Catholic Education, *Lay Catholics in Schools: Witnesses to Faith* (15th October 1982), no 37.

8. Congregation for Catholic Education, *Consecrated Persons and their Mission in Schools*, no. 6; Cf. John Paul II, Post-synodal Apostolic Exhortation *Vita Consecrata*, no. 96: *AAS* 88 (1996), 471–472.

9. *The Catholic School* (19th March 1977); *Lay Catholics in Schools: Witnesses to Faith* (15th October 1982); *Educational Guidance in Human Love. Outlines for Sex Education* (1st November 1983); *The Religious Dimension of Education in a Catholic School* (7th April 1988); *The Catholic School on the Threshold of the Third Millennium* (28th December 1997); *Consecrated Persons and their Mission in Schools. Reflections and Guidelines* (28th October 2002).

called always involves a double dimension, that is to say vertical (communion with God) and horizontal (communion with people). It is fundamental that communion be acknowledged as a gift of God, as the fruit of the divine initiative fulfilled in the Easter mystery.[10]

The Church: Mystery of Communion and Mission

9 God's original plan was compromised by the sin that wounded all relations: between man and God, between man and man. However, God did not abandon man in solitude, and, in the fullness of time, sent his Son, Jesus Christ, as Savior,[11] so that man might find, in the Spirit, full communion with the Father. In its turn, communion with the Trinity rendered possible by the encounter with Christ, unites persons with one other.

10 When Christians say *communion*, they refer to the eternal mystery, revealed in Christ, of the communion of love that is the very life of God-Trinity. At the same time we also say that Christians share in this communion in the Body of Christ which is the Church (cf. *Phil* 1:7; *Rev* 1:9). Communion is, therefore, the "essence" of the Church, the foundation and source of its mission of being in the world "the home and the school of communion,"[12] to lead all men and women to enter ever more profoundly into the mystery of Trinitarian communion and, at the same time, to extend and strengthen internal relations within the human community. In this sense, "the Church is like a human family, but at the same time it is also the great family of God, through which he creates a place of communion and unity through all continents, cultures and nations."[13]

11 As a result, therefore, in the Church, which is the *icon of the love incarnate of God*, "communion and mission are profoundly connected with each other, they interpenetrate and mutually imply each other, to the point that communion represents both the source and the fruit of mission: communion gives rise to mission and mission is accomplished in communion."[14]

---

10. Cf. Congregation for the Doctrine of the Faith, Letter to the Bishops of the Catholic Church *Communionis Notio*, (28th May 1992), no. 3b: *AAS* 85 (1993), 836.

11. Cf. Roman missal, Eucharistic prayer IV.

12. John Paul II, Apostolic Letter *Novo Millennio Ineunte* (6th January 2001), no. 43: *AAS* 93 (2001), 297.

13. Benedict XVI, *Homily at the Prayer Vigil in Marienfeld* (20th August 2005): *AAS* 97 (2005), 886.

14. John Paul II, Post-synodal Apostolic Exhortation *Christifideles Laici* (30th December 1988), no. 32: *AAS* 81 (1989), 451–452.

Educating in Communion and for Communion

12 Because its aim is to make man more man, education can be carried out authentically only in a relational and community context. It is not by chance that the first and original educational environment is that of the natural community of the family.[15] Schools, in their turn, take their place beside the family as an educational space that is communitarian, organic and intentional and they sustain their educational commitment, according to a logic of assistance.

13 The Catholic school, characterized mainly as an educating community, is a school for the *person and of persons*. In fact, it aims at forming the *person in the integral unity of his being*, using the tools of teaching and learning where "criteria of judgment, determining values, points of interest, lines of thought, sources of inspiration and models of life"[16] are formed. Above all, they are involved in the dynamics of interpersonal relations that form and vivify the school community.

14 On the other hand, because of its identity and its ecclesial roots, this community must aspire to becoming a Christian community, that is, a community of faith, able to create increasingly more profound relations of communion which are themselves educational. It is precisely the presence and life of an educational community, in which all the members participate in a fraternal communion, nourished by a living relationship with Christ and with the Church, that makes the Catholic school the environment for an authentically ecclesial experience.

Consecrated Persons and the Lay Faithful Together in Schools

15 "In recent years, one of the fruits of the teaching on the Church as communion has been the growing awareness that her members can and must unite their efforts, with a view to cooperation and exchange of gifts, in order to participate more effectively in the Church's mission. This helps to give a clearer and more complete picture of the Church herself, while rendering more effective the response to the great challenges of our time, thanks to the combined contributions of the various gifts."[17] In this ecclesial context the mission of the

15. Cf. Vatican Council II, Declaration on Christian Education *Gravissimum Educationis* (28th October 1965), no. 3: *AAS* 58 (1966), 731; C.I.C., cann. 793 and 1136.

16. Paul VI, Post-synodal Apostolic Exhortation *Evangelii Nuntiandi* (8th December 1975), no. 19: *AAS* 68 (1976), 18.

17. John Paul II, Post-synodal Apostolic Exhortation *Vita Consecrata*, n. 54: *AAS* 88 (1996), 426-427. For cooperation between lay faithful and consecrated persons see also nos. 54-56: *AAS* 88 (1996), 426–429.

Catholic school, lived as a community formed of consecrated persons and lay faithful, assumes a very special meaning and demonstrates a wealth that should be acknowledged and developed. This mission demands, from all the members of the educational community, the awareness that educators, as persons and as a community, have an unavoidable responsibility to create an original Christian style. They are required to be witnesses of Jesus Christ and to demonstrate Christian life as bearing light and meaning for everyone. Just as a consecrated person is called to testify his or her specific vocation to a life of communion in love[18] so as to be in the scholastic community a sign, a memorial and a prophecy of the values of the Gospel,[19] so too a lay educator is required to exercise "a specific mission within the Church by living, in faith, a secular vocation in the communitarian structure of the school."[20]

16 What makes this testimony really effective is the promotion, especially within the educational community of the Catholic school, of that *spirituality of communion* that has been indicated as the great prospect awaiting the Church of the Third Millennium. Spirituality of communion means "an ability to think of our brothers and sisters in the faith within the profound unity of the Mystical Body, and therefore as 'those who are a part of me,'"[21] and "the Christian community's ability to make room for all the gifts of the Spirit"[22] in a relationship of reciprocity between the various ecclesial vocations. Even in that special expression of the Church that is the Catholic school, spirituality of communion must become the living breath of the educational community, the criterion for the full ecclesial development of its members and the fundamental point of reference for the implementation of a truly shared mission.

17 This spirituality of communion, therefore, must be transformed into an attitude of clear evangelical fraternity among those persons who profess charisms in Institutes of consecrated life, in movements or new communities, and in other faithful who operate in the Catholic school. This spirituality of communion holds true for the Catholic school, founded by Religious families, by dioceses, by parishes or by the lay faithful, which today takes into itself the presence of ecclesial movements. In this way, the educational community

18. Cf. Congregation for the Institutes of Consecrated Life and the Societies of Apostolic Life, *Starting Afresh from Christ* (14th June 2002), no. 28.

19. Cf. Congregation for Catholic Education, *Consecrated Persons and their Mission in Schools*, no. 20.

20. Sacred Congregation for Catholic Education, *Lay Catholics in Schools: Witnesses to Faith*, no. 24.

21. John Paul II, Apostolic Letter *Novo millennio ineunte*, no. 43: *AAS* 93 (2001), 297.

22. *Ibid.*, no. 46: 299.

makes room for the gifts of the Spirit and acknowledges these diversities as wealth. A genuine ecclesial maturity, nourished by the encounter with Christ in the sacraments, will make it possible to develop "whether of the more traditional kind or the newer ecclesial movements [. . .] a vitality that is God's gift,"[23] for the entire scholastic community and for the educational journey itself.

18 The Catholic professional associations form another situation of "communion," a structured aid for the educational mission. They are a space for dialogue between families, the local institutions and the school. These associations, with their break-down at local, national and international levels, are a wealth that brings an especially fruitful contribution to the world of education as regards both motivations and professional points of view. Many associations have among their members teachers and persons in responsible positions both from the Catholic school and from other educational situations. Thanks to the pluralism of their origins, they can carry out an important function of dialogue and cooperation between institutions that differ but which have in common the same educational goals. These associative realities are required to consider how situations change, so adapting their structure and their way of operating in order to continue to be an effective and incisive presence in the sector of education. They must also intensify their reciprocal cooperation, especially in order to guarantee the achievement of their common goals, fully respecting the value and specificity of each association.

19 It is, moreover, of fundamental importance that the service carried out by the associations is stimulated by full participation in the pastoral activity of the Church. The Episcopal Conferences and their continental versions are entrusted with the role of promoting the development of the specificities of each association, favoring and encouraging more coordinated work in the educational sector.

II. A JOURNEY OF FORMATION FOR EDUCATING TOGETHER

20 Educating the young generations in communion and for communion in the Catholic school is a serious commitment that must not be taken lightly. It must be duly prepared and sustained through an initial and permanent project of formation that is able to grasp the educational challenges of the present time and to provide the most effective tools for dealing with them within the sphere of a shared mission. This implies that educators must be willing to learn and develop knowledge and be open to the renewal and updating of methodologies,

23. *Ibid.*, no. 46: 300.

but open also to spiritual and religious formation and sharing. In the context of the present day, this is essential for responding to the expectations that come from a constantly and rapidly changing world in which it is increasingly difficult to educate.

Professional Formation

21 One of the fundamental requirements for an educator in a Catholic school is his or her possession of a solid professional formation. Poor quality teaching, due to insufficient professional preparation or inadequate pedagogical methods, unavoidably undermines the effectiveness of the overall formation of the student and of the cultural witness that the educator must offer.

22 The professional formation of the educator implies a vast range of cultural, psychological and pedagogical skills, characterized by autonomy, planning and evaluation capacity, creativity, openness to innovation, aptitude for updating, research and experimentation. It also demands the ability to synthesize professional skills with educational motivations, giving particular attention to the relational situation required today by the increasingly collegial exercise of the teaching profession. Moreover, in the eyes and expectations of students and their families, the educator is seen and desired as a welcoming and prepared interlocutor, able to motivate the young to a complete formation, to encourage and direct their greatest energy and skills towards a positive construction of themselves and their lives, and to be a serious and credible witness of the responsibility and hope which the school owes to society.

23 The continuous rapid transformation that affects man and today's society in all fields leads to the precocious aging of acquired knowledge that demands new attitudes and methods. The educator is required to constantly update the contents of the subjects he teaches and the pedagogical methods he uses. The educator's vocation demands a ready and constant ability for renewal and adaptation. It is not, therefore, sufficient to achieve solely an initial good level of preparation; rather what is required is to maintain it and elevate it in a journey of permanent formation. Because of the variety of aspects that it involves, permanent formation demands a constant personal and communal search for its forms of achievement, as well as a formation course that is also shared and developed through exchange and comparison between consecrated and lay educators of the Catholic school.

24 It is not sufficient simply to care about professional updating in the strict sense. The synthesis between faith, culture and life that educators of the Catholic school are called to achieve is, in fact, reached "by integrating all the different aspects of human knowledge through the subjects taught, in the light of the Gospel [...and] in the growth of the virtues characteristic of the Christian."[24] This means that Catholic educators must attain a special sensitivity with regard to the person to be educated in order to grasp not only the request for growth in knowledge and skills, but also the need for growth in humanity. Thus educators must dedicate themselves "to others with heartfelt concern, enabling them to experience the richness of their humanity."[25]

25 For this reason, Catholic educators need "a 'formation of the heart': they need to be led to that encounter with God in Christ which awakens their love and opens their spirits to others," so that their educational commitment becomes "a consequence deriving from their faith, a faith which becomes active through love (cf. *Gal* 5:6)."[26] In fact, even "care for instruction means loving" (*Wis* 6:17). It is only in this way that they can make their teaching a school of faith, that is to say, a transmission of the Gospel, as required by the educational project of the Catholic school.

Theological and Spiritual Formation

26 The transmission of the Christian message through teaching implies a mastery of the knowledge of the truths of the faith and of the principles of spiritual life that require constant improvement. This is why both consecrated and lay educators of the Catholic school need to follow an opportune formational theological itinerary.[27] Such an itinerary makes it easier to combine the understanding of faith with professional commitment and Christian action. Apart from their theological formation, educators need also to cultivate their spiritual formation in order to develop their relationship with Jesus Christ and become a Master like Him. In this sense, the formational journey of both lay and consecrated educators must be combined with the moulding of the person towards greater conformity with Christ (cf. *Rm* 8:29) and of the educational community around Christ the Master. Moreover, the Catholic school is well aware that the community that it forms must be constantly nourished and compared with the sources from which the reason for its existence derives: the saving word of

---

24. Sacred Congregation for Catholic Education, *The Catholic School*, no. 37.

25. Benedict XVI, Encyclical Letter *Deus Caritas Est* (25th December 2005), no. 31: *AAS* 98 (2006), 244.

26. *Ibid.*

27. Cf. Sacred Congregation for Catholic Education, *Lay Catholics in Schools: Witnesses to Faith*, no. 60.

God in Sacred Scripture, in Tradition, above all liturgical and sacramental Tradition, enlightened by the Magisterium of the Church.[28]

The Contribution of Consecrated Persons to Shared Formation

27 Consecrated persons who profess the evangelical counsels show that they live for God and of God and become concrete witnesses to the Trinitarian love, so that people can experience the charm of divine beauty. Thus, the first and foremost contribution to the shared mission is the evangelical deep-rootedness of the lives of consecrated persons. Because of their vocational journey, they possess a theological-spiritual preparation that, centered on the mystery of Christ living in the Church, needs to unceasingly progress in step with the Church that progresses in history towards the "complete truth" (*Jn* 16:13). Again within this exquisitely ecclesial dynamic, consecrated persons also are invited to share the fruits of their formation with the laity, especially with those who feel that they are called "[to share] specific aspects and moments of the spirituality and mission of the Institute."[29] In this way, Institutes of consecrated life and Societies of apostolic life involved in education will manage to assure an essential openness to the Church and keep alive the spirit of the Founders and Foundresses, while also renewing a particularly precious aspect of the tradition of the Catholic school. From the very beginning, in fact, Founders and Foundresses paid special attention to the *formation of the educators* and they often devoted their best energies to this. Such formation, then as now, is not only aimed at strengthening professional skills, but above all, at highlighting the vocational dimension of the teaching profession, promoting the development of a mentality that is inspired by evangelical values, according to the specific characteristics of the Institute's mission. Therefore, "formation programs which include regular courses of study and prayerful reflection on the founder, the charism and the constitutions of the institute are particularly beneficial."[30]

28 In many religious Institutes, sharing the educational mission with the laity has already existed for some time, having been born with the religious community present in the school. The development of "spiritual families", of groups of "associated lay people" or other forms that permit the lay faithful to draw spiri-

---

28. Cf. Vatican Council II, Dogmatic Constitution on Divine Revelation *Dei Verbum* (18th November 1965), no. 10: *AAS* 58 (1966), 822.

29. Congregation for Institutes of Consecrated Life and Societies of Apostolic Life, *Starting Afresh from Christ*, no. 31.

30. Congregation for Institutes of Consecrated Life and Societies of Apostolic Life, *Fraternal Life in Community*, (2nd February 1994), no. 45.

tual and apostolic fruitfulness from the original charism, appears as a positive element and one of great hope for the future of the Catholic educational mission.

29 It is almost superfluous to note that, within the perspective of the Church-communion, these programs of formation for sharing in the mission and lives of the laity, in the light of the relative charism, should be designed and implemented even where vocations to the consecrated life are numerous.

The Contribution of Lay Persons to Shared Formation

30 While invited to deepen their vocation as educators in the Catholic school in communion with consecrated persons, the lay faithful also are called in the common formational journey to give the original and irreplaceable contribution of their full ecclesial subjectivity. This involves, first and foremost, that they discover and live in their "life of a lay person [...] a specific 'wonderful' vocation within the Church"[31]: the vocation to "seek the kingdom of God by engaging in temporal affairs and directing them according to God's will."[32] As educators they are called on to live "in faith a secular vocation in the communitarian structure of the school: with the best possible professional qualifications, with an apostolic intention inspired by faith, for the integral formation of the human person."[33]

31 It should be emphasized that the special contribution that lay educators can bring to the formational journey derives precisely from their secular nature that makes them especially able to grasp "the signs of the times."[34] In fact, by living their faith in the everyday conditions of their families and society, they can help the entire educational community to distinguish more precisely the evangelical values and the opposite values that these signs contain.

32 With the gradual development of their ecclesial vocation, lay people become increasingly more aware of their participation in the educational mission of the Church. At the same time, they are also driven to carry out an active role in the spiritual animation of the community that they build together with the consecrated persons. "Communion and mutuality in the Church are never

31. Sacred Congregation for Catholic Education, *Lay Catholics in Schools: Witnesses to Faith*, no. 7.

32. Vatican Council II, Dogmatic Constitution on the Church *Lumen Gentium* (21st November 1964), n. 31: *AAS* 57 (1965), 37.

33. Sacred Congregation for Catholic Education, *Lay Catholics in Schools: Witnesses to Faith*, no. 24.

34. Vatican Council II, Pastoral Constitution on the Church in the Modern World *Gaudium et Spes*, n. 4: *AAS* 58 (1966), 1027.

one way streets."[35] If, in fact, in the past it was mostly priests and religious who spiritually nourished and directed the lay faithful, now it is often "the lay faithful themselves [who] can and should help priests and religious in the course of their spiritual and pastoral journey."[36]

33 In the perspective of formation, by sharing their life of prayer and opportune forms of community life, the lay faithful and consecrated persons will nourish their reflection, their sense of fraternity and generous dedication. In this common catechetical-theological and spiritual formational journey, we can see the face of a Church that presents that of Christ, praying, listening, learning and teaching in fraternal communion.

Formation in the Spirit of Communion for Educating

34 By its very nature, the Catholic school requires the presence and involvement of educators that are not only culturally and spiritually formed, but also intentionally directed at developing their community educational commitment in an authentic spirit of ecclesial communion.

35 It is also through their formational journey that educators are called on to build relationships at professional, personal and spiritual levels, according to the logic of communion. For each one this involves being open, welcoming, disposed to a deep exchange of ideas, convivial and living a fraternal life within the educational community itself. The parable of the talents (*Matt.* 25:14–30) helps us to understand how each one is called to make his or her gifts bear fruit and to welcome the riches of others within the shared educational mission.

36 The shared mission, besides, is enriched by the differences that the lay faithful and consecrated persons bring when they come together in different expressions of charism. These charisms are none other than different gifts with which the same Spirit enriches the Church and the world.[37] In the Catholic school, therefore, "by avoiding both confrontation and homologation, the reciprocity of vocations seems to be a particularly fertile prospect for enriching the ecclesial value of educational communities. In them the various vocations [...] are correlative, different and mutual paths that converge to bring to fulfilment the charism of charisms: love."[38]

---

35. Congregation for Institutes of Consecrated Life and Societies of Apostolic Life, *Starting Afresh from Christ*, no. 31.

36. John Paul II, Post-synodal Apostolic Exhortation *Christifideles Laici*, no. 61: AAS 81 (1989), 514.

37. Cf. Congregation for Institutes of Consecrated Life and Societies of Apostolic Life, *Fraternal Life in Community* (2nd February 1994), no. 45.

38. Congregation for Catholic Education, *Consecrated Persons and their Mission in Schools*, no. 21.

37 Organized according to the diversities of persons and vocations, but vivified by the same spirit of communion, the educational community of the Catholic school aims at creating increasingly deeper relationships of communion that are in themselves educational. Precisely in this, it "expresses the variety and beauty of the various vocations and the fruitfulness at educational and pedagogical levels that this contributes to the life of the school."[39]

Witness and Culture of Communion

38 This fruitfulness is expressed, above all, in the witness offered by the educational community. Certainly in schools, education is essentially accomplished through teaching, which is the vehicle through which ideas and beliefs are communicated. In this sense, "words are the main roads in educating the mind."[40] This does not mean, however, that education is not accomplished in other situations of scholastic life. Thus teachers, just like every person who lives and works in a scholastic environment, educate, or they can also dis-educate, with their verbal and non-verbal behavior. "The central figure in the work of educating, and especially in education in the faith, which is the summit of the person's formation and is his or her most appropriate horizon, is specifically the form of witness."[41] "More than ever this demands that witness, nourished by prayer, be the all-encompassing milieu of every Catholic school. Teachers, as witnesses, account for the hope that nourishes their own lives (cf. *1 Pt* 3:15) by living the truth they propose to their pupils, always in reference to the one they have encountered and whose dependable goodness they have sampled with joy. And so with Saint Augustine they say: 'We who speak and you who listen acknowledge ourselves as fellow disciples of a single teacher' (*Sermons*, 23:2)."[42] In educational communities, therefore, the style of life has great influence, especially if the consecrated persons and the lay faithful work together, fully sharing the commitment to develop, in the school, "an atmosphere animated by a spirit of liberty and charity based on the Gospel."[43] This requires that each one contributes the specific gift of his or her vocation to construct a family supported by charity and by the spirit of the beatitudes.

39. *Ibid.*, n. 43.
40. Benedict XVI, Speech to the Representatives of some Muslim Communities (20th August 2005): *AAS* 97 (2005), 918.
41. Benedict XVI, Address to Rome's Ecclesial Diocesan Convention on the Family and Christian Community (6th June 2005): *AAS* 97 (2005), 815.
42. Benedict XVI, Speech to the Bishops of Ontario, Canada, on their *ad limina Apostolorum* Visit (8th September 2006): *L'Osservatore Romano* (9th September 2006), 9.
43. Vatican Council II, Declaration on Christian Education *Gravissimum Educationis*, no. 8: *AAS* 58 (1966), 734.

39 By giving witness of communion, the Catholic educational community is able to *educate for communion*, which, as a gift that comes from above, animates the project of formation for living together in harmony and being welcoming. Not only does it cultivate in the students the cultural values that derive from the Christian vision of reality, but it also involves each one of them in the life of the community, where values are mediated by authentic interpersonal relationships among the various members that form it, and by the individual and community acceptance of them. In this way, the life of communion of the educational community assumes the value of an educational principle, of a paradigm that directs its formational action as a service for the achievement of a culture of communion. Education in the Catholic school, therefore, through the tools of teaching and learning, "is not given for the purpose of gaining power but as an aid towards a fuller understanding of, and communion with man, events and things."[44] This principle affects every scholastic activity, the teaching and even all the after-school activities such as sport, theatre and commitment in social work, which promote the creative contribution of the students and their socialization.

Educational Community and Vocational Pastoral Activity

40 The shared mission experienced by an educational community of lay and consecrated persons, with an active vocational conscience, makes the Catholic school a pedagogical place that favors *vocational pastoral activity*. The very composition of such an educational community of a Catholic school highlights the diversity and complementarity of vocations in the Church,[45] of which it, too, is an expression. In this sense, the communitarian dynamics of the formational experience become the horizon where the student can feel what it means to be a member of the biggest community which is the Church. And to experience the Church means to personally meet the living Christ in it: "a young man can truly understand Christ's will and his own vocation only to the extent that he has a personal experience of Christ."[46] In this sense, the Catholic school is committed to guiding its students to knowing themselves, their attitudes and their interior resources, educating them in spending their lives responsibly as a daily response to God's call. Thus, the Catholic school accompanies its students in conscious choices of life: to follow their vocation to the priesthood or to consecrated life or to accomplish their Christian vocation in family, professional and social life.

44. Sacred Congregation for Catholic Education, *The Catholic School*, no. 56.
45. Cf. John Paul II, Post-synodal Apostolic Exhortation *Christifideles Laici*, no. 20: *AAS* 81 (1989), 425.
46. Benedict XVI, Address to Seminarians (19th August 2005): *AAS* 97 (2005), 880.

41 In fact, the daily dialogue and confrontation with lay and consecrated educators, who offer a joyful witness of their calling, will more easily direct a young person in formation to consider his or her life as a vocation, as a journey to be lived together, grasping the signs through which God leads to the fullness of existence. Similarly, it will make him or her understand how necessary it is to know how to listen, to interiorize values, to learn to assume commitments and make life choices.

42 Therefore, the formational experience of the Catholic school constitutes an impressive barrier against the influence of a widespread mentality that leads young people especially "to consider themselves and their lives as a series of sensations to be experienced rather than as a work to be accomplished."[47] At the same time, it contributes to insuring strong character formation [. . .] capable both of resisting the debilitating influence of relativism and of living up to the demands made on them by their Baptism."[48]

III. COMMUNION FOR OPENING ONESELF TOWARDS OTHERS

43 The communion lived by the educators of the Catholic school contributes to making the entire educational sphere a place of communion open to external reality and not just closed in on itself. *Educating in communion* and *for communion* means directing students to grow authentically as persons who "gradually learn to open themselves up to life as it is, and to create in themselves a definite attitude to life"[49] that will help them to open their views and their hearts to the world that surrounds them, able to see things critically, with a sense of responsibility and a desire for a constructive commitment. Two orders of motivation, anthropological and theological, form the basis of this opening towards the world.

Anthropological and Theological Foundations

44 The human being, as a person, is a unity of soul and body that is dynamically realized through its opening to a relation with others. A person is formed for *being-with* and *for-others*, which is realized in love. Now, it is precisely love that drives a person to gradually broaden the range of his or her relations beyond the sphere of private life and family affections, to assume the range of universality and to embrace—at least by desire—all mankind. This same drive

---

47. John Paul II, Encyclical Letter *Centesimus Annus* (1st May 1991), n. 39: *AAS* 83 (1991), 842.

48. Sacred Congregation for Catholic Education, *The Catholic School*, no. 12.

49. *Ibid.*, no. 31.

also contains a strong formational requirement: the requirement to learn to read the interdependence of a world that is increasingly besieged by the same problems of a global nature, as a strong ethical sign for the people of our time; like a call to emerge from that vision of man that tends to see each one as an isolated individual. It is the requirement to form man as a person: a subject that in love builds his historical, cultural, spiritual and religious identity, placing it in dialogue with other persons, in a constant exchange of gifts offered and received. Within the context of globalization, people must be formed in such a way as to respect the identity, culture, history, religion and especially the suffering and needs of others, conscious that "we are all really responsible for all."[50]

45 This requirement assumes even more importance and urgency within the sphere of the Catholic *faith*, experienced in the *love* of ecclesial *communion*. In fact, the Church, the place of communion and image of Trinitarian love, "is alive with the love enkindled by the Spirit of Christ."[51] The Spirit acts as an "interior power" that harmonizes the hearts of believers with Christ's heart and "transforms the heart of the ecclesial community, so that it becomes a witness before the world to the love of the Father."[52] Thus, "beginning with intra-ecclesial communion, charity of its nature opens out into a service that is universal; it inspires in us *a commitment to practical and concrete love for every human being*."[53] In this sense, the Church is not an end in itself, it exists to show God to the world; it exists for others.

46 In the same way, inasmuch as it is an ecclesial subject, the Catholic school acts as the Christian ferment of the world. In it, students learn to overcome individualism and to discover, in the light of faith, that they are called to live responsibly a specific vocation to friendship with Christ and in solidarity with other persons. Basically, the school is called to be a living witness of the love of God among us. It can, moreover, become a means through which it is possible to discern, in the light of the Gospel, what is positive in the world, what needs to be transformed and what injustices must be overcome. A vigilant acceptance of the contributions of the world to the life of the school also nourishes and promotes open communion, especially in some educational environments, such as education to peace, to living together, to justice and to brotherhood.

---

50. John Paul II, Encyclical Letter *Sollicitudo Rei Socialis* (30th December 1987), no. 38: *AAS* 80 (1988), 566.

51. Benedict XVI, Encyclical Letter *Deus Caritas Est*, no. 28b: *AAS* 98 (2006), 240.

52. *Ibid.*, no. 19: 233.

53. John Paul II, Apostolic Letter *Novo Millennio Ineunte*, no. 49: *AAS* 93 (2001), 302.

Builders of Open Communion

47 Sharing the same educational mission with a diversity of persons, vocations and states of life is undoubtedly a strong point of the Catholic school in its participation in the missionary life of the Church, in the opening of ecclesial communion towards the world. In this respect, a first precious contribution comes from communion between lay and consecrated faithful in the school.

Lay persons who, because of their family and social relationships, live immersed in the world, can promote the opening of the educational community to a constructive relationship with cultural, civil and political institutions, with various social groups—from the most informal ones to those most organized—present in the territory. The Catholic school also assures its presence in the locality through its active cooperation with other educational institutions, especially with Catholic centers for higher studies, with which they share a special ecclesial bond, and with local bodies and various social agencies. In this sphere, faithful to its inspiration, it contributes to building a network of relationships that helps students to develop their sense of belonging, and society itself to develop a sense of solidarity.

Consecrated persons also participate, as "true signs of Christ in the world,"[54] in this opening to the outside world by sharing the gifts they bear. They must demonstrate especially that religious consecration has much to say to every culture in that it helps to reveal the truth of the human being. The witness of their evangelical life must reveal that "holiness is the highest humanizing proposal of man and of history; it is a project that *everyone* on earth can make his or her own."[55]

48 Another pillar of *open communion* is formed by the relationship between the Catholic school and the families that choose it for the education of their children. This relationship appears as full participation of the parents in the life of the educational community, not only because of their primary responsibility in the education of their children, but also by virtue of their sharing in the identity and project that characterize the Catholic school and which they must know and share with a readiness that comes from within. It is precisely because of this that the educational community identifies the decisive space for cooperation between school and family in the *educational project*, to be made known and implemented with a spirit of communion, through the contribution of everyone, discerning responsibilities, roles and competences. Parents in particular are required to enrich the communion around this project, making the

---

54. John Paul II, Post-synodal Apostolic Exhortation *Vita Consecrata*, no. 25: *AAS* 88 (1996), 398.

55. Congregation for Catholic Education, *Consecrated Persons and their Mission in Schools*, no. 12.

family climate that must characterize the educating community more alive and explicit. For this reason, in willingly welcoming parents' cooperation, Catholic schools consider essential to their mission the service of *permanent formation offered to families*, to support them in their educating task and to develop an increasingly closer bond between the values proposed by the school and those proposed by the family.

49 The Christian-inspired associations and groups that unite the parents of Catholic schools represent a further bridge between the educational community and the world that surrounds it. These associations and groups can strengthen the bond of reciprocity between school and society, maintaining the educational community open to the wider social community and, at the same time, creating an awareness in society and its institutions of the presence and action carried out by Catholic schools in the territory.

50 At an ecclesial level also, the communion experienced within the Catholic school can and must be open to an enriching exchange in a more extensive communion with the parish, the diocese, ecclesial movements and the universal Church. This means that lay persons (educators and parents) and consecrated persons belonging to the educational community must take a meaningful part, even outside the walls of the Catholic school, in the life of the local Church. The members of the diocesan clergy and the lay persons of the local Christian community, who do not always have an adequate knowledge of the Catholic school, must discover it as a *school of the Christian community*, a living expression of the same Church of Christ to which they belong.

51 If lived authentically and profoundly, the ecclesial dimension of the educational community of the Catholic school cannot be limited to a relationship with the local Christian community. Almost by natural extension, it tends to open onto the horizons of the universal Church. In this sense, the international dimension of many religious families offers consecrated persons the enrichment of communion with those who share the same mission in various parts of the world. At the same time, it offers a witness to the living strength of a charism that unites, over and above all, differences. The richness of this communion in the universal Church can and must be shared, for example, through regional or world level formational occasions and meetings. These should also involve lay persons (educators and parents) who, because of their state of life, share the educational mission of the relative charisms.

52 Structured in this way, the Catholic school appears as an educational community in which ecclesial and missionary communion develops in depth and grows in breadth. A communion can be experienced in it that becomes an effective witness to the presence of Christ alive in the educational community gathered together in His name (cf. *Matt* 18:20) and that, precisely for this reason, opens to a deeper understanding of reality and a more convinced commitment to renewal of the world. In fact, "if we think and live by virtue of communion with Christ, then our eyes will be opened,"[56] and we will understand that "real revolution, the decisive change in the world, comes from God."[57]

53 The communion experienced in the educational community, animated and sustained by lay and consecrated persons joined together in the same mission, makes the Catholic school a community environment filled with the spirit of the Gospel. Now, this community environment appears as a privileged place for the formation of young people in the construction of a world based on dialogue and the search for communion, rather than in contrast; on the mutual acceptance of differences rather than on their opposition. In this way, with its educational project taking inspiration from *ecclesial communion and the civilization of love*, the Catholic school can contribute considerably to illuminating the minds of many, so that "there will arise a generation of new persons, the molders of a new humanity."[58]

Conclusion

54 "In a world where cultural challenge is the first, the most provocative and the most effect-bearing,"[59] the Catholic school is well aware of the onerous commitments it is called to face and it preserves its utmost importance even in present circumstances.

55 When it is animated by lay and consecrated persons that live the same educational mission in sincere unity, the Catholic school shows the face of a community that tends towards an increasingly deeper communion. This communion knows how to be welcoming with regard to people as they mature, making them feel, through the maternal solicitude of the Church, that God carries the life of each son and daughter of His in His heart. It knows how to involve young people in a global formation experience, to direct and accompany, in the

---

56. Benedict XVI, Homily during the Eucharistic Celebration in Marienfeld (21st August 2005): *AAS* 97 (2005), 892.

57. Benedict XVI, Homily at the Prayer Vigil in Marienfeld (20th August 2005): *AAS* 97 (2005), 885.

58. Vatican Council II, Pastoral Constitution on the Church in the Modern World *Gaudium et Spes*, no. 30: *AAS* 58 (1966), 1050.

59. John Paul II, Speech to Parents, Students and Teachers of Catholic Schools (23rd November 1991), n. 6: *AAS* 84 (1992), 1136.

light of the Good News, their search for meaning, even in unusual and often tortuous forms, but with an alarming urgency. A communion, finally, that inasmuch as it is based on Christ, acknowledges Him and announces Him to each and everyone as the only true Master (cf. *Matt* 23:8).

56 In presenting this document to those who live the educational mission in the Church, we entrust all Catholic schools to the Virgin Mary, Mother and educator of Christ and of persons, so that, like the servants at the wedding of Cana, they may humbly follow her loving invitation: "Do whatever He tells you" (*Jn* 2:5) and may they, thus, be together with the whole Church, "the home and the school of communion"[60] for the men and women of our time.

The Holy Father, during the Audience granted to the undersigned Prefect, approved this document and authorized its publication.

Rome, 8ᵗʰ September 2007, Feast of the Nativity of the Blessed Virgin Mary.

Zenon Card. Grocholewski, *Prefect*
Msgr. Angelo Vincenzo Zani, *Undersecretary*

---

60. John Paul II, Apostolic Letter *Novo Millennio Ineunte*, n. 43: *AAS* 93 (2001), 296.

THE DOMINICAN TRADITION

Father Thomas C. McGonigle, O.P.

The Dominican Tradition has its origin in the life and ministry of St. Dominic de Guzmán (1170–1221), the son of a Spanish noble, who founded one of the largest Orders in the Catholic Church. Dominic's charismatic vision of a way of responding to the needs of the church in the thirteenth century led to the establishment of the Order of Preachers, popularly known as the Dominicans.

The Thirteenth-Century World of Saint Dominic

The growth of an increasingly literate laity within the urban centers of thirteenth-century Italy and southern France posed a serious pastoral problem for the medieval church. These urbanized men and women experienced a strong dichotomy between the New Testament values of Christian life and the institutional church. The simplicity of Gospel living portrayed in the Acts of the Apostles, with its emphasis on shared common life and the preaching of the Good News of Jesus Christ in poverty, appealed to the hearts and minds of many and seemed to stand in stark contrast to the opulent lifestyle and moral laxity that often marked the clergy.

Because parish priests and the monks of the great abbeys seemed unable or unwilling to respond to their people's needs for forms of Christian life and spirituality more in accord with the apostolic life presented in the New Testament, the laity of the late twelfth and early thirteenth centuries in parts of France and Italy turned away from the institutional church in increasing numbers. Lay movements, such as the Poor Men of Lyons organized by Peter Valdes (d. 1218), who came to be called the Waldensians, offered an alternative form of Christian living that sought to imitate the simple life of the early church by an exact following of the gospel narratives on poverty and preaching.

At the same time the dualist doctrine of the third-century Persian religious thinker Mani (216–276) began to resurface in Western Europe. Medieval followers of his dualism were called Manichees, Cathars, or Albigensians (from the town of Albi in southern France where dualism took hold). The Albigensians rejected most doctrines of the medieval church and taught that salvation was achieved by freeing oneself from everything material through a life of asceticism. The teachers of the movement, the Perfect, lived austere lives with special emphasis on fasting, chastity, poverty, and preaching.

The simultaneous emergence of the Waldensians and the Albigensians created the need for forms of Christian life and spirituality that provided patterns of Gospel living in accord with the traditional teachings of Christianity. Francis of Assisi (1182–1226) in Italy and Dominic de Guzmán (1170–1221) in Spain provided charismatic visions that would capture the ideals of the Gospel in new ways and draw many of the reform-minded men and women of the urban lay movements away from the Waldensians and the Albigensians and back into the medieval Catholic Church.

Saint Dominic, Canon Regular and Itinerant Preacher

Dominic de Guzmán completed his theological studies and was ordained a priest at Palencia in 1196. He became a Canon Regular (a member of a community of priests following the Rule of St. Augustine) of the cathedral of Osma in Spain. In 1203 Dominic encountered the Albigensians of southern France while on a diplomatic mission with his bishop, Diego de Acebes, to arrange a marriage between the son of King Alfonso VIII of Castile and the daughter of the King of Denmark. After the marriage negotiations failed in 1205, Dominic and Diego stopped at the papal court in Rome on their way back to Spain. Pope Innocent III (1198–1216) sent them to be part of the preaching mission against the Albigensians in Languedoc, the south of France. The nine years between 1206 and 1215 he spent preaching among the Albigensians taught Dominic a great deal about the impact of the Perfect on their followers. These years also served as the germinating period for the development of a charismatic vision of a way of living the Gospel in accord with the Christian faith that would appeal to the deepest ideals and needs of the men and women of his time.

Dominic's Vision of the Family of Contemplative Preachers

Dominic was guided by the image of the early Christian community in Jerusalem in the opening chapters of the Acts of the Apostles, which was at the heart of the spirituality he had known as a Canon Regular. He believed that the renewal of Christian society necessitated communities of men and women committed to living the apostolic life. The major component of that apostolic life was to be the preaching of the Gospel by members of communities that lived in evangelical poverty, who were devoted to contemplative prayer and engaged in constant study of the word of God. In Dominic's understanding, preachers were called to be the living reflection of the Gospel they proclaimed. Hence for him the vows of chastity, poverty, and obedience were meant to recreate and transform the preacher into an apostle, a living witness to the crucified and risen Lord, Jesus Christ.

During his early years of preaching in Languedoc, Dominic gathered a group of Albigensian women whom he had converted to form the nucleus of the first community of Dominican nuns. Through a life of contemplative prayer lived in a community dedicated to poverty and mutual service these Dominican women would incarnate the apostolic life and preach the Gospel by their witness to prayer and service. Although the Order of Preachers did not yet have official status, the first community of Dominican women at Prouille in the south of France, the preaching nuns, initiated an evolutionary development in which countless women in the centuries to come in collaboration with their Dominican brothers would fully participate in and help develop the life and ministry of the Order of Preachers, the Dominican family.

The Foundation of the Order of Friars Preachers

After the establishment of the Dominican nuns at Prouille, Dominic continued the implementation of his vision of communities of contemplative preachers living the apostolic life. In the spring of 1215, at the invitation of Bishop Fulk of Toulouse in southern France, Dominic brought the men who were his preaching companions in Languedoc to this important city to establish a formal religious community there under the direction of the bishop. Later in 1215, when Bishop Fulk set out to attend the Fourth Lateran Council in Rome, Dominic accompanied him, hoping to obtain papal approval for his new community of contemplative preachers. In accord with the legislation of the Council, Pope Innocent III promised Dominic that he would approve the founding of the new Order of Preachers after Dominic had chosen one of the already existing Rules of religious life.

As a Canon Regular of Osma, Dominic was already following the Rule of St. Augustine. He supplemented this rule with legislation and customs borrowed from the Premonstratensians, an order of Canons Regular founded by St. Norbert at Premontré in 1120, who supported his own vision of the apostolic life sustained by liturgical prayer. The spirituality of the Canons Regular was that of a community of religious priests who dedicated themselves to carrying out the daily liturgy of the church through the solemn celebration of Mass and the Divine Office and to caring for the sacramental needs of the faithful. Dominic joined these priestly ideals of the Canons Regular to a ministry of preaching in poverty (mendicancy) that flowed from a life of contemplation and study.

In December 1216, Pope Honorius III (1216–1227), the successor of Innocent III, approved Dominic's plan for an order of contemplative preachers exercising the priestly ministry and living in mendicant poverty. They owned no property except for the land on which their religious houses (priories) were built, and they were to work or beg for their daily needs. In the final four-and-a-half years of his life Dominic transformed the sixteen friars living in community at Toulouse into the international Order of Preachers whose lives and ministry would impact history until the present.

The Development of the Order of Preachers

In August 1217, Dominic sent seven friars to Paris to study, to teach, and to found a priory, and four to Spain to preach and establish priories. Three friars remained in Toulouse to continue the ministry they had begun under Bishop Fulk, and two friars went to Prouille to preach in Languedoc and to minister to the spiritual and temporal needs of the preaching nuns. Dominic himself set out for Rome to gain further support from Pope Honorius and to prepare the way for foundations in Italy. The years from 1217 to 1220 saw the growth of the Order through the reception of new members, the establishment of new priories, and the development of the preaching mission of the Order throughout Europe.

Under Dominic's direction, thirty representatives from the twelve priories in Europe gathered for General Chapters at Bologna in 1220 and 1221. The General Chapter of 1220 enacted legislation for preaching, formation of new members, studies, the observance of poverty, and the procedures for General Chapters. Dominic insisted that the Order's laws were not to bind under sin, and that the Priors had the power to dispense from the Order's laws when necessary for the sake of preaching or study.

The General Chapter of 1221 created Provinces as subdivisions of the Order; these would gather the priories of a certain geographic area under the authority of a Provincial, who was responsible to the Master of the Order. The twelve Provinces established by St. Dominic and the General Chapter were Spain, Provence, France, Lombardy, Tuscany, Germany, Hungary, England, Greece, Scandinavia, Poland, and the Holy Land. However, the most significant work of the Chapter, which ended six weeks before Dominic's death, was the formulation of the basic constitutional legislation that would concretize his vision and provide the flexibility for the subsequent development of the preaching mission of the Order.

The Dominican Family

The breadth and universality of Dominic's vision made it possible to incorporate a variety of men and women into the Dominican family. Traditionally the Order of Preachers has been divided into the First Order, the Second Order, and the Third Order.

The First Order, the Friars, is composed of clerical brothers and lay brothers. Clerical brothers are friars who are either priests engaged in ministry or students preparing for the priesthood. Cooperator brothers (formerly called lay brothers) are friars who once cared for the temporal needs of the community but who now also serve in a variety of other ministries, including the diaconate.

The Second Order is composed of contemplative nuns living in cloistered monasteries, usually under the jurisdiction of the local bishop. The Master of the Order also provides oversight and support for the nuns in their contemplative life.

The Third Order, which came into existence at the end of the thirteenth century, is divided into the Third Order Regular and the Third Order Secular. The Third Order Regular was initially composed of women who chose to live Dominican religious life without the strict rules of a cloistered monastery. In the nineteenth century the Third Order Regular also came to include Papal and Diocesan Congregations of Dominican Sisters established to engage in active ministries of service such as education and health care. Members of the Third Order Secular, originally called Tertiaries and now called the Dominican laity, are lay men and women living in the world. Their Rule states that "As members of the Order, they participate in its apostolic mission through prayer, study, and preaching according to the state of the laity."

Dominican Spirituality

The *Fundamental Constitution of the Order* (1968) reaffirms the preaching mission of the Order—"preaching and the salvation of souls"—and the means to attain this mission: (1) the three vows of obedience, chastity, and poverty; (2) community life with the monastic observances; (3) the solemn recitation of the Divine Office; and (4) the study of sacred truth.

The Vows of Obedience, Chastity, and Poverty

The purpose of the three vows within religious life is to free the individual to follow Jesus Christ. From the Dominican perspective the vows of obedience, chastity, and poverty free a man or woman to live the mystery of Jesus Christ the preacher. Dominican friars promise obedience to the Master of the Order, who is chosen by the brothers to hold the place of universal leadership once held by St. Dominic. The Order of Preachers views obedience as a relationship of mutual service between brothers committed to the common mission of preaching the Gospel. The Prior is the superior at the local level, the Provincial is the superior at the regional level, and the Master of the Order is the superior at the international level. Each serves as a focal point of unity and direction in the shared mission of preaching. Dominican obedience is the free choice of placing one's gifts at the disposal of the community, symbolized by the superior, for the sake of fulfilling the common preaching mission of the Order.

In the Dominican tradition the vow of chastity, like the vows of obedience and poverty, is related to the preaching mission of the Order. A Dominican man or woman chooses to live a celibate life within a community of contemplative preachers in order to share the family life of the Gospel community formed by the Holy Spirit through the proclamation and hearing of the word of God. A Dominican lives both in the family of other Dominican men and women committed to preaching and in the family of God's people, which he or she helps to create and sustain through the preaching of the Good News of Jesus Christ.

Since the lay movements of the thirteenth century saw evangelical poverty lived in apostolic simplicity as the guarantor of authentic preaching, the vow of poverty assumed special meaning within the Dominican tradition. Dominican friars were to be itinerant preachers living in mendicant poverty, to give up all possessions and fixed income, and to rely completely on the freewill offerings of the faithful. Each day the friars went out as mendicants begging for alms and their daily bread.

Community Life and the Monastic Observances

As the three vows of obedience, chastity, and poverty were understood as the first means of fulfilling the preaching mission of the Order, so community life with the monastic observances was seen to be the second means. The monastic observances within religious life, which Dominic received from the tradition of Benedictine monasticism, were silence, fasting, abstinence from meat, night vigils, the chapter of faults, acts of penance, and simplicity in religious attire and community life. Within the Dominican tradition the monastic observances provide a disciplined milieu in which contemplative preachers keep the word of God clearly focused in their minds and hearts as they prepare to engage in their ministry of preaching.

The Solemn Recitation of the Divine Office

The solemn recitation of the Divine Office, the Liturgy of the Hours, the third means of facilitating the preaching of the Gospel, centered the worship life of the community on the word of God. As a Canon Regular, Dominic had known the solemn celebration of the eight hours of the Divine Office: Matins, Lauds, Prime, Terce, Sext, None, Vespers, and Compline. With its patterns of hymns, psalms, Scripture readings, and prayers, the Office provided the place where a religious community daily encountered the word of God as it proclaimed the mysteries of salvation in the unfolding of the liturgical year. Daily Mass and the Divine Office constituted the common prayer of the community of contemplative preachers. Gathered together for prayer in common, they experienced the life-giving water of the word of God and the living bread of the Holy Eucharist. This daily nourishment of word and sacrament strengthened and renewed the community of contemplative preachers so that they could share the same living water and bread of life with the people to whom they preached and ministered. The common praise of God and the hearing of the Good News were meant to be joyous occasions of new life and empowerment for ministry, which also would be strengthened by the fourth means of facilitating the preaching mission of the Order, the life of study.

The Study of Sacred Truth

The renewal of Christian life in the thirteenth century with its developing urban centers and its nascent universities not only required preachers who practiced poverty but also preachers who were learned in Scripture and the teachings of the church. For St. Dominic, study was essential to ensure the doctrinal preaching that was necessary to deal adequately with the intellectual challenge to the Catholic faith offered by the Waldensians and the Albigensians. The integral place of study in the Dominican tradition would give the preaching friars a profound role in the development of the great universities of medieval Europe. Every Dominican priory was a school for training contemplative preachers in Scripture and theology. The Dominican Order would provide the church with some of its greatest theologians and speculative thinkers, such as St. Albert the Great, St. Thomas Aquinas, Meister Eckhart, and St. Antoninus.

The vows of obedience, chastity, and poverty; community life with the monastic observances; the celebration of the Divine Office; and continuous study of Scripture and the truths of faith were meant to provide the contemplative basis for Dominican preaching. The fulfillment of St. Dominic's vision of a community of contemplative preachers requires a careful balancing so that both the active-preaching dimension and the contemplative-prayer-study dimension are held in creative tension.

This common framework for understanding the Dominican tradition in terms of the end and the four means was in use from the thirteenth century until 1968. The General Chapter of 1968 kept the traditional understanding for the First Order, but left the Second and Third Orders free to adapt the traditional understanding to their own Dominican experience in their own Constitutions. Hence while the Fundamental Constitution of the Order presents the guiding vision for the whole Dominican family, the Second Order (nuns) and the Third Order Regular (sisters) and Third Order Secular (laity) each have their own Constitutions that articulate their appropriation of the Fundamental Constitution. Thus congregations of Dominican sisters and the Dominican laity in the United States present the Four Elements or Four Pillars in many revised Constitutions in the 1970s: community, prayer, study, and ministry. In these perspectives the vows are subsumed under the larger umbrella of community. The discussion of community includes the vows, prayer and study follow next, and everything is drawn together in ministry.

Independent of the various emphases placed on the guiding vision of St. Dominic, all Dominican men and women commit themselves through vows or promises to live in communities where common prayer and study enable them to preach the Gospel through diverse forms of ministry.

A DOMINICAN PHILOSOPHY OF EDUCATION

Father Philip A. Smith, O.P.

Introduction

Any school's philosophy of education flows from its mission statement. In broad and inspirational terms, that document expresses a school's nature and character, its ideals and values, and its relation to the broader community. A philosophy of education concretizes these aspirations in specific educational goals and objectives that describe its purposes, its expected outcomes and its preferred methods of instruction. Success depends on how well the outcomes match the goals and objectives sought.

Dominican education is necessarily complex because it comes in all shapes and sizes: from elementary to graduate, from preaching to professional. In addition, it embraces not only theology and philosophy but also art and architecture, literature and spirituality, history and health care. It is virtually impossible to fashion a single philosophy of education broad enough to embrace all these efforts. However, some general influences are common to all.

A philosophy of education cannot be created out of whole cloth. Since St Dominic himself stood "*in medio ecclesiae*," the Dominican tradition should be rooted in and shaped by the broader intellectual, spiritual and cultural tradition of the Church from which it emerged. In sketching a philosophy of education, I locate it within the Catholic tradition and continue by exploring themes central to Dominic's vision that apply to education. I trace notable educational developments of the tradition in Thomas Aquinas and then examine Avila's insight of ministry on the "frontiers." I conclude with Providence College's effort to incorporate a Dominican philosophy of education. Other Dominicans could appeal to insights and examples of Dominicans other than Aquinas to fashion different philosophies of education. They would be equally Dominican but tailored to their particular ministries.

The Catholic Tradition

If a Dominican philosophy of education stems from and continues the Catholic intellectual and spiritual tradition, the meaning of "tradition" is important. We cannot appreciate any tradition simply by exploring its origins. Its nature and evolution must be traced as it interacted with the various individuals, schools of thought, religions, cultures and historical events that shaped it. Thus, far from being a sterile relic, the Catholic tradition is the record of the dynamic development of the Church's thought and spirituality, culture and structures over the centuries. Margaret Steinfels offered this helpful description of a tradition:

A tradition is . . . a focus for questioning, a framework for inquiry, a standard for preferring some sets of ideas over others; tradition is the record of the community's conversation over time about its meaning and direction. A living tradition is a tradition that can raise questions about itself.[1]

The Christian community's conversation "about itself" began in the Apostolic Age and was primarily spiritual in nature. As the first generation of believers reflected on the lived experience of their faith, they tried to understand it better by probing its meaning and mysteries: Who was Jesus of Nazareth? What did His message mean? What was the salvation God accomplished in Him? Did His resurrection prove that He was God? If there could be only one God, how could Jesus also be God? How was their faith related to their way of life?

The conversations "about itself" also extended to the intellectual currents of the time. St Matthew sought to discover points of agreement between Christianity and the Jewish scholarly tradition (*Mt* 1:1–17, for example). St Paul used Greek and Roman concepts in his writings and engaged scholars in the Areopagus (*Acts* 22:17–33). St Justin Martyr, a philosopher and a convert to Christianity, defended his faith with philosophical reasoning that the Roman academics at his trial would understand. He made the Catholic intellectual tradition explicit.

As it developed, the Catholic tradition confronted two challenges that are important for this study: firstly, how are truths revealed by faith related to insights discovered by reason? Secondly, how can high moral standards be maintained in a morally lax society? Although the Christian faith originated in Jerusalem, it was lived out in a culture dominated by the intellectual climate of Athens. Justin Martyr found a role for both faith and reason. Faith is the only true philosophy. While reason can probe truths already revealed, the complete truth can be grasped only through faith.[2] An early Church Father, Tertullian, denied any relationship between reason and faith. His famous question, "What has Athens to do with Jerusalem?" has remained the abiding challenge for the Catholic tradition ever since.

The link between faith and daily life posed a second challenge for Christians. They lived in a culture bitterly opposed to their faith and practice, highly pluralistic in its religious beliefs and tolerant of various forms of immorality. Merely being a Christian was enough to arouse suspicion, ridicule or even persecution. The tension between a Catholic way of life and public perception of it has always posed a problem for the tradition.

---

1. Margaret Steinfels, "The Catholic Intellectual Tradition," *Origins* 25/11 (24 August 1995): 272.

2. Justin Martyr, *The Fathers of the Church,* (New York: Christian Heritage, Incorporated, 1948). Justin Martyr sets forth, at length, his understanding of the relation of philosophy and faith in several works, especially in "The First Apology," "The Second Apology," and his "Dialogue With Trypho."

The tradition developed through the community's conversations about itself, the influences of historical events and social movements and the insights of theologians and philosophers. Also influential were the examples of martyrs and saints, the teaching of Synods and Councils, the emergence of Schools and universities and contributions of religious men and women. The Dominican Order played an important role in this development.

St Dominic's Framework for a Philosophy of Education

Any Dominican approach to education must be rooted in and reflect Dominic's spirit and vision. Since he left virtually nothing in writing, we must rely largely on other historical sources to discover the outlines of what might be called his philosophy of education. Dominic had a very clear vision for his Order, what Dominicans should study and how they should be formed. His vision was influenced by his temperament, education and experience.

Study was always important to Dominic. At fourteen, he entered the prestigious school at Palencia where he studied liberal arts and theology, especially sacred scriptures, for the next decade. Although respected as learned, Dominic was more admired for his sanctity, compassion and generosity of spirit. While he was a student, Spain suffered a severe famine. Jordan of Saxony relates that Dominic "was deeply moved by the plight of the poor, and resolved, in . . . his compassion . . . to do as much as possible to remedy the needs of the poor who were dying."[3] He sold all his books to get money to aid the poor and feed the hungry. Impressed by Dominic's life and learning, Bishop Diego of Osma invited him to join his Cathedral Chapter in 1196.

A few years later, accompanying Bishop Diego on his diplomatic missions, Dominic was shocked and saddened by what he saw: the clergy too often poorly educated and lax, the Church threatened by ignorance and the popular Albigensian movement, and ordinary believers confused and spiritually hungry. These journeys were for Dominic defining experiences.

Albigensianism, rooted in dualism, proclaimed two equal and opposing gods. The good god, the savior, created the invisible world and spiritual beings who are incorruptible and indestructible. The evil god created the visible material world, including the human body which is corruptible and evil because it is material and imprisons the soul. The body, continued through sexual reproduction, remains defiled.

To avoid contamination, the elite Albigensians, the 'Perfecti', embraced extreme asceticism and poverty: they vowed sexual abstinence and refused to

---

3. Jordan of Saxony, *On the Beginnings of the Order of Preachers* (Dublin, Ireland: Dominican Publications, 1982), numbers 6–7, 10.

eat foods that involved sexual procreation.[4] Most people were incapable of such exalted lives. However, they could be saved by receiving the 'consolamentum', a sacrament administered by the *Perfecti* at the time of death. Albigensianism and the *Perfecti* were attractive alternatives to Christians who viewed some of the clergy as worldly, unlearned and insensitive. The *Perfecti*, however, were well informed, practiced what they preached, and were compassionate to the weaknesses of the majority.[5]

Albigensianism struck at the heart of Dominic's Christian beliefs. It undermined the goodness of creation and the sanctity of marriage by driving a wedge between spirit and matter, mind and body, sexuality and procreation. It demonized the human body and the incarnation; rendered the crucifixion and resurrection meaningless and distorted the salvation offered by Jesus. Dominic was convinced that the cure for this spiritual malaise was nothing less than a deep conversion of mind and heart, achievable only by informed and zealous preaching. Dominic felt called by God to preach to those who had abandoned Christianity for Albigensianism.

Dominic was consumed with the need to preach. We know little about his preaching except that sometimes it moved both his listeners and himself to tears. However, we know he used more than one method. He preached at every opportunity, in different places and to all classes of people: at Mass, in Church, in private homes. Throughout southern France, he participated in public disputations with *Perfecti* on doctrinal issues. On one occasion, he argued all night with an inn-keeper who had converted to Albigensianism, winning him back to the Church. Obviously, he was more concerned that the gospel be preached in a way that touched minds and hearts rather than about the particular method used.[6]

For Dominic, study was always devoted to the service of truth and the preaching of the gospel. However, he soon realized that knowledge alone was not enough. Discouraged papal legates, sent to preach against Albigensianism, had pointed to the stark contrast between the *Perfecti's* knowledge and example and the clergy's ignorance and laxity. In response, Dominic, and later his companions, identified with the poor and inspired them by preaching like the Apostles: humbly, barefooted and mendicant.[7] His preaching was successful

---

4. Guy Bedouelle, OP, *Saint Dominic: The Grace of the Word* (San Francisco: Ignatius Press, 1987): 172–4. Bedouelle cites a long passage from the Inquisitor, Jacques Fournier, on the doctrine. Later, Fournier became Pope Benedict XII. The citation is clear, informative and concise.

5. Bedouelle, *Saint Dominic*, 175–6.

6. Benedict Ashley, OP, *The Dominicans* (Collegeville, Minnesota: The Liturgical Press, 1990), 18–21.

7. HM Vicaire and Leonard von Mott, *St Dominic: A Pictorial Biography* (Chicago: Henry Regnery Company, 1957), 25–7.

only when the example of his life matched the power of his words. His work, penance, and fasting took their toll. Worn out, he died by the age of fifty.

Dominic's vision for his Order unfolded gradually and reflected his preaching experience in the company of his small band of early companions, at first around the Prouille monastery near Fanjeaux, and later in Toulouse. Here, we must mention briefly the important contributions of the nuns at Prouille through their hospitality, prayers and spirituality. Dominic had a special affection for them, returning there often for physical rest and spiritual renewal. The record of how these early "Preachers of Toulouse" became in 1216 and 1217 "champions of the faith and true lights" for the whole world, under papal protection, is documented in the various sources.[8] We need note here only that the "Order of Preachers" existed for the purpose of saving souls. Their mission was to refute error and to preach the truths revealed by God, by both word and example, to everyone according to need. Once the Order's mission was firmly established, Dominic turned his attention to the intellectual and spiritual education of his new friars. This is as close as he came to a philosophy of education.

Dominic always saw an essential connection between serious study and good preaching. For successful preaching, sanctity of life needed to be enlightened by doctrine. He studied the Letters of Paul and the Gospel of Matthew until he almost knew them by heart. Humbert of Romans, echoing Dominic, reminded his brothers that study, while not the end of the Order, was essential to preaching and laboring for the salvation of souls. Study, also a means of sanctification, should be a prayerful search for truth leading to self-knowledge and a deeper understanding of the scriptures; it could also be a penitential exercise.

Dominic's program of study or curriculum was narrow. He did not want his students to "study the books of pagans and philosophers," though they may consult them in passing. In addition, they 'shall not learn secular sciences, even the so-called liberal arts ... everyone ... shall read only theological books' (*Distinctiones* II, XXVIII). He was educating not scholars as such but preachers, knowledgeable in scripture and theology and virtuous in life. He feared that secular knowledge would get in the way of preaching. Within decades of Dominic's death, however, "teaching" was included within the scope of the "preaching" mission. Some Dominicans studied liberal arts and philosophy at the universities, and truth in the service of the gospel was sought wherever it could be found.

---

8. For example, William A Hinnebusch, OP, *The History of the Dominican Order*, vol. 1 (New York: Alba House, 1965), 39–40; *Early Dominicans: Selected Writings*, edited by Simon Tugwell, OP (New York: Paulist Press, 1982), 88; *St Dominic: Biographical Documents*, edited by Francis C. Lehner, OP (Washington, DC: The Thomist Press, 1964), 197–202. Lehner includes a translation of Pope Honorius III's text.

Dominic was convinced that intellectual and spiritual preparation for preaching could not be separated. According to Jordan of Saxony, Dominic grasped information through the "humble intelligence of the heart." He wanted his followers' lives to preach as eloquently as their words. Hence, study should be marked by silence and meditation, strengthened by prayer and penance, and supported by a religious community committed to regular observance and fraternal charity.

Nor did Dominic take preaching preparation for granted. Candidates were to be carefully examined about their readiness: questions were to be asked about "what grace of preaching they have from God" and about their quality of life and commitment (*Distinctiones* II, XX).

Dominic was indeed a powerful "light of the world" because his light had its source in God's eternal Word, "a light that shines in the dark, a light that darkness could not overpower" (*Jn* 1:5). Dominic's era is far removed from ours, yet aspects of his vision and spirit are as inspirational for us today as they were for followers in his time. These include: his passion for truth and preaching; his witness in action to what he proclaimed in word; his integration of study and spirituality; his insistence that preachers be well prepared; his respect for human dignity; his love and compassion for all people, even his enemies. Above all, he showed that we can transform the minds and hearts of others only by loving and respecting them and having compassion on them.

The Dominican tradition reflects the dynamic development of Dominican ideas and spirituality, culture and structures over the centuries. It flourished through the Order's conversations about itself: through General Chapters and teachings of the Order's Masters, through the insights of saints, martyrs and scholars, through academic institutions. The contribution of Thomas Aquinas to this tradition is fundamental, both because he gave academic structure to Dominic's vision and because he is the patron saint of Catholic education.

The Dominican Tradition: St Thomas Aquinas

Few theologians or philosophers have received such acclaim as Thomas Aquinas. A saint and genius, he was as renowned for sanctity as he was admired for scholarship. His books are so profound that they occupy the shelves of any worthwhile library in the world. I reflect now on one aspect of Thomas that should have special meaning for educators: his life as a teacher.

From the time he began teaching at Paris in 1252 until he finished at Naples in 1273, Aquinas always studied, taught and wrote. On hearing he was to be made a cardinal, he prayed that God would let him die first for that would mean an end of teaching. God took him at his word! In his study and writing, Thomas developed or refined a number of themes that have become distinctive features of Dominican education, especially of the liberal arts tradition. I comment on four: the relation of faith and reason, the role of philosophy, the goodness of creation, and his methodology.

The Relation of Faith and Reason

In his encyclical, *Fides et Ratio*, Pope John Paul II noted Thomas' unique contributions to discussions about the integration of faith and reason.[9] Aquinas argued that faith and reason are distinct but inseparable sources of truth, and both must be respected. Faith illuminates reason but does not destroy it. For example, human reason can develop a philosophy of the human person according to the norms of human inquiry. However, by introducing questions about God, revelation, creation and redemption, faith broadens the framework and deepens the discussion by enlightening the mind to possibilities that transcend reason. Together, faith and reason can fashion a synthesis that is both true to faith and intellectually defensible. Aquinas saw faith and reason as one in the pursuit of all truth, whether human or divine.

Aquinas assumed that philosophy and theology were distinct disciplines but could be harmonized. The question of God is a case in point. As a philosopher, he believed that human reason could discover certain truths about the existence and nature of God.[10] He also believed that all creation was called into existence by God's word and was intelligible because it bore the divine imprint. Since "the heavens declare the glory of God," (*Ps* 19:1) Aquinas could reason from "the things [God] has made" to God's "everlasting power and deity" (*Rom* 1:19–20). As a believer, Aquinas also heard deep within himself God's further Word, God's eternal Son, through whom everything was created and in whom everything found its meaning. In the human Jesus, Aquinas moved far beyond the vestiges of divinity he discovered in creation and could gaze into the very face of God.

Imitating Dominic, Aquinas made his own the truth he taught and wrote about. Whether from faith or reason, knowledge was not an abstract truth to be known intellectually but a reality to be pondered and lived. Like 1 John, he "came to know the Word, who is life" (*1 Jn* 1:1). Such an intimate experience of God can be achieved only by those who have the depth of faith and humility of heart to accept God's call to conversion. For Aquinas, Christianity was a way of love that risked everything to follow Jesus, a way that forced him to his desk to study and write and to his knees before the cross.

Although Aquinas' conversion was life-long, it may have peaked in the

---

9. Pope John Paul II, *Fides et Ratio,* numbers 43–4.

10. Thomas Aquinas, OP, *Summa Theologica,* Part I, question 2, articles 1 and 2. Future references to the *Summa* will be in an abbreviated form.

famous experience that occurred while he was saying Mass on 6 December 1273. He emerged from the incident transformed, unable or unwilling to talk about it. He may have experienced a religious encounter with God so powerful that everything else paled in comparison. He never said what happened. Pressed for an explanation, he would only say: "All I have written seems to me so much straw compared to what has been revealed to me." Never again would he write or dictate a word.

The Role of Philosophy

Given the importance of reason, it is not surprising that Aquinas embraced philosophy and philosophical reasoning. In this, he differed from Dominic who had concerns about studying the works of pagan philosophers. Aquinas accepted truth, whatever its source. He transformed much of Western theology by philosophical insights drawn from Greek, Arab and Jewish scholars. His impact on the Catholic and Dominican traditions is so profound that it is simply impossible to understand either tradition without philosophy. It is necessary for understanding the human person and human behavior and for developing a systematic approach to reality. Aquinas' unity of the human person[11] is at the heart of Dominican education. Education is embraced not only by the mind but the whole person. The integration of the liberal arts with specialized disciplines and the relation of spiritual and moral growth to intellectual development flows directly from a philosophy of education addressed to the entire person.

The Goodness of Creation

Aquinas echoed Dominic's insistence on the goodness of the human person and of all created reality. Creation was good when it came from the hand of God,[12] and human persons were created in the image of God,[13] blessed with the power to know and the freedom to love. Although flawed by sin, the human person still retains the image of God, enjoys the ability to reason, is capable of living ethically and is open to recreation through grace. Aquinas made the human person as an image of God the very center of his theology because that image was the source of human dignity as it would later be the basis of human rights.

Aquinas' legacy of the human person as an image of God and the goodness of creation is long and rich. For example, two Spanish Dominicans, De Vittorio and Las Casas, appealed to the dignity of the human person to defend the rights

---

11. Aquinas, *Summa*, I, q. 76.
12. *Ibid.*, I, q. 5, a. 3.
13. *Ibid.*, I, q. 93.

of Native Americans against exploitation by colonials. In contemporary times, the dignity of the person and the goodness of creation have an enormous influence on issues such as human rights and the common good, life and death, hunger and homelessness, poverty, health care and environmental concerns.

Method

Aquinas' method was important for Dominican education. In his *Summa Theologica*, he probed for truth by asking questions about God and the central Christian doctrines. He died before he completed the *Summa*. That the *Summa* remain unfinished was providential because a method that sought truth by posing questions about inexhaustible mysteries can never be completed. After the manner of Aquinas, each generation of Dominicans must continue the spiritual and intellectual tradition in a way suited to its own time and place. Each generation is called to search for truth by asking its own questions about God and the mysteries of faith in light of the "signs" of its own times.

The Tradition of the Frontiers

The Avila General Chapter (1986) urged Dominicans to minister on the "frontiers," understood not as spatial reality but as the outer edge of a living tradition. Dominic was very much on the frontiers of his time. He lived in a society and church undergoing cultural and social upheaval. He founded his Order specifically to address the threat to Christianity posed by the Albigensian heresy. Yet, based on his preaching experience, he changed and expanded the frontiers of his Order, moving beyond Toulouse to the outer boundaries of Christianity and beyond and from lapsed Christians to all people. The Avila Chapter identified five frontiers: life and death, humanity and inhumanity, Christianity and world religions, religious experience and secular ideologies, the Catholic tradition and other Christians. Subsequent chapters elaborated on these by urging engagement across other divides, including those between women and men, rich and poor.[14]

This list is neither exhaustive nor easily adapted to an educational mission. However, while frontiers will not dictate the content of an educational program, they can shape attitudes and responses. They suggest that the most pressing issues facing education today emerge from our broader social and cultural context. In that sense, the current challenges are not so much frontiers *of* education as they are frontiers *for* education. Dominic discovered the spiritual needs of people through faith. We must do the same. The Vatican II taught that "faith throws a new light on everything and makes known the full ideal God

---

14. Bologna, 1998, Chapter 2; Providence 2001, n. 79.

has for (all people), thus guiding the mind toward solutions that are fully human."[15] By thus "reading the signs of the times," we will discover the "frontiers" of our society and the educational needs of our students.

Education on the current frontiers will be marked by continuity and change. Continuity is crucial because Dominican educators stand heir to an incredibly rich intellectual and spiritual legacy rooted in Dominic. If today's Dominican women and men are to be true to his spirit and vision and that of the Dominicans who have continued and helped shape his legacy, they must make Dominic's story their own by embodying its beliefs and values, insights and memories. However, change is equally important. Contemporary Dominicans cannot merely repeat the past without reference to our own historical and cultural situation. Our educational challenge, then, is to "read the signs of the times," bringing the richness of our tradition to bear on the issues emerging from our particular culture's frontiers.

Current Dominican educational efforts will differ because we minister on different frontiers and educate students with diverse needs. All share the philosophy of education rooted in and shaped by the Dominican tradition. However, some Dominicans may select particular aspects of the tradition to meet the special educational needs of their students. From the perspective of higher education, I choose Thomas Aquinas; from other educational perspectives such as art, spirituality, canon law, or health care, other Dominicans might find insights and examples of different Dominican saints and scholars more helpful for their ministries.

In applying our legacy to current frontiers, we must never forget that educating on the frontiers is not enough by itself. The papal legates, preaching on the same frontiers as Dominic, were unsuccessful because their lifestyle was at odds with their message. Dominic's somber reminder to his followers that success in ministry would hinge on the credibility of their lives applies equally well to Dominican educators today. I now offer a brief overview of how Providence College tries to incorporate the Dominican intellectual and spiritual tradition into its educational mission.

Providence College: Liberal Arts, Catholic and Dominican

In this abridged version of its mission statement, Providence College is:

> A . . . liberal arts, Catholic institution of higher education. Committed to fostering academic excellence . . . the College provides a variety of opportunities for intellectual, social, moral and spiritual growth . . . and actively

---

15. Pope Paul VI, *Gaudium et Spes*, 1965, n. 11.

cultivates intellectual, spiritual, ethical and aesthetical values within the context of the Judeo-Christian heritage. These values are nurtured by the unique tradition of the Dominican Order.

The College . . . recognizes the unity of the human family . . . from its one Creator . . . encourages the deepest respect for the essential dignity, freedom and equality of every person.

Providence retains its commitment to the liberal arts despite widespread social resistance to the very idea of the liberal arts. Many in contemporary society would rephrase Tertullian's question, "What does Athens have to do with Jerusalem?" and ask, "What does a liberal arts education have to do with career preparation, business schools, research universities, or coping with a market-driven economy where education is reduced to a commodity?" Providence offers a liberal arts education marked by both breadth and depth and avoids the trap of confusing information with learning or credentialing with education. The core curriculum provides the breadth. Its centerpiece is the Development of Western Civilization Program, a team-taught approach designed to educate students about the ideas, individuals and events that have helped shape our present world. More specialized fields of study in the majors and academic programs supply the depth.

What does the adjective "Catholic" add to the liberal arts to make Providence distinctive? First, it is important to note that the quest for academic excellence is the coin of the realm. In any academic institution worthy of its name, studies should be undertaken, scholarship pursued and truth sought for its own sake. The Church's mission of evangelization is carried out through teaching, research and service. However, evangelization cannot be a substitute for scholarship. If an academic institution fails in its proper function as an academy, it would undermine any role that academics might play in the mission of the Church. It could well deepen the prejudice already existing among some that scholarship and belief, Catholic and university, faith and reason are contradictions in terms.

The unique identity of Providence as "Catholic" and "Dominican" is found in witnessing to what it means to be religious in the thought, words and actions peculiar to the academy. Lip service is not enough. The College strives to have its religious character permeate the life and work of the campus, reflecting a philosophy of education broader than academics and an understanding of religion broader than a creed. The College weakens its credibility if it proclaims "truth" as its motto but engages in deceptive practices, or if it proclaims that every person is an image of God but treats members of the community and others with disrespect. The College makes its distinct Catholic contribution to higher education and the community by committing itself at the very heart of its mission to the philosophical, theological, spiritual and moral dimensions of the questions it addresses.

The specific form that the liberal arts take at Providence is influenced by the Dominican philosophy of education that addresses the whole person. The curriculum stimulates intellectual pursuits, broadens historical and cultural perspectives, hones powers of judgment and discrimination, improves analytical and communication skills and creates a love of learning that will be life-long. However, knowledge alone is not enough. It should lead to good moral choices. Providence has always tried to link the transmission of knowledge to the cultivation of character. It seeks graduates who are not only knowledgeable but also morally good. The College believes that it will influence the thinking and values of society primarily by shaping the insights and morals of its graduates.

Just as faith cannot be separated from reason in the Dominican tradition, neither can the quest for academic excellence be separated from its Catholic and Dominican character. The College "actively cultivates intellectual, spiritual, ethical and aesthetical values within the context of the Judeo-Christian heritage." This educational philosophy should be a transforming experience for students. It links academic excellence and religious values, insights of reason and influence of faith, intellectual development and spiritual growth, psychological maturity and moral responsibility for others, especially the less fortunate.

However, we must take to heart St Dominic's admonition that the brothers' lives preach as eloquently as their words. Having a wonderful philosophy of education, an excellent curriculum and superb learning goals will not by themselves create a transforming experience for students. If the curriculum does not come alive in the classroom, it will remain sterile, incapable of either exciting or transforming. Faculty members must make the ideas and values embodied in the curriculum their own and communicate them to students with dedication and expertise, love and compassion. When they reach out to students in this way, they model what it means to be an educated person, how academic excellence and spiritual values can be one in seeking truth and serving others.

Conclusion

I conclude with two stories from our classical and religious traditions. The first comes from *The Odyssey* and recounts the wanderings of the Greek hero, Ulysses, during the decade following the fall of Troy. *The Odyssey* traces the adventures of Ulysses on his journey back to his homeland. According to one interpretation, Ulysses is driven to return home because he is homesick and nostalgic for everyone and everything he had known in his former life. He journeys back toward a familiar and comfortable past where he was secure and at home.

The second story, the saga of Abraham, comes from our biblical tradition. He is called by God to leave home, friends, familiar surroundings, even his homeland and set out on a journey without security, a road map or even a clear destination. He is guided only by faith and God's promise of descendants as numerous as the stars in the sky. At each stop on his journey, Abraham set up an altar to God, reflecting his belief that God was with him even in an alien land. His altars also became markers for those who follow him. It was not that way with Abraham. The altars were behind him; ahead, the way was uncharted. Abraham commits everything and goes from place to place led by an interior voice telling him to "leave here" and "go there," and guided only by a vague promise that "I will show you." This is a journey, not back to a comfortable and secure past, but forward to an unknown yet promising future.

The Dominican educational tradition combines aspects of both stories. Like Ulysses, we have roots in the past that shape our identities and ministries, influence our beliefs and values. We cherish our roots and are nourished by them, but we cannot live in the past. That would be to freeze the tradition, rob it of vitality, drain it of hope and reduce it to an heirloom rather than a living fountain. Like Abraham, we are bearers of a promise to shape the minds and hearts of our students. Rooted in Dominic's vision, the promise has been enriched by centuries of tradition, is lived out on the frontiers of the present but open to the future. As educators, we are committed to guiding our students on both journeys: to experience the depth and richness embodied in our tradition and expressed in our missions; and to grasp the promise and possibility of a future different from the past, marked by the spirit of Dominic but with its own special memories and traditions.

Our particular educational journeys will differ, depending on our specific missions. However, all Dominican education should be marked by the quest for academic excellence, by fidelity to our intellectual and spiritual traditions and by concern for those in the society where we labor. Above all, we should be known for nurturing our students, fostering their love of knowledge, sharing their dreams, cultivating their character and shaping their hopes. We need not fear the future or the challenges that might emerge from our frontiers. The God who inspired the founding of our Order and who shepherded it through difficult times over the centuries still abides in our midst and will sustain us in the future. I conclude with a quotation from the Senegalese poet, Baba Dioun, which beautifully sums up our philosophy of learning and teaching:

> *In the end*
> *We will conserve only what we love*
> *We will love only what we understand*
> *And we will understand only what we have been taught.*

THE HEALING WORK OF TEACHING:
THOMAS AQUINAS AND EDUCATION

Father Vivian Boland, O.P.

Dominicans of a certain age will be familiar with the expression *sana doctrina* and will know that it was regularly used for the teaching of Thomas Aquinas (1225–1274). It was usually translated into English as "sound doctrine" but it could also be translated as "healthy teaching." Thomas believed that Jesus of Nazareth was the most excellent of teachers.[1] His compassion for the harassed and dejected moved him to teach them many things.[2] Along with his work of feeding the hungry, healing the sick, and casting out demons, Jesus taught. His teaching is the bread of life, the truth that sets free, and the wisdom that gives life.[3]

We know that Thomas had to fight to become a Dominican. For reasons that remain unclear his family opposed his decision. But eventually he was able to join the preaching friars and to place his exceptional gifts at the service of their mission. That mission, in its original context, was to counter the unhealthy teaching of the Albigensians with the healthy teaching of the gospel. In practice this meant a sustained defense by the early generations of Dominicans of the goodness of the created order. How else could they speak seriously about central Christian truths like the incarnation of the Word, the bestowal of grace in the sacraments, and the resurrection of the body? How else could they be faithful to the teacher of life, truth and wisdom?

Thomas played his part in that mission particularly through his theology of creation and of the human person. For him the creation itself is all about teaching. It is a lesson in the goodness of God illustrated by the creation and redemption of the world. He says that the end of creation is truth because the origin of creation is mind.[4] He is thinking, of course, of the mind of God. But he speaks of other minds too, created they may be, but still capable of appreciating truth and participating at their own level in God's work of teaching. He speaks about angelic intelligence and the forms of communication in which it might be involved. He speaks about human intelligence and the forms of communication in which it might be involved. And this is where he considers the question of whether one human being can teach another.

---

1. Thomas Aquinas, *Summa Theologiae*, III, 42, 4.
2. *Mk* 6:34.
3. *Jn* 6:32–51; 8:31–6; *Matt* 11:25–30.
4. Thomas Aquinas, *Summa Contra Gentiles*, I, 1.

Texts on Teaching

In the two texts in which he discusses this question at some length, Thomas positions his understanding of teaching between two other views that he rejects.[5] On one side was the idea that there is a common mind for the human race, a sort of collective consciousness, into which we are plugged as long as we are alive and which continues when we pass on. The threat to individual immortality is one reason why Thomas was unhappy with this but it is not his immediate concern in these texts. His immediate concern is that this view would mean that the individual human would not, strictly speaking, be a person, even in this world. He believed that the reality and dignity of being a person are seen in the fact that each individual comes to know the truth and to choose the good. Responsibility cannot be passed to some more general spirit or guiding force: it belongs to each one individually. The knowledge each person attains is that person's knowledge. The enjoyment of truth each person attains is that person's enjoyment of truth. The decisions and commitments each person makes are that person's decisions and commitments. If it is done for us or even through us by some power that is beyond ourselves, then it is not we who are doing it at all.

The second view that Thomas rejects, he associates with Plato. In this view we are born with an implicit knowledge of everything and need stimulation from the outside world only to bring back to memory what the soul has always known. It is true that Thomas follows Aristotle in accepting that there are first principles of reasoning, both speculative and practical, that are part of the equipment of human intelligence. He is thinking of principles like "a whole is greater than its parts," or "the good is to be sought and the evil is to be avoided." Once experience begins we know these principles and see that they are true. But he does not agree with Plato's idea that knowing is remembering, not just because he cannot accept Plato's theory of separated forms but because he believes Plato's way of describing the process of human knowing empties our empirical experience of its reality and meaning.

Thomas developed his understanding of teaching as a middle position between these two views. For him they were both unhealthy because they took something away from the reality, and therefore from the goodness, of the created order and its activities. The first assigned the effective power of knowing to an agency beyond us. The second regarded our current experience as accidental to the process of knowing. Thomas's teaching is that the student really grows in

---

5. The main texts are *Quaestiones Disputatae de Veritate,* 11, 1 and *Summa Theologiae,* 117, 1. Other texts in which he discusses teaching are in II *Sentences* 9, 1, 2 ad 4; *Summa Contra Gentiles,* II, 75 and *On the Unity of the Intellect Against the Averroists,* chapter 5 (Leonine XLIII, lines 186–206, Marietti §258).

knowledge through experience and that the knowledge in which she grows she can call her own.

In working out the details of his account of teaching Thomas uses ideas from Aristotle's philosophy, ideas such as potentiality and actuality, principal and instrumental causality, extrinsic and intrinsic causality, nature and art. At the same time his understanding is fundamentally a Christian, theological one. It is true that Augustine is more explicitly present in the earlier text on teaching[6] but he remains a significant background presence in the later text too.[7] Thomas agreed with Augustine that, in one sense, God is the only real teacher because God equips us to know the truth. At the same time, and in another sense, human teachers really do something for their students. Thomas sees it as part of the wonder of creation: with some creatures God shares the power to effect things.

For Thomas teaching means placing the imagination at the service of understanding. He was himself a good teacher and his preferred analogy for what the teacher does is the work of the medical doctor. Just as the medic cannot replace nature but can assist it in various ways, so the teacher cannot replace the student's intellectual processes but can assist them in various ways. A human being cannot assist another human being in the way that God can, by making them brighter, for example, through strengthening the light of intelligence itself. But a human being can assist another human being to see things he/she had not seen before. This involves not only presenting the student with new things to consider but also pointing out connections that the student, left to himself/herself, might not see. The teacher cannot do the students' understanding for them and so the students' appreciation of truth is not identical with the teacher's appreciation of truth. And for Thomas this means that a real change comes about through teaching.

Thomas treats explicitly of teaching within his metaphysics of creation, then, explaining how created minds meet in the process of communicating truth and goodness, and thereby collaborating in God's government of the world. A close study of these texts is the best way to see how Aquinas understands teaching and learning.[8] There are, however, other ways in which he teaches us about his understanding of education. One is through the way he himself studied and taught. Another is in the sustained pedagogical concern revealed in his written works. We shall consider each in turn.

---

6. *Quaestiones Disputatae de Veritate*, 11, 1.

7. The reference to 'signs' in *Summa Theologiae*, 117, 1 and 3 brings Augustine, *De Magistro*, i–ii, to mind.

Practicing Teaching

Thomas is a great scholastic, a man of his time, and followed the standard medieval practices of reading (*lectio*), disputation (*disputatio*), and oral repetition (*repetitio* or *praedicatio*), practices that still hold much interest for the educationalist. Then, as now, teacher and students together read through great classical texts, in Thomas's case beginning with the Bible and then the works of theologians and philosophers. This practice gives us much of our pedagogical terminology: lecture, lecturer, lector, lectern, and lesson. The reading together of classical texts remains a basic element of any educational system and is a practice that is supported by philosophers who are otherwise radically different in their understanding of education.

Master and students engaged secondly in disputations where questions were considered dialectically, and positions were refined through the presentation of evidence and in the progress of logical argument. This allowed them to move beyond the reading and interpretation of texts while drawing on what they had read. The disputed question remained a standard part of university education in Europe until the eighteenth century and was still practiced in the neo-scholastic schools of the twentieth century, albeit in more formalized ways. On occasion, though, it retained something of the vitality one imagines in discussions at Plato's Academy or at the annual disputations in thirteenth century Paris. The Irish Dominican Fergal O'Connor, for example, was an exceptional exponent of this method of teaching: he "saw actual dialogue, live and unscripted with face-to-face others, as the very best medium in which thinking is learned."[9]

Thomas believed the best teaching is done not through texts but orally and that the best teachers imprint their teaching directly on the hearts of their students. The third element of scholastic method was repeating or proclaiming. The student was required to speak back what he had learned not just because writing materials were scarce, and in order to impress it on his memory, but

---

8. Jacques Maritain, *Education at the Crossroads* (Yale University Press: New Haven and London, 1943 and 1971) paraphrases Thomas's text on pages 29–32 but the whole book is informed by Thomas's understanding of teaching. For a recent reappraisal of Maritain's work and of other aspects of what St Thomas has to say about education see Daniel McInerny, editor, *The Common Things: Essays on Thomism and Education* (Washington DC: American Maritain Association, The Catholic University of America Press, 1999). Brian Davies and Patrick Quinn offer reflections on the text of Thomas but without drawing attention to the context: Brian Davies OP, "Aquinas and the Academic Life," *New Blackfriars* 83 (2002): pp. 336–46; Patrick Quinn, "Aquinas's Views on Teaching," *New Blackfriars* 81 (2001): pp. 108–20.

9. Joseph Dunne, "Figures of the Teacher: Fergal O'Connor and Socrates" in *Questioning Ireland: Debates in Political Philosophy and Public Policy*, edited by Joseph Dunne (Dublin: Attracta Ingram and Frank Litton, Institute of Public Administration, 2000), pp. 13–33. The quotation is from page 26.

also because the tasks for which people were being prepared were the tasks of teaching and preaching, of communicating with a view to building community, as Thomas puts it in his commentary on Aristotle's *Politics*.[10]

At first sight, an article of the *Summa Theologiae* looks very different from the dialogue form used by Plato, Boethius, and many others. On reflection, though, it can be seen that each article is in fact a stylized dialogue in which a number of voices are heard. The initial arguments are real arguments, not just objections, as if they made no contribution to the final resolution. Very often Thomas agrees with aspects of the initial arguments and he certainly allows these other voices to guide his own thinking. So even when written down, his way of learning and teaching is dialectical. Each article contains a short discussion or debate leading to a nuanced conclusion.

Thomas is open to many voices speaking about the matters that concern him. The range of sources he employed, his enthusiasm for new texts and for fresh translations of old ones, his anxiety to interpret texts in the fairest possible way, his reception of the thought of others which is always benign but never naïve, above all his respect for the truth and obedience to it: all of this informs a method of studying and teaching that we can describe, once again, as healthy. His confidence that 'the truth is strong in itself, and nothing can prevail against it'[11] allowed him to pursue knowledge and truth with great freedom and courage. He quoted with approval the view attributed to Saint Ambrose, that any truth, no matter by whom it is said, is from the Holy Spirit.[12]

The Reflective and Creative Practitioner

While using to great effect the standard practices of reading, disputation and repetition, Thomas also expressed dissatisfaction with them. In the prologue to the *Summa Theologiae* he highlights their limitations and says he wants to construct his own work according to "a sound (implying 'sounder') educational method". What he proposes, it seems, is a pedagogical order determined by the subject matter itself of Christian theology. This refers not to the order of the Creed or to the way in which Peter Lombard's *Sentences* had been structured, far less to the way the *summae* of moral theology and canon law had been put together, but rather to the way in which revelation has happened, in

10. For a fuller account of the significance of these comments in the *Politics* commentary see my chapter "Boring God: Theology and Preaching," in Michael Monshau OP, editor, *The Grace and Task of Preaching* (Dublin: Dominican Publications, 2006), pp. 52–70.

11. *Summa Contra Gentiles*, IV, 10.

12. *Summa Theologiae*, I, II, 109, 1 ad 1; *Commentary on the Gospel of John*, 1, lectio 1 (Marietti §§103–4).

words to the way in which God as teacher has taught humanity and for the purpose for which God's teaching has been made.

Mark D. Jordan has recently gathered a series of articles in which he argues that the reception of the thought of Aquinas has been distorted by a more or less complete failure on the part of his readers to see his pedagogical concerns: "I hold that rewriting Thomas erases a decisive feature of his texts, namely, their pedagogical structure."[13] Leonard Boyle set this discussion off in the now classic lecture on the setting of the *Summa*[14] in which he drew attention to the fact that its originality is above all pedagogical. Thomas is given the freedom to experiment with curriculum and teaching method, and proposes something revolutionary: that moral theology be firmly placed within an account of creation and redemption. In this he is thinking not only about how to present theology in a material way but is thinking also of the students studying theology for particular spiritual and pastoral purposes. The truth of theology is a matter of human salvation or beatitude, Thomas says in the opening question of the *Summa*, and Fergus Kerr has shown how beatitude is a theme that structures the *Summa*.[15] Jordan's work alerts us to the fact that Thomas returns to beatitude again and again not simply because it is another key theme of Christian theology but because it is what students of Christian theology enter into precisely through their study of Christian theology. The *Summa Theologiae* is a book that requires, for its proper reception, a way of living.

Boyle already argued that the Dominicans for whom the work was intended did not get the point of Thomas's experiment. Jordan agrees, saying that on educational grounds the *Summa Theologiae* is a hybrid genre, fully suitable for neither university nor pastoral use "because it means to reform both."[16] Elsewhere he put it like this:

> The *Summa* is read whole when it is enacted as a single theological teaching, with morals at its center and the Passion of Christ as its driving force, before a community committed to sanctification through mission, with the consolations of sacraments and liturgy, in the illumination of contemplative prayer.[17]

---

13. Mark D. Jordan, *Rewritten Theology: Aquinas After His Readers*, (Oxford: Blackwells), 2006. The quotation is from page 6.

14. *The Setting of the Summa Theologiae of Saint Thomas* (Toronto: Pontifical Institute of Medieval Studies, 1982).

15. Fergus Kerr, *After Aquinas: Versions of Thomism* (Oxford: Blackwells, 2002), pp. 128ff.

16. Jordan, *Rewritten Theology*, p. 10.

17. "The *Summa's* Reform of Moral Theology—and its Failures," in *Contemplating Aquinas: Varieties of Interpretation*, edited by Fergus Kerr OP (London: SCM Press, 2003), p. 53.

One is tempted to say that we are dealing here with a post-modernist reception of Aquinas for which pedagogy is central. At the same time many of the points made by Jordan are found already in *The Intellectual Life*, Sertillanges' invaluable and "entirely Thomistic" introduction to the theology and practice of study. And in the study circles organized by Jacques Maritain something similar was recognized: the text of Aquinas was read in a setting that included prayer and a community life as well as study and conversation.[18]

The teacher has the task of creating structures for handing down the discipline with which he is concerned. Creating those structures for theology, Jordan says, is like creating regimes for teaching virtue.[19] In fact one might have thought that a consideration of teaching would be found in the moral part of the *Summa* that deals with human actions, virtues, relationships and professions. Instead, as we have seen, Thomas speaks of it in relation to creation. But there is much of relevance to education in what he says about virtue. Because the acquisition of knowledge is a significant part of human experience and the communication of knowledge is a significant activity of human society, all the virtues will be seen to touch on it. This is true of what he calls intellectual virtues, the dispositions that are directly concerned with science and wisdom. Among the moral virtues also there is, for example, a virtue of truthfulness that is a form of justice, docility that is a part of prudence, and patience and perseverance that are sub-virtues of courage. There is also the special virtue of *studiositas* that is a form of temperance. Like other human desires, the desire to know is good, but it needs to be kept focused if the balance of a human life is not to be distorted by the opposing vice of curiosity.[20]

And So Back to Christ

For Thomas human flourishing can only come about through the living of a theological life. Wisdom, the tasted knowledge of truth-goodness-beauty that human beings seek, is found, he believed, in the knowledge of Jesus Christ. He is the most excellent of teachers who in his own person and life has shown us

---

18. A.G. Sertillanges OP, *The Intellectual Life: Its Spirit, Conditions, Methods* translated from the French by Mary Ryan, with a new foreword by James V Schall SJ, The Catholic University of America Press, Washington DC, 1998. For "entirely Thomistic" see page xxix. For Maritain's study circles see *The Common Things*, pp. 139–43.

19. Jordan, *Rewritten Theology*, p. 193.

20. *Summa Theologiae*, II, II, pp. 166–7. On *studiositas* see Liam Walsh OP, "St Thomas and Study," in The Renewal Papers: Papers from the Renewal Programme of the Irish Dominican Province 1993, St Mary's, Tallaght, 1994, 58–89 [also published in La Formazione Integrale Domenicana al Servizio della Chiesa e della Societ, Edizioni Studio Domenicano, Bologna, 1996, pp. 223–52] and Gregory M Reichberg, "*Studiositas: The Virtue of Attention*," in *The Common Things*, edited by McInerny, pp. 143–52.

the way of truth by which we come to our full flourishing.[21] Through the virtues of faith, hope and charity, and the Spirit's gifts of knowledge, understanding, fear and wisdom, we already live the eternal life.[22]

An indispensable element in any teaching, Thomas believes, is the conversation of teacher and student, and the appeal to imagination through signs, especially language. This is how Jesus taught his disciples, taking them to himself as
his pupils and friends, and revealing to them all that he had learned from the
Father.[23] The climax of his life is also the climax of his work as a teacher. The
cross of Jesus, the glory of the only Son, is his greatest act of teaching. Thomas
refers to Augustine's extraordinary image: Jesus hanging on the cross is like a
teacher on his chair, *sicut magister in cathedra*.[24] From that chair he poses a
question for his disciples, gives a sign to illustrate his teaching and reveals the
love that binds him to them. The lesson given by this most excellent of teachers
is for the life of the world, for the healing of the nations.

21. *Summa Theologiae*, III, prologue.

22. *Jn* 17:3: "This is eternal life, that they know you the only true God and Jesus Christ whom you
have sent." For Thomas's understanding of how we possess this knowledge see his questions on the
Spirit's gifts that perfect the activities of the theological virtues: *Summa Theologiae*, II, II, 8--9, pp. 19
and 45.

23. See Michael Sherwin OP, "Christ the Teacher in St Thomas's *Commentary on the Gospel of
John*," in *Reading John with St Thomas Aquinas: Theological Exegesis and Speculative Theology*, edited
by Michael Dauphinais and Matthew Levering, (Washington DC: The Catholic University of America Press, 2005), pp. 173–93.

24. *Commentary on the Gospel of John*, 19, lectio 4 (Marietti §2441).

ABOUT THE EDITORS

Sister Matthew Marie Cummings, O.P. is a member of the Dominican Sisters of Saint Cecilia of Nashville, Tennessee and is professor of education at Aquinas College in Nashville. She holds a Doctor of Education degree, as well as a Master of Science degree, in Instruction and Curriculum Leadership from the University of Memphis. In addition, she has a Master of Arts in Religious Studies from Notre Dame Institute; a Bachelor of Arts in Elementary Education from Belmont University; and an Associate of Arts degree from Aquinas College. A national speaker on the integration of technology in classroom instruction, curriculum, and the development of professional dispositions in the pre-service teacher, Sister Matthew Marie also sponsors the Aquinas College Student Chapter of ASCD.

Sister Elizabeth Anne Allen, O.P. currently serves as the Vice President for Academics at Aquinas College in Nashville, Tennessee. A member of the Dominican Sisters of Saint Cecilia, she holds a Doctor of Education degree in Education and Policy Studies from the University of Memphis. With teaching and administrative experience on elementary, secondary and collegiate levels; Sister has a Master of Arts and a Bachelor of Science degree in History from Middle Tennessee State University; a Master of Arts in Religious Studies from Notre Dame Institute; and a Master of Education degree in Administration from the University of Southern Mississippi. Sister presents professional development sessions nationally on a variety of educational topics including the dignity of teaching and Catholic identity.

www.ingramcontent.com/pod-product-compliance
Lightning Source LLC
Chambersburg PA
CBHW070410100426
42812CB00005B/1695